studying
management
critically

edited by
mats alvesson and hugh willmott

studying
management
critically

SAGE Publications
London • Thousand Oaks • New Delhi

SAGE Publications Ltd
6 Bonhill Street
London EC2A 4PU

SAGE Publications Inc
2455 Teller Road
Thousand Oaks, California 91320

SAGE Publications India Pvt Ltd
B-42, Panchsheel Enclave
Post Box 4109
New Delhi 110 017

British Library Cataloguing in Publication data

A catalogue record for this book is available
from the British Library

ISBN 0 7619 6736 2
ISBN 0 7619 6737 0 (pbk)

Library of Congress Control Number available

Typeset by C&M Digitals (P) Ltd., Chennai, India
Printed in Great Britain by TJ International, Padstow, Cornwall

Contents

Notes on Contributors

Mats Alvesson

got his PhD in 1984 and works currently at Lund University in Sweden. Apart from critical theory, major research interests include cultural perspectives on organizations, gender, leadership (or rather 'eadership'), identity, knowledge work, professional organizations and qualitative methodology. Recent books include *Reflexive Methodolgy* (2000, with Kaj Sköldberg), *Doing Critical Management Research* (2000, with Stan Deetz), *Postmodernism and Social Research* (2002), *Understanding Organizational Culture* (2002) and *Knowledge work and Knowledge-intensive Firms* (in press).

Gibson Burrell

is Professor of Organisation Theory and Head of the Management Centre at the University of Leicester. He was previously employed at the Universities of Lancaster, Warwick and Essex, which all allowed him spaces and places to do what he wanted. Some of his material has even been read. He has returned to the University of Leicester in which he was a student *à la recherche du temps perdu.* There is no escaping, for some, the draw of 1960s architecture.

David Cooper

is the Certified Accountants of Alberta Chair in Accounting in the Department of Accounting and MIS at the University of Alberta, and Director of the School of Business PhD Program. He obtained a BSc (Econ) from LSE and his PhD from the University of Manchester in 1979. David has written or edited seven books and about fifty articles in academic and professional journals such as *Accounting, Organizations and Society, Administrative Science Quarterly, Contemporary Accounting Research, Organisation Studies, Accounting Management and Information Technology* and *Accounting, Auditing and Accountability Journal.* He is interested in power and rationality in organizations and society and these issues have been explored in a variety of contexts: management control systems in mining, implementation of new budgeting, information and costing systems in hospitals, the history of the accounting profession and their codes of ethics, the regulation of the accounting profession, and strategic and performance measurement in government. He is a joint editor of the international research journal, *Critical Perspectives on Accounting* and a member of the Editorial Boards of seven other journals.

Karen Dale

is a Lecturer at the University of Essex. She was previously at Warwick University, and has worked in the National Health Service and local government. She has published a number of articles in the areas of gender and equality, and the body and organisation. Her book, *Anatomising Embodiment and Organisation Theory,* was published in 2001. Currently she is working on a book on architecture, space and organisation with Gibson Burrell, and has already published on the topics of space, utopias, aesthetics and anaesthetics.

Stanley Deetz

Ph.D., is Professor of Communication at the University of Colorado, Boulder, where he teaches courses in organizational theory, organizational communication and communication theory. From 1984–97 he was a professor at Rutgers University, chairing the department during the 1980's. He is a Fellow of the International Communication Association and served as its President, 1996–97. He has held visiting appointments at the University of Texas, Arizona State University, the University of Iowa, and the Copenhagen Business School. He is co-author of *Leading Organizations through Transition* (2000) and *Doing Critical Management Research* (2000); and author of *Transforming Communication, Transforming Business* (1995) and *Democracy in an Age of Corporate Colonization* (1992); as well as editor or author of eight other books. He has published nearly one hundred essays in scholarly journals and books regarding stakeholder representation, decision making, culture, and communication in corporate organizations and has lectured widely in the U.S. and Europe.

Linda C. Forbes

is Assistant Professor of Organizational Behavior and Management at Franklin & Marshall College, Lancaster, Pennsylvania, U.S.A. Her interests include cultural studies and organizational symbolism, environmental philosophy and history, and varieties of qualitative inquiry. Her current work draws on symbolic organization theory as a framework for analyzing the greening of organizational cultures. She recently published: 'The Institutionalization of Voluntary Organizational Greeting and the Ideals of Environmentalism: Lessons About Official Culture From Symbolic Organization Theory' in *Organizations, Policy, and the Natural Environment* (2002). She is a Feature Editor for the journal, *Organization & Environment: International Journal for Ecosocial Research* where she recently published an article on the legacy of the early conservationist and first Chief of the US Forest Service, Gifford Pinchot.

John Forester

is Professor and immediate past Chair of the Department of City and Regional Planning at Cornell University. A Ph.D. from the University of California at Berkeley, his research interests include the micro-politics and ethics of planning practice, including the ways planners work in the face of power and conflict. His most recent books include *The Deliberative Practitioner: Encouraging Participatory Planning Processes,* (1999), co-edited with Raphaël Fischler and Deborah Shmueli, and *A collection of oral histories, Israeli Planners and Designers: Profiles of Community Builders* (2001). For the past decade he has been producing first person voice 'profiles' of planners, mediators, and participatory action researchers in the US and abroad. Along with several edited collections on planning, policy analysis, and critical theory, his earlier work includes *Planning in the Face of Power* (1989), *Making Equity Planning Work: Leadership in the Public Sector* (with Norman Krumholz, 1990), and *Critical Theory, Public Policy, and Planning Practice* (1993).

John M. Jermier

is Professor of Organizational Behavior and of Environmental Science and Policy at the University of South Florida, Tampa, Florida, U.S.A. Most of his work has focused on critical studies of organization and management and his current interests include power and politics in organizations, environmental philosophy and literary ecology, and research methodology. He is founding editor and current senior editor of the journal, *Organization & Environment: International Journal for Ecosocial Research.* He served as guest editor (with Steve Barley) of a special issue of *Administrative Science Quarterly* (1998) concerned with critical perspectives on organizational control and is past chair of the Organizations and the Natural Environment Interest Group of the America Academy of Management.

Richard Laughlin

M.Soc.Sc. Accounting (Birmingham) 1973, Ph.D. Accounting (Sheffield) 1985, F.C.A. (Chartered Accountant – Associate 1969, Fellow 1979), F.R.S.A. (Fellow of the Royal Society of Arts, 1993). He worked as a trainee and manager in a professional accounting practice and as a consultant accountant before joining the University of Sheffield in 1973. He worked at the University of Essex 1995–1998 and is currently a Professor of Accounting in The Management Centre at King's College, London, University of London where he has been Head of Department until recently. He has a range of publications in accounting, management, organisation and political science, related to methodological issues and to understanding the organisational and human effects of changes in accounting, finance and management system in organisations and society with particular emphasis on the health and education sectors of the public sector. He is on the Editorial Boards of a number of journals as well as being Associate Editor of the *Accounting, Auditing and Accountability Journal.*

David L. Levy

is Professor of Management at the University of Massachusetts, Boston. His research examines the intersection of business strategy and politics in the development of international governance. Recently, he has studied the response of multinational corporations in the oil and automobile industries to the emerging greenhouse gas regime, and is co-editing, with Peter Newell, a book on the political economy of international environmental governance (forthcoming). He is an advisor in the development of the Massachusetts Climate Change Action Plan and works with a state program to support the development of the renewable energy sector.

Joanne Martin

is the Fred H. Merrill Professor of Organizational Behavior at the Graduate School of Business, Stanford University. She holds a B.A. from Smith College, a Ph.D. from the Department of Psychology and Social Relations at Harvard University, and an Honorary Doctorate in Economics and Business Administration from the Copenhagen Business School. She recently received the Distinguished Educator award from the Academy of Management and the Centennial Medal for contributions to society from the Graduate School of Arts and Sciences at Harvard. She serves on the Board of Directors of CPP, Inc., a test and book publisher, and on the Advisory Board of the International Centre for Research in Organizational Discourse, Strategy, and Change for the Universities of Melbourne, Sydney, London, and McGill. She has published many articles and five books including *Cultures in Organizations: Three Perspective* (1992) and *Organizational Culture: Mapping the Terrain* (2002). Her current work focuses on gender and culture.

Glenn Morgan

is Reader in Organizational Behavior at Warwick Business School, the University of Warwick. He has previously worked at Manchester Business School and the Manchester School of Management, UMIST. His current research interests lie in the comparative study of economic organisations and multinationals. Recent edited collections included G. Morgan, P.H. Kristensen and R. Whitley eds. (2001) *The Multinational Firm*, with S. Quack, G. Morgan and R. Whitley (eds) (2000), *National Capitalisms, Global Competition and Economic Performance.* He has published in a range of journals including *Organization Studies, Journal of Management Studies, Sociology and Work, Employment and Society.* He is currently Co-Editor of the *Journal Organization.*

Martin Parker

is a Professor in the Management Centre at the University of Leicester. He holds degrees in authropology and sociology from the Universities of Sussex, London and Staffordshire and previously taught at Staffordshire and keele Unversities. His writing is usually concerned with organisational theory and the sociology of culture. His most recent and relevant books for his chapter are the edited *Ethics and Organisation* (1998), *Utopia and Organisation* (2000), the authored *Organisational Culture and Identity* (2000) and *Against Management* (2000).

Michael Power

is P.D. Leake Professor of Accounting and a Director of the ESRC Centre for the Analysis of Risk and Regulation (CARR) at the London School of Economics, where he has worked since 1987. Holding degrees from the Universities of Oxford, Cambridge and London, he is a fellow of the Institute of Chartered Accountants in England and Wales (ICAEW) and an associate member of the UK Chartered Institute of Taxation. He has been a Faculty member of the European Institute for Advanced Studies in Management, Brussels and a Coopers & Lybrand Fellow. He has acted as an advisor to the National Audit Office and the Cabinet Office in the UK, and has been a visiting fellow at the Institute for Advanced Study, Berlin (1996/6) and All Souls College, Oxford (2000). Research interests focus mainly on the changing relationship between financial accounting, auditing and risk management. In addition to *The Audit Society: Rituals of Verification* (1999), recent publications include *Accounting and Science* (1996) and *The Audit Implosion: Regulating Risk from the Inside* (2000). He is currently working on *Visions of organizational control: constructing the new risk management* (forthcoming).

Hugh Willmott

is professor of organization theory at Judge Institute of Management Studies, Cambridge University and a visiting professor at the University of Lund. He is currently working on a number of projects whose common theme is the changing organization and management of work, including projects in the ESRC Virtual Society and ESRC Future of Work programmes and an ICAEW funded study of strategic reorientation. He has published widely in social science and management journals including Sociology, Sociological Review, Administrative Science Quarterly, Academy of Management Review, Accounting, Organizations and Society and Journal of Management Studies. His more recent books include *Making Sense of Management: A Critical Introduction* (1996, co-authored), *Management Lives* (1999, co-authored), *The Re-engineering Revolution* (2000, co-edited), *The Body and Organizations* (2000, co-edited) and *Managing Knowledge: Critical Investigations of Work and Learning* (2000, co-edited). He has served on the editorial boards of a number of journals including *Administrative Science Quarterly. Organization, Organization Studies and Accounting,* and *Organizations and Society.*

Chapter 1

Introduction

Mats Alvesson and Hugh Willmott

This collection presents a series of critical reflections upon key themes, topics and emergent issues in management studies. Written by specialists in their respective fields, it provides an informed overview of contemporary contributions to the study of management. Shared by its contributors is a concern to interrogate and challenge received wisdom about management theory and practice. This wisdom is deeply coloured by managerialist assumptions – assumptions that take for granted the legitimacy and efficacy of established patterns of thinking and action. Knowledge *of* management then becomes knowledge *for* management in which alternative voices are absent or marginalized. In contrast, critical perspectives on management share the aim of developing a less managerially partisan position. Insights drawn from traditions of critical social science are applied to rethink and develop the theory and practice of management.

The predecessor to this volume – *Critical Management Studies* (1992) – arose from a small conference held in 1989. This event brought together scholars from Europe and North America to connect critical work that was emerging on both sides of the Atlantic. Since then, the field has grown and diversified, spawning various conferences (notably, the biennial Critical Management Studies Conference) and workshops and the establishment of journals (e.g. *Organization, Electronic Journal of Radical Organization Theory, Tamara*) that are supportive of Critical Management Studies as well as special issues (e.g. *Academy of Management Review, Administrative Science Quarterly*) and regular contributors to longer established journals (e.g. *Journal of Management Studies, Human Relations, Management Learning*). In North America, the Critical Management Studies Workshop (CMSW) has met annually at the Academy of Management Meetings and is now a special interest group of the Academy. In recent years, Critical Management events have been held in Japan, Brazil, Australia and elsewhere and there have been conferences, journals and collections that provide vehicles for Critical Management in different specialisms (e.g. accounting, marketing).

CRITICAL THEORY AND BEYOND

The tradition of Critical Theory, established in Frankfurt in the 1930s (see Alvesson and Willmott, 1996: Ch. 3, for a brief history and discussion), was, in the earlier volume, the chief, though by no means exclusive, inspiration for its contributors. Influential thinkers in this school include Horkheimer, Benjamin, Adorno, Marcuse, Fromm and, most recently, Jürgen Habermas. The influence of the Frankfurt School tradition is apparent in the work of writers such as Lasch (1978, 1984) and Sennett (1998). Critical Theory (CT) proceeds from an assumption of the *possibilities* of more autonomous individuals, who, in the tradition of the Enlightenment, in principle can master their own destiny in joint operation with peers – possibilities that are understood to be narrowed, distorted and impeded by conventional managerial wisdom. CT aspires to provide an intellectual counterforce to the ego administration of modern, advanced industrial society. CT apprehends how employees in large bureaucracies, and consumers of mass goods, are affected by corporations, schools, government and mass media; and how personalities, beliefs, tastes and preferences are developed to fit into the demands of mass production and mass consumption, thereby expressing standardized forms of individuality. CT challenges the domination of this instrumental rationality, which tends to reduce human beings to parts of a well-oiled societal machine (Alvesson, 2003; Steffy and Grimes, 1992).

Critical Theory provides *a* (not the) *critical-constructive* intellectual counterpoint to mainstream management studies. In Parker's (2002: 9) words, it contributes to 'a cultural shift in the image of management, from saviour to problem'. The principal strength of Critical Theory resides in its breadth, which offers an inspiration for critical reflection on a large number of central issues in management studies: notions of rationality and progress, technocracy and social engineering, autonomy and control, communicative action, power and ideology as well as fundamental issues of epistemology. In comparison to orthodox Marxism, CT has been rather more alert to the cultural development of advanced capitalistic society, including the growth of administration and technocracy (Alvesson and Willmott, 1996) and offers an incisive perspective for the understanding of consumerism and ecological issues (see, for example, the chapters by Morgan, and Jermier and Forbes in this volume).

During the 1990s, other streams of critical and disruptive thinking (e.g. varieties of feminism) – many of them collected under the umbrella headings of 'postmodernism' and 'poststructuralism' – have emerged and developed within the field of management to complement and challenge analyses guided by Critical Theory. Notably, the thinking of Michel Foucault has been important in providing an alternative, critical voice – in both style and substance – to the vision of Critical Theory. His ideas have, for example, questioned the humanist concept of autonomy ascribed to subjects and challenged the assumption that knowledge can be cleansed of power

(Foucault, 1980). Given the diverse critical traditions of analysis that are now being deployed to interrogate management theory and practice, then the current challenge is perhaps to appreciate commonalities and continuities in different strands of critical thinking rather than becoming preoccupied with differences and detained by schisms. The unqualified dismissal of rival approaches in favour of a single, 'enlightened' conception of Critical Management Studies is, in our view, likely to be diverse and counterproductive in terms of any aspiration to scrutinised and change the theory and practice of management.

Critical Theory comprises an important, but by no means a single dominant, strand of Critical Management Studies (CMS) that continues to be an inclusive, pluralistic 'movement' wherein a diversity of critical approaches – from non-orthodox forms of labour process analysis, through varieties of Critical Theory to deconstructionism (Derrida) and approaches that have broader affinities with many contemporary social movements (e.g. feminism, environmentalism, postcolonialism, etc.) – is accommodated. This diversity has grown during the past decade (see Fournier and Grey, 2000 for a discussion of this). This volume does not try to cover all varieties of Critical Management Studies, but incorporates some of its most influential currents. So, rather that being religiously attached to Critical Theory, in the sense of the Frankfurt tradition, a way forward could involve recognizing and even celebrating, rather than minimizing, key and very probably irreconcilable differences in the conception of what it means to 'think critically'. These differences are evident in the respective writings of Critical Theorists, such as Habermas, and poststructuralists like Foucault. In principle, they provide a rich and diverse source of inspiration that can enrich rather than confound critical studies of management (Alvesson and Deetz, 2000). If this tack is taken, then it is acknowledged that CT has limitations that should be confronted, rather than be regarded as remediable or inescapable shortcomings. More specifically, it is relevant to recognize the tenuousness of efforts to establish secure foundations for CT's truth claims – in the consciousness of autonomous individuals or in the structure of language. Challenging the normative ideals to which Critical Theory appeals, and that it seeks to provide with rational foundations, Foucault has commented that

> The thought that there could be a state of communication which would be such that the games of truth could circulate freely, without obstacles, without constraint and without coercive effects, seems to me to be Utopia. (Foucault, 1988: 18)

Foucault, of course, has a point, but inspiration from Foucault as well as Habermas may be a way of avoiding either Utopia or Dystopia – by maintaining a potentially productive tension between scepticism and inspiration for the development of alternative management practices. The difference between Foucault and Habermas is substantial, but their ideas seem to encourage productive debates (Kelly, 1994). There are arguably shared interests between Foucault and a large part of the Frankfurt School, in particular Adorno (Bernstein, 1994). It is worth noting that Foucault himself late in life, when he learned about German Critical Theory, expressed himself very positively about the Frankfurt School and emphasized his affinity:

> it is this form of philosophy that, from Hegel, through Nietzsche and Max Weber to the Frankfurt School, has founded a form of reflection in which I have tried to work. (Foucault, 1994: 148)

We refrain here from commenting more extensively upon the relationship, critiques and debates between CT and other forms of critical analysis (see Alvesson and Willmott, 1996). Instead, we underscore our belief that there is less point in stressing theoretical rigour and orthodoxy than in welcoming inspiration from a variety of theories and ideas that share 'enough' affinities to advance and extend critical studies of management.

CONTRIBUTIONS TO THIS VOLUME

More than half of the present volume comprises commissioned chapters that cover new topics and themes (see table below). The inclusion of more new rather than revised chapters is signalled by a modification of the book's title, rather than its replacement or just labelling it the second edition.

The collection has a number of potential readerships and uses. For researchers committed to studying management critically, it provides an overview of work from a variety of perspectives and across a range of topics, subdisciplines and themes. For academics interested to learn more about the field, the collection offers a comparatively accessible point of entry into a range of areas so that specialists can readily appreciate what is distinctive about studying management critically. For teachers, it provides a series of resources that could be used to complement established courses by providing students with a taste of non-mainstream approaches to particular topics. It could also be

Revised and updated from *Critical Management Studies*	Commissioned Contributions for *Studying Management Critically*
Introduction	Burrell and Dale: Space
Deetz: HRM	Jermier and Forbes: Environmentalism
Forester: Methodology	Levy, Alvesson and Willmott: Strategy
Morgan: Marketing	Martin: Feminism
Power, Laughlin and Cooper: Accounting	Parker: Ethics

adopted selectively as a supplementary text for advanced studies of areas covered by the collection. Or it could provide the basis for advanced under-graduate or postgraduate courses and modules in Critical Management Studies. For more reflective practitioners (including researchers and teachers in their organizational work), the collection offers access to ideas and perspectives that, by providing alternative, non-managerialist frameworks of interpretation, can be valuable in broadening their repertoire of theoretically informed ways of making sense of their experiences and moving in directions that are informed by the concerns addressed by critical studies of management.

A brief overview of each of the following chapters provides an outline of the volume's scope and focus. Stanley Deetz (Chapter 2) addresses how modern corporations have a variety of stakeholders with competing interests within and between each of them. Many have documented the way arbitrary advantages are given to management and the questions this raises for a democratic society. Deetz argues that a productive analysis of these issues must consider the politics involved in the construction of the human subject and his/her knowledge. He contends that the basic democratic issue is not the representation of stakeholder interests, but the social production of stakeholders and their interests. Human resources management is seen to provide the most explicit treatment of the recruitment, development and regulation of the human subject in the workplace. Drawing upon Foucault's analysis of power as discipline, this chapter offers insights into the everyday, practical manner by which power is deployed and potential conflicts sup-pressed through human resources management.

John Forester (Chapter 3) probes a transcript from a staff meeting of urban planners in a small municipality's city hall to challenge/refute the view that Critical Theory, and especially Habermas's theory of communica-tive action, has little relevance for the analysis of empirical cases and has less to say about how we might explore the work of managers and administra-tors. Forester shows how we might develop an empirically grounded, pheno-menologically sensitive, and politically critical sociology by appropriating and building upon Habermas's action theory and his analysis of speech acts in particular. Much more than claims about any 'truth' of the matter is at stake in organizational and political interaction. Actors construct and contest agendas and identities alike; they use humour and irony to do actual work; and they not only continually negotiate relations of status and authority, but they shape each other's imaginations and commitments as well.

Joanne Martin's contribution (Chapter 4) explores the affinities and divergences between feminist theory and Critical Theory. Although they both focus on social and economic inequalities and share an agenda of promoting system change, these fields of inquiry have developed separately and sel-dom draw on each other's work. This chapter identifies areas of common interest and assesses the validity of critiques of feminist theory – such as claims that it focuses on privileged women and does not challenge existing hierarchical arrangements. It is suggested that these critiques fail to recognize and address much contemporary feminist scholarship, and it is argued that synergies between Critical Theory and feminist theory could and should be better appreciated and further explored.

David Levy, Mats Alvesson and Hugh Willmott (Chapter 5) present a critique of strategic management, contending that it needs to be taken seriously as the exercise of power in contested social networks of firms, governmental agencies, and non-governmental actors such as labour and environmental groups. Building on prior critiques of the strategy literature, the chapter draws from Gramsci to offer a historical materialist perspective on struggles for influence within social and economic networks. The Gramscian perspective is seen to facilitate and enrich attempts to integrate strategy, dynamics and agency within institutional theory and social movement theory. If power lies in the strategic coordination of resources rather than mere possession of them, then a strategic conception of power offers the opportunity for subordinate groups to develop coalitions capable of challenging dominant groups and effecting change at the corporate, industry or issue level.

Glenn Morgan's chapter on marketing (Chapter 6) notes how the dominant paradigm in marketing embraces various versions of positivism and, ethically, has identified itself with 'the needs of the consumer'. Marketing aims to provide a scientific approach to uncovering what consumers as individuals 'really, really want'. An effect of this, Morgan contends, is to corrode other potential forms of collective identity, particularly around ideas of citizenship. Critiques of marketing emanating from the Frankfurt School, postmodernism and Foucault-inspired research are then reviewed before commending an approach that conceives of marketing as a set of practices and technologies with specific origins and effects which constitute the subjectivity of the 'consumer' and the objectivity of the 'market' in distinctive ways. Such an approach, Morgan contends, offers the possibility of developing an empirical and theoretically informed critique of marketing.

Michael Power, Richard Laughlin and David Cooper (Chapter 7) identify accounting as a pervasive force in modern society that is strongly connected to pressures for globalization and economic rationalization as it affects decision-making by governments, corporations and individuals. Accounting claims to represent reality – to tell us 'true costs' and 'the bottom line' – and, in so doing, it helps to constitute what is seen as legitimate performance. It would seem that if control of complex modern societies is to be secured, then ever more elaborate forms of economic calculation are required, of which accounting is a dominant instance. In this chapter, some central elements of Habermas's work are reviewed in order to explore the role and function of accounting. In particular, its role as a steering medium and its potential for enabling or distorting communication is considered. Critical Theory, it is suggested, can play a part in recovering the public dimension of accounting's legitimacy and to comprehend its possible effects on society.

John Jermier and Linda Forbes (Chapter 8) note how negative environmental trends are, in unprecedented ways, 'spiking' – simultaneously and in combinations – adding credence to the hypothesis of a looming, global environmental crisis. The crisis has many causes and few apparent solutions but increasingly responsibility for solving environmental problems is being placed in the domain of organizations and their managers. The chapter examines existing approaches to organizational greening and to help generate more systematic, critical thinking in this emerging and crucial area of management studies. Critical Theory is deployed to analyse the conceptual adequacy and political content of existing approaches to greening. Jermier and Forbes conclude that existing approaches to greening do not go far enough in addressing concerns for nature. While they do not seem to undermine other forms of green politics, they should not be seen as the vanguard of the environmental movement or as a substitute for regulatory and adversarial initiatives.

Gibson Burrell and Karen Dale (Chapter 9) explore the relationship between real material architectures and the creation of social, specifically organizational, spaces. Through the work of Critical Theorists such as Adorno and Benjamin, they go further than considering the power relations embedded in architectural and spatial arrangements. Drawing in particular on the concepts of 'representational space', as delineated by Lefebvre, along with Benjamin's writing on 'phantasmagoria', they consider how spatial arrangements have been central to the construction of certain organizational categories and of the life experiences of these groups. The focus is upon the development of factory design for mass production, giving special consideration to the influence of Albert Kahn, and on the growth of large-scale bureaucracy, taking the buildings of the architectural practice of Skidmore, Owings and Merrill (SOM) as an exemplar. They conclude by asking, if we can recover the material and embodied conditions of organization, whether it is possible to create emancipatory organizational spaces.

Martin Parker (Chapter 10) notes how the rise of business ethics has involved making a series of claims about expertise and legitimacy. Does this mean that businesses were not ethical before business ethics? What expertise do professional ethicists have that ordinary mortals do not? And, perhaps most importantly, will business ethics actually make businesses ethical? These questions are addressed in this chapter, but there is a further question: What is 'Critical Management Studies' to make of business ethics? Business ethics texts are interrogated in order to expose some of their conventional assumptions, and absences. Business ethics is re-viewed through the lens of Horkheimer's Critical Theory and Adorno's quasi-deconstructive 'negative dialectics', as well as a more conventional form of economic determinist Marxism. It is argued that these approaches are critical in some sense, and Marxist in some sense, yet they position the subjects and objects of criticism in very different ways. Finally, these understandings are returned to Critical

Management itself to open up the possibility that the differences between business ethics and Critical Management Studies are not so great as is often assumed, or perhaps hoped.

RETHINKING MANAGEMENT DISCIPLINES

How are the disciplines of management and the activities of management academics commonsensically understood? We suggest that this understanding typically assumes a devotion to the (scientific) improvement of managerial practice and the functioning of organizations. In this vision of management practice and theory, questions directly and indirectly connected to efficiency and effectiveness are made central; and knowledge of management is assumed to be of greatest relevance to managers. Accordingly, in the mainstream literature on management, exemplified in its door-stopping, jaw-dropping textbooks, managers are routinely presented as carriers of rationality and initiative (for example, in many versions of strategic management and corporate culture). 'Better management' – by which is meant the transfer of responsibility for 'getting things done' to an elite of technocrats – is increasingly commended as the solution to diverse political and social, as well as economic, problems. Other agents – employees, customers, citizens – are then cast as objects or instruments of managerial action. Where technocracy is in the ascendancy, knowledge based on science and placed in the hands of an army of engineers, administrators, managers, psychologists and computer specialists is viewed as the best or even the only possible way of effective problem-solving. Images and ideals of 'professional management' which emphasize the skilled employment of neutral and objective techniques – from accounting and personnel appraisal to conflict and knowledge management – exemplify this technocratic understanding of knowledge and social affairs. Against this, Critical Management insists on the political nature of what is seemingly neutral or technological, and highlights the dangers of technocracy for human autonomy and responsibility.

In the conventional narrative of management, the assumption is that managers perform valuable functions, and proceed in a (professional, impartial) way that fulfils the common interests of workers, employers, customers and citizens alike. Absent from this rosy picture is an appreciation of how managerial action is embedded in wider, politico-economic institutional arrangements that operate to steer and constrain as well as enable managerial action. Contributors to this collection survey and advance a body of knowledge that questions the wisdom of taking the neutrality or virtue of management as self-evident and unproblematical. Critical thinking about management reflects and advances the understanding that management is too potent and potentially corrosive in its effects upon the lives of employees, consumers and citizens to be represented through, guided by, and shrouded in, a narrow, instrumental form of means–ends rationality. By drawing upon critical traditions of social theory, it is possible to advance a different, broader understanding of the work of administrators and managers. For example, in his study of planners, Forester notes how

> Critical Theory gives us a new way of understanding action, or what a planner does, as attention-shaping (communicative action), rather than more narrowly as a means to a particular end (instrumental action)....we can understand structures of action, e.g. the organizational and political contexts of planning practice, as structures of selective attention, and so systematically distorted communication. (Forester, 1985: 203)

In this way, the insights of critical thinking may then be taken into account in counteracting communicative distortions in the private sector. Profit motives and the more contradictory relations between participants in corporations may of course amplify and compound the difficulties that constrain its application. Even so, Forester's analysis of planning is informed by the insights of Critical Theory (CT) – 'pragmatics with vision' (1985: 221; see also his chapter in this volume) – and demonstrates how CT has much relevance for everyday organizational action.

Critical Management Studies draw and build upon numerous earlier contributions that have addressed management as a historical and cultural phenomenon that merits serious critical examination (e.g. Anthony, 1977; 1986; Bendix, 1956; Child, 1969; Jackall, 1988; Knights and Willmott, 1986; MacIntyre, 1981; Reed, 1989; Watson, 1994). In general, these works have derived their inspiration from Weber, from moral philosophy or from Marx's analysis of the labour process, and make limited reference to Critical Theory. Yet, it was Horkheimer, a highly influential Director of the Frankfurt-based Institute of Social Research, the institutional origin of the School, who identified white-collar employees, among which may be included many managers and supervisors, as a social group that demanded urgent critical examination (Horkheimer, 1989). In setting out his vision of Critical Theory, Horkheimer contrasts it with a view of scientific study that assumes a seemingly objective, instrumental relationship to its 'objects' (e.g. managers), and that contrives to reserve the exercise of value judgements for conduct in other spheres (e.g. politics). Rejecting this (bourgeois) division of science and politics – which fuels a technocratization of management based upon the understanding that 'good practice' can be objectively determined by using scientific methods – Horkheimer contended that

> The scholarly specialist 'as' scientist regards social reality and its products as extrinsic to him [sic] and 'as' citizen exercises his interest in

> them through political articles, membership in political parties or social
> science organizations, and participation in elections....Critical think-
> ing, on the contrary, is motivated today by the effort really to transcend
> the tension and to abolish the opposition between the individual's pur-
> posefulness, spontaneity, and rationality, and those work-process rela-
> tionships on which society is built. Critical thought has a concept of
> man [sic] as in conflict with himself until this opposition is removed.
> [Critical] theory never aims simply at an increase in knowledge as
> such. Its goal is man's [sic] emancipation from slavery. (1976: 220, 224)

Contributors to this volume vary in their affinity with Horkheimer's specific formulation of critical thinking and, more specifically, to the conception and methodology of emancipatory action commended by Critical Theorists. Those of a more sceptical disposition would doubtless question, for a variety of reasons, whether 'emancipation from slavery' can ever be fully accomplished and/or whether CT provides the intellectual resources for its realization. This scepticism is also part of the Frankfurt School tradition and was strongly expressed in the later works of Horkheimer and, in particular, Adorno (see Parker's contribution to this book). Nonetheless, there would be widespread agreement with Horkheimer's broad concern to problematize the idea (and associated practice) of (social) scientists as people who can remove or disembed themselves from their life and responsibilities as human beings and citizens. In critical thinking, (social) scientific practice is conceived to have an ethico-politico dimension that is at the core, rather than the periphery, of its operation and effects. Accordingly, the activity of the social scientist is framed in terms of a practical rationality that, in contrast to technical rationality, does not study managers (for example) in a way which separates politics/ethics from the production of knowledge. Instead of proceeding by examining and striving to perfect the means of organizing work (for example) independently of an (unacknowledged) articulation and pursuit of certain ends, attention is directed from the outset to the interrogation of ends and their inextricable connectedness to means. In this process, there is an appreciation of how the 'objects' of managerial and scientific interests are formed within particular, historical and cultural contexts. These 'objects' are not given but, rather, are shaped by relations of power and domination that, in principle, can be transformed to develop very different 'objects'. Instead of confining change to reform within the status quo, Critical Management challenges the necessity of its current boundaries and anticipates the possibility of future forms of management that transgress and redraw them.

BROADENING THE AGENDA OF MANAGEMENT STUDIES

Working within different specialist fields of management, the interest of the contributors to this volume flows from a disillusionment with traditional forms of management theory and practice in which, as Horkheimer notes, the actions of scientists *qua* observers of social practices (e.g. managerial practice) is distanced, or alienated, from their lives as participants in the social world. Management is simply too important an activity and field of inquiry to be left to the mainstream thinking of management departments, business schools and, increasingly, corporate universities and sponsored courses. Saying this, we are not denying that mainstream texts and practices can be 'well intentioned' in their concern to eliminate inept and self-serving practices. Sometimes these purposes may be partially fulfilled, yet their broad effect, and often their intent, is probably the creation of (more) compliant, controllable employees and customers. So much management theory and practice is tunnel-visioned and dangerous – practically as well as intellectually, ecologically as well as culturally. As a counterweight to technical (or technocratic) images and ideals of management – in which a narrow focus on the improvement of means–ends relationships is predominant – there is a strong case for advancing sociological, historical, philosophical and critical studies of management. It is in the light of these considerations that the force of Habermas's concern to recognize and renew the emancipatory impulse of science can be felt:

> Science as a productive force can work in a salutary way when it is suffused by science as an emancipatory force, to the same extent as it becomes disastrous as soon as it seeks to subject the domain of praxis, which is outside the sphere of technical disposition, to its *exclusive* control. The demythification which does not break the mythic spell but merely seeks to evade it will only bring forth new witch doctors. (Habermas, 1974: 281)

Many contemporary advocates of critical thinking, including some contributors to this volume, would doubtless question the apparent ease with which adherents of Critical Theory are able to see through 'the mythic spell(s)' produced within bourgeois culture. Nonetheless, they would broadly sympathize with the spirit of Habermas's intent to subject scientific practice – which includes knowledge of management – to wider forms of accountability. Generally speaking, diverse forms of Critical Management scholarship share the view that technical knowledge (means) should be subordinated to, and guided by, the domain of praxis – so that science is used critically and reflexively as a resource for, rather than a master, of social development.

The contributions to this volume share Habermas's commitment to break the mythic spell of conventional management theory and practice to which people in organizations, managers included, are routinely subjected. Instead of assuming the neutrality of management theory and the impartiality of management practice, each contribution challenges the myth of objectivity and argues for a very different, critical conception of management in which research is self-consciously motivated by an effort to discredit, and ideally eliminate, forms of management and organization that have institutionalized the opposition between the purposefulness of individuals and the seeming givenness and narrow instrumentality of work-process relationships. The task of critically examining management perspectives becomes more urgent in the context of the increasing social, political and ecological implications of decisions made by managers within modern corporations, as Deetz has argued:

> The modern corporation has emerged as the dominant means of institutionalizing working relations. In achieving dominance, the commercial corporation has eclipsed the state, family, residential community, and moral community. This shadowing has hidden or suppressed important historical conflicts among competing institutional demands. Corporate practices pervade modern life by providing personal identity, structuring time and experience, influencing education and knowledge production, and directing entertainment and news production. (1992: 2)

To the extent that management has a 'productive' role to play in organizational work – and it would be unwise (and certainly inconsistent with Critical Theory) to assume or exaggerate its vital importance (Carter and Jackson, 1987; Pfeffer and Salancik, 1978) – it is not restricted simply to facilitating the innovation, production and distribution of valuable social goods. Companies and management are also implicated in 'producing' people-workers, customers, as well as citizens in other capacities. That is to say, they shape, are involved in, and promote, needs, wishes, beliefs and identities. Advertisements and other forms of consumer marketing maintain and reinforce gender stereotypes, problematize identities and make self-esteem precarious. That they foster a materialistic and egoistic lifestyle is a comparatively obvious aspect of corporate activity (Alvesson, 1994; Lasch, 1978; Pollay, 1986). Companies – and thus their leading actors – bear some responsibility for unemployment as well as employment, for pollution and ecological disasters, for psychic and social problems associated with the (often low) quality of work and for the exploitation of workers. Companies and top managers selectively promote or even block socially beneficial innovations (Egri and Frost, 1989) as they labour tirelessly to advance their own careers and increase their benefits packages, pensions and share options. As Deetz (1992, and Chapter 2 in this volume) stresses, corporations and their executives can act, through lobbying and agenda-setting, as a powerful force that undermines democratic accountability in modern Western society: the technocracy of management subverts the democracy of citizens.

PRISING MANAGEMENT OPEN

Closely associated with the notion of critical studies of management is the ideal of representing other interests and perspectives than those immediately associated with a managerial position (the manager managing people and activities). There are a number of groups that have a legitimate interest in being represented in the illumination and development of management functions, processes and discourses. Management is not the sole preserve of (predominantly male) managers: subordinates, customers and citizens in general have a legitimate interest in management. So is also the case with groups marginalized in management practice and theory, such as females and members of ethnic minorities. For example, the significance of gender relations has been seriously neglected in management and organization studies. Only quite recently have feminist voices been heard, but even then they are often restricted to issues of access to existing professional/managerial career tracks (Marshall, 1984). To an increasing extent, broader issues are being addressed and deeper critiques of management theory and practice are being addressed (see e.g. Alvesson and Billing, 1997; Calás and Smircich, 1996; Martin in this volume). Also ethnic groups outside White Anglo-Saxon Protestants need to be considered in the context of dominant notions of management and leadership ideals that frequently bear subtle imprints of a particular cultural and/or postcolonial tradition (see A. Prasad, 2003; P. Prasad, 1997). A careful scrutiny of managerial discourse and practice in terms of voices that not only speak loudly, but also quietly or cannot yet be heard is an important task for Critical Management Studies.

Turning to consider management as a technical function, we can point to a number of activities that at the present time, and for the foreseeable future, will be undertaken. These include the physical and intellectual labour of production and distribution, including the planning and coordinating of activities. Engagement in productive activity necessarily involves the performance of a variety of tasks and processes that can be (narrowly) conceived and examined as technical functions. Yet, their particular organization – which includes the issue of who is to occupy positions of authority within the division of labour and who is to derive greatest advantage (symbolic as well as material) from this *social* division – is inescapably a matter of politics that cannot be determined neutrally by an impartial appeal to the requirements of an impersonal, technical logic. Or, rather, when such appeals are made, they are heard by Critical Management as involving more or less conscious efforts to defend or advance sectional interests in the name of an avowedly rational and universal interest.[1]

In the world of work, there are recurrent struggles over the question of whose purposes, or interests, work (production) is to serve – owners, managers, producers, consumers? Equally, there are struggles over how work is organized – autocratically, bureaucratically, democratically? These struggles may not take the form of collective actions and disputes that challenge the status quo. But they exist nonetheless as owners endeavour to exert tighter control over corporate management, and not least when employees, including managers (except possibly at the very highest level), manoeuvre to circumvent hierarchical control; and as consumers (citizens) lobby to influence the specification and manufacture of products that are safe and healthy. Studies of management that take little or no account of such struggles are intellectually shallow and politically naïve as well as ethically problematic. To deal with these issues, the technical functions of management require organization and control in ways that do not systematically privilege the ends of those who currently own, control and manage modern organizations. In principle, the ideal of democracy could be extended from the political (parliamentary) to the economic sphere by facilitating much greater participation in decision-making, and making those who undertake the management functions more widely accountable for their actions. As Deetz (1992) points out, however, this must be addressed more deeply than in terms of empowerment and access to formal participation, as dominant discourses tend to constitute forms of subjectivities that act in accordance with, rather than challenge, dominant social codes and interests.

Critical analyses of management draw back from conceiving of those occupying management positions as mere functionaries. Representing them in this way serves to legitimize their position and facilitate their control, but it does not produce credible social science. Managers are not sensibly represented as ciphers who serve the predetermined needs of some higher entity (e.g. capital or the state). Different groups of managers struggle over positions and privileges, and conflict over their competing claims to possess superior knowledge and skills (Armstrong, 1986; Chalmers, 2001). Nor are managers adequately conceived as selfish agents who act exclusively in accordance with their own personal interests. 'Self-interest' is part of the picture, but most managers to some extent act upon feelings of responsibility for the corporate whole and/or various interest groups: consumers, shareholders, employees, the ecological environment and so on. At the very least, managers are routinely obliged to rationalize and legitimize their actions by reference to wider considerations, obligations that risk a discrediting of personal and corporate reputations if they are not at least partially fulfilled – as the recent scandals of Enron and WorldCom (among many others) have borne witness. Caught between contradictory demands and pressures, managers encounter ethical problems; they run the risk of dismissal; they are 'victims' as well as perpetrators of discourses and practices that (un-) necessarily constrain ways of thinking and acting (Jackall, 1988). Managerial ideologies – notably a belief in managers' prerogative to manage – tie them to ideals and identities that, paradoxically, limit their options as they simultaneously appear to secure for them a position of relative power and influence (see Knights and Willmott, 1999; Nord and Jermier, 1992). Critical social science is of direct relevance to managers in interpreting such experience, and it is therefore not entirely surprising to find that managers, who are of course also citizens, are not necessarily unreceptive, as individuals, to its concerns.

At the same time, it is important to recognize that others, including employees who are the subordinates of managers, are sometimes entranced with, and supporters of, an extension of managerialism. Employees may be more critical of what they regard as the incompetence of their supervisors than of the *social* division of labour out of which hierarchies and elites are produced. Managers are not alone in endorsing managerial ideologies or advocating the expansion and refinement of technocracy. Workers may favour similar ideals – means as well as (assumed) outcomes. An important role for critical social science is to relate what is perceived to be a manifestation of individual, technical incompetence to a system that institutionalizes the non-accountability of managers to their subordinates. The central problem of management resides in the social relations of production which *systematically* foster and sustain very limited forms of relating and communicating between those who occupy positions within the horizontal and vertical divisions of labour. Exercises designed and controlled by managers to improve levels of 'involvement' and 'participation' among employees, for example, are frequently limited in their effectiveness as employees are excluded from, or assigned a managerially defined 'bit part' in, the design and operation of these programmes – an exclusion that stems from the desire of managers and owners to retain control as well as from the suspicion or indifference of employees towards such programmes.

A non-technocratic agenda for management studies requires that management theory and practice be examined in a critical light – that is, a light that considers not only means–ends relationships, but also the ends and institutionalized conditions of management discourse and action. Issues of power and ideology are to be taken seriously – a move that pays attention to various interest groups and perspectives that are under-represented or silenced in mainstream writings and in corporate talk and decision-making. For these groups, there exist issues and ideals other than the effective utilization of resources in order to attain certain (economic) ends. Their concerns extend, for example, to workplace democracy, quality of work, gender equality (absence of gender domination), respect for ethnic diversity, environmental protection, informed and independent consumption, and so on. In sum, Critical Management has an agenda for research, teaching and organizational practice that understands management as a political, cultural and ideological phenomenon, and addresses managers not only as managers but as people, and is attentive to other social groups (subordinates, customers, clients, men and women, citizens in other capacities) whose lives are more or less directly affected by the activities and ideologies of management. It is important to recognize that managers are not only carriers of more or less repressive rationalities and exploitive or patriarchial relations, but also as subjects caught in complex, difficult situations, with responsibilities for economic results, but also worker safety, customer satisfaction and so on. Scholarship and research that takes the difficult work situation of many managers seriously has a place within the broad church of Critical Management Studies (Thomas and Linstead, 2002; Watson, 1994).

A RESEARCH AGENDA FOR CRITICAL STUDIES
IN AND OF MANAGEMENT

Initially guided by Critical Theory (CT) as a primary source of inspiration, yet subsequently open to other thinking that complements and/or stands in a position of 'fruitful tension' to CT, a number of foci for critical studies of management can be identified: resisting technicistic and objectivistic views; drawing attention to asymmetrical power relations and discursive closures associated with taken-for-granted assumptions and ideologies; exploring the partiality of shared and conflictual interests; and paying careful attention to the centrality of language and communication. We briefly examine these below.

Developing a non-objective view of management
techniques and organizational processes

In opposition to traditional social science and management studies, critical studies of management proceed from a 'non-objectivist' understanding of ontology and epistemology (Alvesson and Deetz, 2000; Burrell and Morgan, 1979). Social reality then appears as much more arbitrary and precarious than is indicated by commonsense management theory and management techniques. The presumptions that knowledge products and techniques can mirror reality, and thus turn it into an object for efficient action, are questioned. Instead of suggesting that knowledge more or less exactly reflects corporate economic reality, accounting, for example, is understood to be inescapably implicated in creating that reality (see Power, Laughlin and Cooper, in this volume). Instead of responding to people's diverse needs and wants, marketing produces (people as) consumers as it divides them into market segments, thus producing social stereotypical categories (such as gender and youth) (see Morgan, in this volume). Instead of 'leadership' simply responding to a psychological or functional 'need' to have an authority figure who provides direction and defines key meanings, leadership may be seen as creating 'leader-dependent' subjects (Alvesson, 2003). Needless to say, management's role in the social construction of social and economic reality is not omnipotent, and to some extent it must adapt techniques and actions to a pre-existing socio-historical reality. But any claim, however qualified, that management is essentially a matter of grasping and manipulating elements of objective reality (such as structures or cultures) through efficiency-enhancing techniques is viewed as a mystification that is practically as well as intellectually deficient.

Exposing asymmetrical power relations

The practices and discourses that comprise organizations are never politically neutral. Sedimented within asymmetrical relations of power, they reproduce structures in which there is differential access to valued material and symbolic goods. Top management is routinely privileged in decision-making and agenda-setting, and in defining and shaping human needs and social reality. This is strongly emphasized in the strategic management literature, most of it singling out top management as the only actors worth considering (see Levy, Alvesson and Willmott, in this volume). An objective of studying management critically is to challenge the centrality and necessity of the dominant role of elites in defining reality and impeding emancipatory change. By questioning the rationality of elite structures, critical studies of management seek to reduce the disadvantages of groups other than those of the managerial elite in determining the practices and discourses that comprise organizational realities. As is clear from the writings of Foucault and other poststructuralists, power neutralization is, at best, a very tricky project, and at worst, a matter of self-deception. This is because, in common with all kinds of knowledge, critical studies exert a disciplining effect upon subjectivity (see Burrell and Dale, in this volume). In the development of methodologies for change, the issue of power must be taken seriously and handled in a 'constructive' way, something that some critical studies of management have done at least to a limited extent (e.g. Knights and Murray, 1994) .

Counteracting discursive closure

Related to the problems of objectivism and power is the commitment to explore critically taken-for-granted assumptions and ideologies that freeze the contemporary social order. What seems to be natural then becomes the target of 'de-naturalization': that is, the questioning and opening up of what has come to be seen as given, unproblematic and natural (see Martin, in this volume). This can also be formulated as a counteracting of discursive closure. Whereas earlier versions of Critical Theory tended to operate with the notion of false consciousness, the implicit idea of a 'true' consciousness is rejected: 'ideology' 'is best seen as drawing attention to arbitrary representational practices rather than a false or class consciousness', as Deetz (in this volume) notes. Expert cultures, such as those of management specialisms, are 'socially structured silences' that 'exhaust the space of possible discourse' (Power, Laughlin and Cooper, in this volume). The role of Critical Management is thus one of encouraging 'noise' to break these silences – to trigger critical comments and inspire dialogue (Alvesson and Deetz, 2000).

Revealing the partiality of shared interests

Another vital focus for Critical Management Studies concerns the dynamic partiality of consensus and shared interests. This understanding is positioned between traditional consensus (including weaker forms of pluralism theory) and more pronounced conflict assumptions (such as in Marxism and other types of radical theory). In opposition to traditional Marxist understandings, critical studies of management do not assume the primacy of a fundamental contradiction between capital and worker interests, nor is (higher-level) management lumped together with capital (see Martin, in this volume). Nonetheless, attention is drawn to contradictions in society and organizations, and to latent social conflicts (see, for example, Levy, Alvesson and Willmott, in this volume). These are related by recognizing the political nature of techniques and seemingly objective descriptions. For example, the colonization of the lifeworld (cultural meaning patterns) by the system's formalized media (Power, Laughlin and Cooper, in this volume) is critically examined; and in this way conflict is reviewed as a potentially constructive, liberating force.

Especially in Habermas's (1984) idea of communicative rationality, it is suggested that conflictual matters can quite often be brought into the open and resolved through dialogue in which participants explore each other's validity claims and let the force of the better argument decide (see Forester, in this volume). As many commentators have pointed out, this model for handling social conflicts has clear limitations (e.g. Bubner, 1982; Deetz, 1992; Thompson, 1982) and it must be appreciated that arriving at arguments and opinions that all concerned agree to be the best possible ones (i.e. most truthful, most normatively appropriate) is a rarely fulfilled ideal. Nevertheless, the prospect in principle of this outcome, encouraged by the opening of an arena for comparatively free debates created by societal modernization (e.g. the discrediting of religious dogmas and authoritarian states), makes appropriate a focus on the partiality of shared interest as well as conflicts (see Levy, Alvesson and Willmott, in this volume).

Appreciating the centrality of language and communicative action

An interest in communication is to some extent inherent in all the areas mentioned above, but such an interest can also be a central focus of investigation. Communication is central to all structures and actions – however instrumental or self-evident they may appear. Establishment of facts, appeals to norms of legitimacy, inner dispositions expressed by a speaker and the framing of attention – all are involved in everyday statements and claims (Forester, in this volume). Studies of management informed by Critical Theory examine their organization to discern forces that distort processes of communication. An interest not only in communicative action – which involves speakers as well as listeners, as Forester emphasizes – but also in language which carries historically established meanings and distinctions that tend to create a certain version of the social world, resonates with the emancipatory concerns of Critical Theory. This latter perspective understands language not as representational – able to refer to external objects through containing a fixed meaning or at least making clarified meanings possible – but as inherently ambiguous and constitutive. Language viewed in this way, as Deetz (in this volume) stresses, is not about how people use language to accomplish goals as much as how language constitutes the identity of groups, their relations and their priorities. From this standpoint, and especially when informed by poststructuralism, studies of management strive to open up representations in a way that has unsettling and potentially emancipatory consequences.

A MANAGERIAL TURN IN CRITICAL THEORY?

Habermas's efforts to ground critique in the presuppositions of language rather than the structure of consciousness have been described as a 'linguistic turn'. Can the contributors to this volume be characterized as proponents of a 'managerial turn'?

At the most fundamental, metatheoretical level, the answer must be in the negative. The concern of critical students of management is not to change the basis or direction of critical theorizing but, rather, to apply it to the mundane but socially significant world of management. In this respect, they may be seen to exemplify the broad intent of Critical Theory: to combine the respective strengths of theoretical and empirical modes of investigation. The empirical focus is upon the theory and practice of management, principally in its contribution to the organization and development of modern (e.g. advanced capitalist) societies and the lives of everyone engaged in their future formation. The theoretical focus ensures that the taken-for-granted world of management is examined critically, with the intent that the opposition between science and politics – individuals as neutral observers/managers and as engaged citizens – is debunked and overcome.

So, rather than a 'turn', the concern of Critical Management is to recall the commitment of critical thinking in a way that makes an appeal and poses a challenge. This challenge is directed to critical thinkers, including Critical Theorists who have largely disregarded the empirical realm of management, as well as to management academics and practitioners who have marginalized or disregarded traditions of critical thinking. From critical thinkers is sought an understanding of their deep appreciation of the philosophical foundations of critical thinking to enrich the study of the mundane, empirical world of management. The relevance of critical thinking – from Habermas's complex theory of communication to the insights into social relations yielded by feminist and poststructural analyses – could no doubt be better appreciated if those most familiar with its complex features were to apply it to the study of management. From management academics and practitioners is sought a reconstruction of management theory and practice that is informed by an engagement with critical theoretic traditions. The present volume is intended as a further stimulus to this project.

NOTE

1 Typically, managers are obliged to justify their existence by demonstrating their added value. Yet the demonstration of their value in the language of universal benefit barely conceals their sectional interests – as functional specialists or as an elite within organizations – in developing or sustaining arrangements that, they anticipate, will secure their (institutionalized) position of comparative privilege. A key skill in the management game is to pursue sectional interests – of management as a whole or (functional and product) divisions within management – while appearing to be fully committed to the organization as a whole – for example, by mediating between, or synergizing, the claims or contributions of diverse social groups (Pfeffer, 1981).

REFERENCES

Alvesson, M. (1994) Critical Theory and consumer marketing. *Scandinavian Journal of Management*. 10(3): 219–313.
Alvesson, M. (2003) Critical organization studies. In B. Czarniawska and G. Sevon (eds), *Nordic Lights*. Malmš: Liber/Oslo: Abstrakt.
Alvesson, M. and Billing, Y.D. (1997) *Understanding Gender and Organization*. London: Sage.
Alvesson, M. and Deetz, S. (2000) *Doing Critical Management Research*. London: Sage.
Alvesson, M. and Willmott, H. (1996) *Making Sense of Management: A Critical Analysis*. London: Sage.
Anthony, P. (1977) *The Ideology of Work*. London: Tavistock.
Anthony, P. (1986) *The Foundations of Management*. London: Tavistock
Armstrong, P. (1986) Management control strategies and inter-professional competition: the cases of accountancy and personnel management. In D. Knights and H.C. Willmott (eds), *Managing the Labour Process*. Aldershot: Gower.
Bendix, R. (1956) *Work and Authority in Industry*. New York: Wiley.
Bernstein, R.J. (1976) *The Restructuring of Social and Political Theory*. Oxford: Blackwell.
Bernstein, R.J. (1994) Foucault: critique as a philosophical ethos. In M. Kelly (ed.), *Critique and Power: Recasting the Foucault/Habermas Debate*. Cambridge, MA: MIT Press.
Bubner, R. (1982) Habermas' concept of Critical Theory. In J.B. Thompson and D. Held (eds), *Habermas, Critical Debates*. London: Macmillan.
Burrell, G. and Morgan, G. (1979) *Sociological Paradigms and Organizational Analysis*. London: Heinemann.
Calás, M. and Smircich, L. (1996) From the woman's point of view: Feminist approaches to organization studies. In S. Clegg, C. Hardy and W. Nord (eds), *Handbook of Organization Studies*. London: Sage.
Carter, P. and Jackson, N. (1987) Management, myth and metatheory: from scarcity to postscarcity. *International Studies of Management and Organization*. 17(3): 64–89.
Chalmers, L. (2001) *Marketing Masculinities: Gender and Management Politics in Marketing Work*. Westport, CT: Greenwood Press.
Child, J. (1969) *British Management Thought*. London: Allen & Unwin.

Deetz, S. (1992) *Democracy in an Age of Corporate Colonization: Developments in Communication and the Politics of Everyday Life.* Albany: State University of New York Press.

Egri, C. and Frost, P.J. (1989) Threats to innovation; roadblocks to implementation: the politics of the productive process. In M. Jackson, M.P. Keys and S. Cropper (eds), *Operational Research and the Social Sciences.* New York: Plenum.

Forester, J. (1985) Critical Theory and planning practice. In J. Forester (ed.), *Critical Theory and Public Life.* Cambridge, MA: MIT Press.

Forester, J. (1989) *Planning in the Face of Power.* Berkeley: University of California Press.

Foucault, M. (1980) *Power/Knowledge.* New York: Pantheon.

Foucault, M. (1988) The ethic of care for the self as an ethic of freedom. In J. Bernauer and D. Rasmussen (eds), *The Final Foucault.* Boston, MA: MIT Press.

Foucault, M. (1994) The art of telling the truth. In M. Kelly (ed.), *Critique and Power: Recasting the Foucault/Habermas Debate.* Cambridge, MA: MIT Press.

Fournier, V. and Grey, C. (2000) At the critical moment: conditions and prospects for Critical Management Studies. *Human Relations.* 53(1): 5–32.

Habermas, J. (1974) *Theory and Practice.* London: Heinemann.

Habermas, J. (1984) *The Theory of Communicative Action, Vol. I: Reason and the Rationalization of Society.* Cambridge: Polity Press.

Horkheimer, M. (1976 [1937]) Traditional and Critical Theory. In P. Connerton (ed.), *Critical Sociology.* Harmondsworth: Penguin.

Horkheimer, M. (1989) The state of contemporary social philosophy and the tasks of the Institute for Social Research. In S.E. Bronner and D.M. Kellner (eds), *Critical Theory and Society.* London: Routledge.

Jackall, R. (1988) *Moral Mazes: The World of Corporate Managers.* Oxford: Oxford University Press.

Kelly, M. (ed.) (1994) *Critique and Power: Recasting the Foucault/Habermas Debate.* Cambridge, MA: MIT Press.

Knights, D. and Murray, F. (1994) *Managers Divided.* London: Wiley.

Knights, D. and Willmott, H.C. (eds) (1986) *Managing the Labour Process.* Aldershot: Gower.

Knights, D. and Willmott, H.C. (1999) *Management Lives: Power and Identity in Work Organizations.* London: Sage.

Lasch, C. (1978) *The Culture of Narcissism.* New York: Norton.

Lasch, C. (1984) *The Minimal Self.* London: Picador.

MacIntyre, A. (1981) *After Virtue.* London: Duckworth.

Marshall, J. (1984) *Women Managers: Travellers in a Male World.* Chichester: Wiley.

Nord, W. and Jermier, J. (1992) Critical social science for managers? Promising and perverse possibilities. In M. Alvesson and H. Willmott (eds), *Critical Management Studies.* London: Sage.

Parker, M. (2002) *Against Management.* Oxford: Polity.

Pfeffer, J. (1981) Management as symbolic action: the creation and maintenance of organizational paradigms. In L.L. Cummings and B.M. Staw (eds), *Research in Organizational Behavior,* Vol. 3. Greenwich, CT: JAI Press.

Pfeffer, J. and Salancik, G.R. (1978) *The External Control of Organizations: A Resource Dependence Perspective.* New York: Harper & Row.

Pollay, R.W. (1986) The distorted mirror: reflections on the unintended consequences of advertising. *Journal of Marketing.* 50 (April): 18–36.

Prasad, A. (ed.) (2003) *Postcolonial Theory and Organizational Analysis: A Critical Engagement.* New York: Palgrave.

Prasad, P. (1997) The protestant ethic and the myth of the frontier: cultural imprints, organizational structuring and workplace diversity. In P. Prasad et al. (eds) *Managing the Organizational Melting Pot.* Thousand Oaks, CA: Sage.

Reed, M. (1989) *The Sociology of Management*. Hemel Hempstead: Harvester Wheatsheaf.

Sennett, R. (1998) *The Corrosion of Character: The Personal Consequences of the Work in the New Capitalism*. New York: Norton.

Steffy, B. and Grimes, A. (1992) Personel/organization psychology: a critique of the discipline. In M. Alvesson and H. Willmott (eds), *Critical Management Studies*. London: Sage.

Thomas, R. and Linstead, A. (2002) Losing the plot? Middle managers and identity. *Organization*. 9: 71–93.

Thompson, J.B. (1982) Universal pragmatics. In J.B. Thompson and D. Held (eds), *Habermas: Critical Debates*. London: Macmillan.

Watson, T. (1994) *In Search of Management*. London: Routledge.

Chapter 2

Disciplinary Power, Conflict Suppression and Human Resources Management

Stanley Deetz

Concepts from Critical Theory have been widely used to support studies of social arrangements and practices in work organizations. Many studies have identified systems and practices of unwarranted control and decisional asymmetry and the costs of these for people, organizations and host societies. Other studies have fostered the development of wider and more open participation in the productive codetermination of the future. Much of this work has focused on power, ideology and symbolic/cultural practices (for review see Alvesson and Deetz, 1996). As this volume, as well as others, demonstrates, these studies range in focus from macro to micro and investigate a variety of material and symbolic resources and practices. One central concern has been an understanding of the relations among power, discursive practices and conflict suppression as they relate to the production of individual identity and corporate knowledge. Critical and postmodern scholars have approached these relations in various ways. At other places I have compared and contrasted these approaches (Deetz, 1992, 1996). Here I wish to look more narrowly at the politics of person/personal structured around Foucault's conception of 'disciplinary' power in relation to the theory and practice of human resource management

Understanding the relations among power, discursive practices and conflict suppression requires a relatively new conception of political processes of everyday life (see Deetz, 1992). The political battles of the last several years, in at least the Western world, can be seen as waged over the content of the subjective world not just its expression and subsequent impact on decisions. Such conflicts, however, often remain obscured and misrecognized. As Baudrillard (1975) argued, the issues cannot be attributed to economic distributions and speaking opportunities within the existing mode of representing interests, but the fight must be against the monopoly of the 'code' itself. With such a view, scholars' concerns have shifted to examining alternative codes. Such analyses have demonstrated that 'free' and autonomous expressions often suppress alternative representations and thus hide the monopoly of existing codes.

Traditional critical analyses have shown that work organizations have often been guilty of economic exploitation. Various reproduced ideologies can make it difficult to see and discuss such exploitations. But decisional asymmetry can also be seen as subtle, arbitrary, power-laden manners of world, self and other constitution requiring no structure of exploitation nor ideological cover. With such a conceptual shift, contemporary critical analyses more often focus on systems that develop each subject's active role in producing and reproducing domination. Fostering more democratic communication in these terms must look to the formation of knowledge, experience and identity, rather than merely their expression. The development of the conceptual shift to a politics of meaning and identity construction, however, is often limited through linguistic and social forces, including the borrowing of most conceptions of power, domination, freedom and democracy from political theories concerned with the relation of the individual to the modern state. This can be seen in 'negotiated order' theories, for example. In most of these conceptions the free agent, knowledge and decision-making are based on eighteenth-century conceptions of the individual and reason, views which both help sustain managerial domination in corporations and hamper the development of alternatives.

Modern human resources management (HRM) is clearly in the culture and meaning business, its focus is on the production of a specific type of human being with specific self-conceptions and feelings. And, equally importantly, much of the work promotes concepts of the person that make the critical investigation of the person and his or her experience less likely and seeming necessary. The very notions of free contract, social relations and agency as well as personal identity as a manager, secretary, or worker that are core to HRM can be seen as corporate productions and reproductions needing investigation (Jacques, 1996).

Laclau and Mouffe summarized the three assumptions regarding people that are fundamental to contemporary social relations: 'the view of the subject as an agent both rational and transparent to itself; the supposed unity and homogeneity of the ensemble of its positions; and the conception of the subject as origin and basis of social relations' (1985: 115). These are clearly manifest in contemporary organizations. The first is necessary for the illusion of freedom that allows the subject to be conceptualized as freely subordinating him/herself in the social contract of the corporation and having choices based on self-interests there. The second sets out the hope of a well-integrated work environment where the work relations fit without conflict into other institutions and coexist with the democratic processes and the basis for consensual decision-making and mutual understanding. And finally, the individual is conceptualized as the fundamental site of meaning production choosing specific relations with others, hence the personal itself is protected from the examination necessary if it were seen as an arbitrary historical social production resulting from certain social arrangements. Each of these conceptions is misleading and reproductive of forms of domination. As an outcome of such assumptions, HRM relies on the rationality of the work contract for justification of control over people but functions primarily to manage the extra-rational requirements of the person to achieve the efforts and commitments not specified in the work contract while at the same time hiding these extra-rational activities from political analysis (see Baldamus, 1961).

The most common conceptions of the human character and the communication process are thus 'imaginary', that is, they are constructed as real within particular social/historical systems of domination. And corporate processes like those organized as HRM actively support and reproduce these images. If we understand this imaginary nature, we can displace the constructed-as-presumed-free subject as centre and origin of meaning and better understand how the subject is produced. And if discourse itself is understood as power-laden rather than neutral and transparent, we can better reveal the sites of power deployment and concealment. This chapter will provide a reconception of power in regard to cultural formations, an analysis of possible hidden antagonisms in discourse and the manner of the suppression of conflict among them, and a description of the role of organizational analysis in the recovery of antagonism and member agency.

CORPORATIONS AS COMPLEX POLITICAL SITES

Concern with the representation of interests in corporations has provided useful initial conceptions for examining the politics of corporate practices. Critical Theory's concern with interest representation is an essential step towards a more basic conception possible from recent works. From a Critical Theory perspective, organizational processes and products fulfil certain human needs, hopes and wants. These together can be described as the interests or 'stake' that various parties (managers, workers, consumers, suppliers and the wider society) have in the organization (Deetz, 1995). Beyond these work-related distinctions, interest differences can often be demonstrated in groups divided by gender, ethnic and racial considerations.

The advantages given to management arise from neither rational nor open consensual value foundations, nor are they simply acquired through management's own strategic attempts. They are produced historically and actively reproduced through discursive practices in corporations themselves. Such discursive practices range from the choice of specific vocabularies producing and distinguishing people and events in specific ways to telling stories and giving instruction and orders. Even the conception, practices and legal standing of 'ownership', which is often used to justify specific systems of control, is not 'natural' but an outcome of specific historical processes.

The managerial advantages and prerogative can be seen as taking place through historically produced, economic-based structures *and* systems of discursive monopoly – domination of the 'code' and speaking opportunities. In modern corporations such an advantage is not so much conceptualized as a right or as legitimate but is unproblematically reproduced in routines and discourses. As such this privilege is treated as normal, natural and neutral. The presumed neutrality makes understanding the political nature of organizations more difficult. Order, efficiency and effectiveness as values aid the reproduction of advantages already vested in an organizational form. Concepts of organizational effectiveness tend to hide possible discussion of whose goals should be sought and how much each goal should count.

Critical Theorists have argued that workers and the general society have interests in work that are only partially and indirectly shared by management and owners. These include the quality of the work experience and work environment, mental health and safety, the skill and intellectual development of the worker, the carryover of thinking patterns and modes of action to social and political life, and the production of personal and social identity (Alvesson, 1987). Organizational life could be an explicit site of political struggle as different groups openly develop and try to realize their own interests but the conflicts there are often routinized, evoke standard mechanisms for resolution, and reproduce presumed natural tensions (e.g., between workers and management). The essential politics thus become invisible.

The work site could be considered a polysemic environment where the production of the individual or group interests could itself be seen as an end product (or temporary resting place) in a basic conflictual process defining personal and group identity and the development and articulation of interests. But such potential conflicts are often suppressed in normalization of organizational knowledge, identity formation and decisional practices aided by human resource professionals. The production of the conflicts that exist and the lack of other equally plausible ones more signify a type of discursive closure than ideology or false consciousness. The possible development of alternative interests and the subsequent tension between them is often suppressed in organizational practices and discourse through representational marginalization, reduction of alternative interests to economic costs, socialization of members, and the shift of responsibility to the individual. The human resources division of organizations plays a key role within these moves.

Under such conditions what might be accepted as legitimate power differences are best represented as a system of domination, since the empirical manifestation is that of free consent but yet structures are reproduced which work against competitive practices and fulfilment of the variety of interests. The human interior is itself a construction where under different historical processes and forms of discourse, wants and preferences would be different. With such a view, what is taken as legitimate consensual processes are more often evidence of domination and suppressed conflict than of free choice and agreement. Compliance and consent are often a result of clear member understanding of the material conditions for their success but in systems contrived against them. As Przeworski (1980) and DuGay (1997) argued, the desire to live well and to engage in a consumption-based society provides pressure towards active consenting participation in the corporate system.

The concern expressed here is not just managerial domination, but the corporate development of the obedient, normalized mind and body which is held up against equally legitimate but unrealized alternatives. The critical interest is in describing the ways by which both managers and workers become obedient in their own structurally prescribed manner (Burrell, 1988: 227). While managers and sometimes owners gain in these structures, the structures are not simply or directly owing to those gains. Rather it is a set of practices and routines which constitute identities and experiences and in doing so provide unproblematic asymmetries, privileged knowledge and expertise located in some and not others, and in doing so instantiate inclusions and exclusions in decisional processes (Knights and Willmott, 1985).

Critical research is to reclaim conflicting experiences through describing the practices and routines by which alternatives are disregarded or rendered invisible. The understanding of the processes by which value conflicts become suppressed and certain forms of reasoning and interests become privileged requires an investigation into the politics of meaning, language and personal identity.

THE DISCURSIVE POLITICS OF IDENTITY

The politics of identity and identity representation is the deepest and most suppressed struggle in the workplace and, hence, the 'site' where domination and responsive agency are most difficult to unravel. Conceptions that place experience within individuals, present language as a neutral transparent representation, and treat communication as if it were simply a transmission process make it difficult to carefully describe these processes. The position here differs greatly from this. As recent social theory has shown, conceptualizing the individual as the original site of meaning and decisional choices is misleading. Rather, each individual exists with produced identities placed in an already meaningful world. The psychological subject with experiences and the presumed objective world to be described arise out of a set of discursive and non-discursive practices which constitute the subject and produce a world of distinguished objects (Knights and Willmott, 1989). Central to understanding the workplace is an understanding of these practices. Prior to any analysis focusing on managers, workers or women and their various interests and reasoning processes is a concern with how these classifications and identities come to exist at all and how actors themselves are enticed to embrace them and use them as personal resources (see Holmer-Nadesan, 1996, 1997). This leads further to questions regarding how they are reproduced as meaningful, how they are utilized in producing certain types of conflicts and their resolutions, and how they preclude other interests and conflicts within and among the various groupings.

With identities come interests and relations with other identities, but the first identities are not fixed but are themselves arbitrary social productions. Social groupings and their interests, types of rationality, and the concept of profit are social productions. Each is produced as distinguished from something else. The questions posed for Critical Theory are thus not how do these things exist, have power, or explain organizational behaviour, but rather how do they come to exist, coexist and interrelate in the production and reproduction of corporate organizations and work in the process of potential inner and outer colonization?

Several questions arise that are of concern. Which personal/relational identities are produced in the modern corporation? How are these identities specified with particular forms of interests and types of knowledge? How are these identities discursively and non-discursively inscribed, interrelated and reproduced? How do such identities become naturalized and reified so as to be taken for granted and suppress the conflict with potential competing identities? How do activities within HRM contribute to these processes?

POWER, IDENTITY AND CONTROL

The task of the critical scholar rests in developing a vocabulary so that we, and the wider society, may better understand these processes, discuss them critically, and learn new ways of thinking and acting together (Alvesson and Deetz, 2000; Deetz, 1992). The questions posed here already initiate a new vocabulary, and require relative new ways of thinking and talking about organizations for their answer. Most centrally, as scholars following Foucault have argued, concepts of power and control need to be reconsidered if we are to open new and more democratic discussions in organizations.

In Western societies few topics have commanded as much critical attention as the twin issues of freedom and the exercise of power. Foucault (1980b), perhaps better than anyone else, has demonstrated that it is frequently because of these discussions rather than an inattention to power that we have failed to understand its presence and manners of deployment. So too in corporate organizations the attention to inter-group conflict, coalitions, regulations and rights have often led us further from understanding power and control. Most conceptions and analyses of power in organizations have been derived from political scientists. Each of these conceptions was primarily designed to discuss power in relation to the influence different people or groups have in political processes or the rights of individuals in opposition to possible state domination. This I believe to be true in the Critical Theory tradition. Discussions of leadership, coalition formation, special interests, and authority in corporations are often only distinguished from similar 'public' process by scale and the special applicable rights. Similarly, discussions of loyalty and collective priorities closely parallel conceptions developed for the relation to the state.

Foucault has shown how each of these conceptions is tied to sovereign rights as expanded in a 'juridico' discourse. Since power is conceived as restrictive of individual freedom, the question 'by what right or necessity is the rule made?' serves as a fundamental issue for the exercise of power. This was the case, for example, in Weber's conception of 'Herrschaft' (by what authority or rule) and 'Dominium' (the state of achieving supremacy). The legitimacy of governance of this sort required specific conceptions of human beings such as those suggested by Laclau and Mouffe (1985). But governance may be achieved by other means also.

Following Foucault (1980b), disciplinary power rather than sovereign power is of utmost significance. The state or central administration still has much power but it is limited if only because power in its 'sovereign' form is experienced today as restriction and oppression. In corporations a kind of sovereign power exists and can be described as parallel in character to that of the state. But attention to this can be misleading and often conceals more pervasive and subtle procedures of power and the sites of its deployment. As seen in relation to HRM, in modern corporations control and influence are dispersed into norms and standard practices as products of moral, medical, sexual and psychological regulation – Foucault's disciplinary power. Foucault's conception of disciplinary power allows a description of the enabling as well as constraining constitutive capacity identified as power.

Disciplinary power resides in every perception, every judgement, every act. In its positive sense it enables and makes possible, and negatively it excludes and marginalizes. Rather than analysing power in the organization as if it were a sovereign state, the conception of power has to be reformed to account for this more massive and invisible structure of control. Administration has to be seen in regard to order and discipline if its power is to be understood.

Disciplinary power for Foucault is omnipresent as it is manifest and produced in each moment. Power is thus not dispersed in modern society to citizens who argue and vote, but spreads out through lines of conformity, commonsense observations, and determinations of propriety. Disciplinary power is evidenced in the production of a normalized body and response which is produced, reproduced and supported by arrangements of the material world which result in coordination and consent, not only regarding how the world is but how it should be. The focus on order with accompanying surveillance and education shifts control away from the explicit exercise of power through force and coercion and places it in the routine practices of everyday life. What is of interest then is not so much the powerlessness of the state, which presumably represents the will of the people, but the organization of these innumerable sites of power through other institutions and the complicity of the state in these hidden power relations.

Disciplinary power has been present in corporations from their outset. Perhaps the clearest case is the development of the assembly line. The assembly line transformed an explicit authority relation between the worker and supervisor into a partially hidden one. Rather than the supervisor having to tell the worker how hard or fast to work and dealing with the question, 'by what right?', the movement in the line already accomplished it. In doing so the functional relation changed. This can be seen in Edwards' (1979) conception of the assembly line in terms of 'technical control'. The assembly line extended and enabled a particular worker capacity; instead of being restrictive of the worker, it facilitated an accomplishment. The assembly line, like the new organization, was a new tool extending collective bodies' capacity to produce. But it was also a new kind of tool. Rather than being subjugated to the body's rule, it subjugated the body into an extension of itself – a docile, useful body. Like any technology, it 'subjects' the individual in a particular way. While there was still no doubt that authority and explicit power kept the worker at the line and that it was the company's decision to implement work in this way, the relation to the supervisory could also change. Through training the worker could keep up with the line with less effort, thus the supervisor could be on the side of the worker in the worker's complicity with the systems that controlled him or her. The management interest in suppressing and routinizing conflict could be realized often with the full involvement of the worker. While new forms of resistance are made possible, they are also made less likely by the complicity and new form of surveillance. Piece-rate payments on up through the various worker participation programmes merely extend this basic model (Burawoy, 1979). Systems such as these do not lend themselves well to ideological criticism. They are not filled with false needs or hidden values. Rather it is the truth and naturalness of the domination, the *free* acceptance, that make it so powerful.

DISCIPLINE AND IDENTITY

The interest here is in how discipline occurs in the discursive practices of specific work environments. The focus is on how the individual comes to have a determinate identity at work with particular experiences. Discursive practices include:

1   The organizational vocabulary which involves the linguistic constitution of identities through systems of distinctions.

2   The presence of specific subject positions in organizational talk that the individual takes on as his or her own.

3 Subject positions embedded in institutional structures and practices that
   further provide the point of view from which the individual has experiences.

Language as a system of distinction

The most common misleading conception of language is that it represents an
absent, to-be-recalled, object. Rather language is primarily constitutive rather
than representational. The character of the object and expression arise
together. As a system, language holds forth the historically developed dimensions of interests – the attributes of concern or the lines along which things of
the world will be distinguished. Language holds the possible ways we will
engage in the world and produce objects with particular characteristics. Thus
when we consider language from a political point of view within organizations, the interest is not primarily in how different groups use language to
accomplish goals, the rationality in language usage, nor how the profit motive
influences language use. The concern is with the dimensions utilized to produce classifications and thus produce groups and their relations. And further,
we must understand how representational conceptions of language themselves aid in making classification and identity production appear neutral and
based in natural divisions rather than choices with distinct political effect.
    Every linguistic system, because it is a system of distinction, puts into
place certain kinds of social relations and values – that is, certain things that
are worthy of being distinguished from other things – and puts into play the
attributes that will be utilized to make that distinction. For example, whenever we distinguish between men and women, in using a description that
notes gender, we claim that distinction along the line of gender is important
and valuable to this society and that particular attributes can be used to
make that distinction (Hollway, 1984). Both the choice of distinction based
on gender and the choice of attributes are arbitrary. They are chosen in choosing
the signifying system. The words 'man' or 'woman' does not simply represent something real out there. It puts into play a way of paying attention to
the 'out there'. The employment is not neutral. The distinction performs a
production of identity for the subject as a woman or man and of the persons
as objects with certain rights and characteristics. As the chain of signifiers
webs out, the female can be upheld as a mother in a kinship system, a wife in
a marital relation, and so forth. In each case, each individual so constituted is
both advantaged and disadvantaged in the way institutional arrangements
specify opportunities and constraints. But the distinction remains arbitrary.
The signifiers are arbitrary in the sense that at the next moment, distinction
on the basis of gender can be overlooked, irrelevant, or difficult and in the
sense that the system of relations among signifiers could be different.
    To many it appears self-evident that men and women are different and
that therefore the distinction is important. But such 'self-evidence' guides

attention away from the political consequences of making the distinction and the choice of sites where it is deployed. Each distinction enters into the play of power in the organization in important and conflicting ways. On the one hand many would wish that the gender distinction would become irrelevant in the place of work so that the identity of people constituted as women, as well as pay and routine treatment practices, would be based on other dimensions of distinction and other constituted identities. Yet rendering gender invisible would exclude the possibility of women organizing and working towards distinct group interests which arise in a gendered society. Thus the distinction socially separates women, marginalizes female experience and provides a unitary identity that denies personal complexity and internal identity conflict. Yet it also provides a ground for resistance and retains a place for conflict of a different sort. The same type of analysis can be applied to each identity produced in the corporation. The double effect of representational practices is a key issue in any emancipatory project in corporations. First we must understand the systemic nature of distinction and then move to develop the complexities of alternative practices within the discursive system.

Gender distinction is only one of many critical distinctions in the workplace, for example, worker/manager, facts/opinions, private/public information, rational/irrational, and expert/non-expert. Understanding the importance of the gender issue reminds us of the multitude of classificatory activities having political implications and protected by their seeming self-evidence and other-worldliness. Further, each of these becomes interwoven in a complex of signifiers, for example, gender becomes tied to forms of understanding and knowledge, private and public becomes critical to various forms of expertise and proprietary information. Moreover, occupational classification is only one of many signifying practices that has significance for gender politics, such as stories, jokes and dress codes – each implements distinctions and a chain of signifiers. Far less has been done about these things than about gender and occupational classification. If people could work back through the systems of distinctions they implement, they would often find a gap between what they reflectively think and feel and what they unwittingly express. The point is not to determine what they 'really' or freely think. But recalling the arbitrariness of such constructions is a step in understanding the plurality of equally plausible subject articulations momentarily out of the reach of proclaimed 'naturalness and self-evidence'. It is this self-evidence and presumed transparency of language that must be given up to understand power and the politics of experience.

The production of subject identity

The individual being born into an ongoing system, acculturated into it, and finally selected into a work organization, largely takes on socially available identities. While freedom and agency may be possible, the individual's capacity to be articulate about the interlaced systems and their alternatives is usually fairly limited (Giddens, 1991). More often active consent to try to fit in to acquire choices within systems exceeds the capacity to choose systems (Willis, 1977). The social attempt actively to suppress conflict reduces the moments when choice might be perceived. With the passive acceptance of existing systems and one's own identity in it come unobtrusive social and organizational control and active compliance.

Direct forms of domination or control are unnecessary to the extent that the individual takes the imaginary construction of self as if it were real. The individual feels relatively free and in control. But, as Weedon suggested,

> The crucial point...is that in taking on a subject position, the individual assumes that she is the author of the ideology or discourse which she is speaking. She speaks or thinks as if she were in control of meaning. She 'imagines' that she is the type of subject which humanism proposes – rational, unified, the source rather than the effect of language. It is the imaginary quality of the individual's identification with a subject position which gives it so much psychological and emotional force. (Weedon, 1987: 31)

The consideration of alternative meanings and alternative subjectivities poses a threat to the individual's claimed identity, thus an individual may reject the possibility of freedom that still resides. The individual may protect the constructions as natural and one's own even though they are not, and reject alternatives as mere constructions and potentially unnatural and ironically politically motivated (see Deetz, 1998; Knights and Willmott, 1985, 1989). The first political act is forgotten as attention is paid to the second. As such, the individual is not simply identifying with those in power; that power is the subject.

The subject as mediated through language is always produced. There is no place out of the formation to claim an independent subject. The individual experiences a particular world, one that is the product of socially inscribed values and distinctions like the subject itself. Only on the basis of this does the individual claim personal beliefs or values or come to share them with others. The possible subjectivities are a particular way of being in the world, a social sharing prior to any individual taking it on as his/her own. Systems of thought and expression contain embedded values that constitute a particular experience through the making of distinction and relations through perception. The very ordinariness of common sense hides implicit valuational structure of perceptual experience. Each discourse and attended technology constitutes ways of knowing the world, privileges certain notions of what is real, and posits personal identities. Specific discourses posit specific subjects, have an epistemology, and structure value choices. Further these are embedded in material institutions beyond linguistic discourse.

Institutions as discursive practices

Everyday life is filled with institutional artefacts, routines and standard practices. Each implements values and establishes a subject point of view. Institutional practices are concretized (sometimes literally) in the construction of buildings, the laying of sidewalks, the writing of legal codes, the placement of postings and signs, the development and implementation of technologies, and the development of stories, jokes and vocabularies. Cultural researchers have long noted the presence of such features. Unfortunately, they are often treated as expressive of the individual or culture and in so doing their constitution of the subject and world is lost. Institutional forms are textual, they are human creations which, like language, position a subject and direct the construction of particular experiences with particular conflicts and opportunities for alternative perceptions.

The relation among institutional arrangements produces a complex subject, a subject who is at once dispersed among many and competing institutions and unified as an integrated identity across inter-relatable institutions. The desire for or expectation of autonomy in certain institutions can create dependency in others. For example, to the extent that freedom and the pursuit of happiness are institutionally inscribed as a leisure activity outside of work, dependency and control become acceptable and even necessary characteristics of the place of work towards a greater promise of leisure. The worker may demand greater work, presumably for his or her own interest. Not only across institutions but the modern workplace itself evidences such dispersion and provides a set of practices that unify, thus suppress, the potential conflicts. The very complexity frequently hides the one-sidedness of the matrix and stops exploration of possible identities that would be constituted in different institutional arrangements. The task of working out these relationships at any particular corporate site or for the more general corporate experience is great. The subject is subject to a range of institutional and discursive practices, some of which conflict. There is never one linguistic expression in one institutional arrangement but many.

HUMAN RESOURCES AND CONTROL OF
IDENTITY PRODUCTION

If the subject and the subject's world are an arbitrary production remarkably integrated and appearing necessary and unproblematic, we must account for its accomplishment, the complexity of the formation, and the political gains and losses in particular formations. Clearly this production is not in any simple sense intentional or singular in origin. The subject and subject's world result from a complex array of intentional activities, institutional practices retained from a past, accidents and unintended consequences. Invading and unravelling the tangle can be accomplished from many angles. Understanding the function of HRM elucidates key portions of this in contemporary organizations.

To a large extent the conceptional development of HRM parallels what Foucault describes as the move from sovereign to disciplinary power. Two portions of this are significant. HRM was to provide a knowledge-based system of managing to replace an authority-based one. And, HRM was to provide orderly scientific knowledge to replace common sense. Thus power passes from based in position to knowledge, and the knowledge to be preferred comes from professionals. HRM thus became a system standing alongside managers and other employees disciplining both. And the content of HRM knowledge increasingly focused on the management of the employees' insides – their values, commitment and motivation – and less on the supervision of their behaviour (Kochan et al., 1986).

Of course this characterization highlights an overall thrust at the expense of the complexity of HRM. HRM did not arrive on the scene full blown and intact. Its origins were multiple, often reactive and ad hoc (Guest, 1987; Niven, 1967). Often its issues are defined so broadly as to encompass all of organizational behaviour and much of management itself (see Lewin et al., 1997). And clearly, HRM differs as it is developed in different industries and cultural settings (see Begin, 1997). But as Townley (1993) argued, what makes all of these diverse understandings of the same thing, rather than about different things, is its 'functionalist' orientation:

> In HRM, connotations of goal-directed activity, inputs and outputs, stability, adaptability, and systems maintenance predominate. From this perspective HRM is the black box of production, where organizational inputs – employees – are selected, appraised, trained, developed and remunerated to deliver the required output of labor (Townley, 1993: 518)

Even where issues of the quality of the life of workers are clearly added to this, the conception of the functional maintenance of systems is expanded but rarely changed (Begin, 1997; Legge, 1998). Clearly, the focus on resource management is based on 'creativity in acquiring, using and creating resources' (Constantin and Lusch, 1994). To list people as a 'resource' is a particular world understanding that creates positive husbandry of employees and configures their worth functionally. Whether HRM is conducted in US companies or elsewhere, it functions to advance a kind of 'American' dream of personal growth, increased opportunities and entrepreneurial individualism (Guest, 1990: 390).

Thus, the type of systems functionalism advanced by HRM is not a dehumanizing mechanical one achieved through explicit control, but a specific form of humanizing largely dependent on managed will and unobtrusive controls – i.e., discipline. Through HRM, the willing assent of employees is engineered through the production of the normalcy of specific beliefs and practices. Rather than visible control by elites, HRM professionals become 'organic intellectuals' (in Gramsci's [1971] sense), producing a variety of cultural forms that express and shape values, actions and meanings, and reproduce hidden forms of domination. Some of the outcomes are intentional and many others are important consequences without self-conscious intent.

The site of HRM's discipline is the myriad everyday institutional activities and experiences that culminated in 'common sense', thus hiding the choices made, and 'mystified' the interests of dominant groups. Dominant group definitions of reality, norms and standards appear as normal rather than political and contestable. HRM professionals are 'symbolic elites' (in Bourdieu's [1977] sense) defining the preferred representational systems in the organization. When Foucault discusses discipline he develops psychiatrists, doctors and wardens as controllers of discourse. Their definitions of deviance and normalcy can be seen as expressions of power that often arbitrarily support certain ways of life as normal and others as pathological. The preferenced knowledge of HRM functions in this same way.

In the modern organization, disciplinary power exists largely in the new 'social technologies of control'. HRM experts and specialists operate to create '*normal*ized' knowledge, operating procedures, and methods of inquiry, and to suppress competitive practices. Like Gramsci's (1971) organic intellectuals, in the strongest cases the outcome of their activities is a hegemonic social cohesion lacking the conflicts and differences that characterize an open world context. But unlike Gramsci's conception, in contemporary organizations the effect is neither simply coherent nor primarily accomplished through values and ideological consent. Foucault (1980a) usefully reconceptualizes hegemony as a free-floating set of conflicts and incompatibilities but which yet maintain asymmetrical relations. Power relations arise out of aims, objectives and strategies but there is no simple key to determing the network of power.

For example, no management group can control the actions let alone the thoughts of other groups. The presence of fear (warranted or not), assumptions of knowledge differences, principles of least effort, wanting rewards, and so forth must be provided by the controlled groups. However, these are not usually knowingly so, and such things are not formed outside of specific power relations which are often supported by other institutions. The explicit and unilateral display of authority more often denotes the breakdown of power relations rather than the presence of them. It is the last resort of normal power relations.

Another key aspect of Foucault's conception of disciplinary power relevant to understanding the function of HRM is in the presence of new forms of surveillance. While the worker was always watched, disciplinary control allows a new form of surveillance, self-surveillance. Self-surveillance uses norms backed by 'experts' for areas previously in the 'amateur' realm.

Foucault (1977) developed Bentham's 'panoptic' prison design as the root vision of this new self-surveillance. In Bentham's design a single guard house stood with a view into each cell but the prisoner could never tell when he or she was being watched. The surveillance, hence, could be more complete than from any number of guards walking the cell block; the prisoner imagined being watched constantly. Certainly this is a feeling enforced in the modern organization, particularly at the managerial levels. Whether or not it is true, the employee can never tell who might use what against him or her or when a statement will come back to cause their own demise. And the wider the group participating in decision-making, the fewer people who are safe confidants. Worker participation programmes, for example, can move the work group from interest solidarity to member self-surveillance. No cohort in resistance exists when everyone/anyone can be a member of the 'management team'. The implicit lawyer at the side censors discussion today as well as the fear of eternal damnation did in a past time. In such a configuration, managers are not simply controllers but are controlled as much as any other group.

The human resources specialist and human resources management practices provide a special type of elite or expert in the contemporary organizations. Gradually industrial and occupational psychologists have become more sensitive to the constructed and relational nature of identity and its relation to HRM (Hollway, 1991; Legge, 1995; Rose, 1990; Townley, 1993). As Townley argued, HRM,

> constitutes a discipline and a discourse, which organizes an analytical space – the indeterminacy between promise and performance. HRM serves to render organizations and their participants calculable arenas, offering, through a variety of technologies, the means by which activities and individuals become knowable and governable. (1993: 526)

Core to the human resources function is to provide and police the vocabularies of attention and division in the workplace. This includes partitioning the organization into functions, ranking, differential pay and job classification. To the extent that both members and work processes are produced in specifiable ways through processes of distinction, skill inventories, performance appraisal systems and various other assessments and measurement forms become central (Townley, 1993). Rose (1990; Miller and Rose, 1995) shows the importance of psychology as a discourse in 'dividing' individuals and rendering them inscribable and calculable. The complex history enabling psychological discourse to arise in this way is beyond the scope of this chapter, but the costs from it to the possibility of open democratic participation are clear. The potential attention to processes of person and work construction often become eclipsed by the attempt to conform and accomplish the ascription well. The implicit values and hierarchies become reified and suppress potential discussions and conflicts.

The individual's identity in this discourse becomes connected to the vocabulary and divisions of the work function in the organization. The member's attributes are rewritten and assessed in terms of the attributes of the job (Hollway, 1991). As such, 'desirable' personal attributes can be defined and measured. The produced individual is now open to examination and comparison to others. Selective recruitment, training, evaluations and rewards are rendered both possible and seemingly objective. As Holmer-Nadesan (1997) showed, 'personality testing' is both a core process and illuminating exemplar in the activities of governing the individual and his or her experience.

The complicity of humanistic, cognitive and behavioural psychology in these processes should not be underestimated. Psychology has provided the study of the individual, especially the prediction and control of the individual. Fostered by the massive research support of the military and professional drive of therapy, it has been the ideal provider of the tools of the new 'discipline' of corporations. The prospect of a well-integrated worker appropriately matched to the job, and the job to the individual, bespoke of the harmony of managerial hope. And it also provided the motives and confidence of self-manipulation by the upwardly mobile employee. The centred-self who knows who he or she is and what he or she wants provides the trustworthy person in control (well subject*ed*/sub*jected*). The testing/training programmes provided the mechanism of correction in systems oriented to control rather than autonomy. And significantly, the human self-understanding as malleable and values as subjective and learned, discredited competing voices and glorified the secular and modern. The 'helping profession' could define healthiness based on social integration and lack of personal conflict, disqualifying radical voices and the fragmentation within and without. Adjustment and retooling could put problems within the person or at least the solutions to them within the person. Both the individual and corporation could be seen as gaining at once. The corporation is active in the production of unitary personal identity armed with a science of the person. And all this is done in the realm of a value-neutral social research, a discipline at its best.

The vocabulary of psychology provides for surveillance of the life of the person beyond explicit words and actions. With the battery of psychological (and chemical) tests – experts in attitudes, culture and bodily fluids – the corporation assesses the purity of one's mind and soul. But more importantly, employees self-assess on the corporation's behalf. The fear of someone seeing beneath the surface to detect a doubt or disloyalty or the fear that one's own gender or belief structure won't cut it, conspire to enforce the norms. The New Age self-manipulations are often far deeper and more extreme than Huxley could have imagined or that any corporation could explicitly require.

As my own empirical research (1998) shows, many individuals are not just governed from the outside. The individual is given a vocabulary for self-management. The individual with the help of this new knowledge can now monitor and act on the self, thereby working to remove defects and acquire capacities to match the qualities of the job. One's own mind, body and soul now become conceptualized as the negative control and constraint rather than the contrived nature of the organization. The now enlightened individual acts on the self on behalf of the company, even turning to the company, and specifically Human Resources, for help in this self-improvement. And in doing so, he or she displays newly prized skills in adaptation and continuous learning.

In several ways the 1960s move of the 'backstage' (the hidden social order negotiation talk, professionalized by Goffman and the ethnomethodologists) into the open, has provided new areas of surveillance, especially this self-surveillance. For example, when common practices are totally taken for granted in traditional societies, they discipline invisibly and completely, but they are also protected from manipulation by this same invisibility. As common practices are revealed as mere social conventions, a measure of freedom is acquired, since they can be enacted or not or even openly negotiated. But as such they may be trained or manipulated. Goffman may have made visible the invisible disciplinary processes of cultural inscribed face work, but in doing so he initiated an industry of 'facial' surveillance and 'facial' production in the form of image management. Similarly in corporations, performance appraisals, which are designed to enable employee input into the formation of objectives, turn to open the personal to public appraisal. Not only is one's work being appraised, but one's hopes, dreams and personal commitments. Most employees learn to bring these under prior assessment by their own private/public eye.

RECOVERING CONFLICT IN DISCOURSE AND AGENCY

The discipline afforded by HRM both enables and disables. The enablements, which are the primary focus of HRM writings, primarily regard the increased control over and productivity of employees and the increased capacity of employees to succeed in the corporate system. The disablements remain relatively invisible. They arise primarily from the reduction of potentially meaningful conflicts. The presence of such conflicts could lead to broader assessment of the organizational system itself, greater creativity and innovation in fulfilling social and economic values in decision-making, greater representation of diverse organizational stakeholders, more employee choice in definitions of success, and greater productive tensions among identities acquired from competing institutions.

Thus far, the focus in this chapter has been on constraints enacted with HRM, but positive programmes towards greater democracy are possible. A positive critical programme needs to display the potential, show how it is constrained, and offer new openings. For example, as argued, an individual is 'subjected' in a variety of discourses and such formations may be contradictory and competitive in particular sites. A woman with a young child and holding a position in a corporation is produced as a subject in both family and corporate discourses. To the extent that these offer conflicting images and behavioural scripts, she will experience considerable tension. This tension can productively display each image as partial and as a construction, but more often the conflict and tension are suppressed by various means of 'articulating' (in the double sense of expressing and providing an interface) the discourses, thus providing an integrated identity to the corporation's advantage (Martin, 1990). The male counterpart, being subjected in different discourses, has different potential tensions with different articulated unities. The complexity and diversity of the individual are channelled to specifiable identities and conflicts within dominant discourses. The political implication of the production of roles and approved, understandable conflicts, is thus overlooked and the individual becomes the site of felt conflict and resolution. The production of the modern corporate form in a period of white, Western, male domination posits a cluster of 'normal' roles, identities and discourses constituting them. The conflicts that males, as well as females and other groups, experience are articulated with the individual but have external origins. HRM works to treat such conflicts as personal defects and suppresses productive tensions rather than investigates or critiques organizational practices (e.g., Martin, 1990).

From a critical standpoint, any hope for an openly formed, responsive agent in the modern corporation arises in the recovery of suppressed conflicts within the organizational site. Identifying the gaps and incompleteness of the produced order is key to this. The free subject cannot be conceptualized as a thinking, choosing or reflecting one. The illusionary 'free' subject as a part of the disciplinary practice must be rejected. But neither is the subject determined by any condition of *necessity* in the disciplinary formation. The subject may be forgetful of the constitutive process and there may be active conditions of concealment, but each is partial and incomplete. The recovery of the subject as agent is not in recovering the subject as unitary and rational, but as responsive. Responsiveness can be seen as a reclaiming of the processual quality of subjectivity as it is produced in relation to something that is concretely other over and against reification. The concrete 'other' is that which exists prior to reduction to categories and normal scripts. The complexity of the self is dependent on the preservation of the complexity of otherness and the indeterminacy that comes with its demands to be more than that which is already determinant. Agency is not dependent on a newfound internal will, but a recovery of the demand on the outside, of 'otherness'. It is fostered by communicative processes that perpetually recover a space for exceeding personal and systemic restraints and distortions, a communicative practice outlined in Habermas's many works but aimed at the recovery of conflict rather than a new consensus.

In order to describe how disciplinary power is dispersed and organized in particular corporations, the various members, discourses and sites of discourse including but also beyond HRM need to be analysed. Research and professional practices need to show both how conflicts are suppressed and how to make aspects of life and the world contestable again (see Deetz, 1995). Included in this examination would be relative access to speaking forums and information (as equality of opportunity), social relations (a critique of historically derived asymmetries), personal experience (as conflictual rather than unitary), and the claim of the subject matter (a critique of the reduction of the otherness of the external world to any single description).

Laclau and Mouffe (1985) helped accomplish this in their development of the concept of articulatory practices. They argued that the contingent conditions of each experience within totalizing formation allow a distinction between 'elements' and 'moments'. In total domination an element would have no meaning outside its moment of discursive articulation, but while each articulation is of elements in a totalizing relation, it does not exhaust the possibilities of other articulations. In other words the element is always left open to different and further articulations, hence domination is always incomplete. Quoting Laclau and Mouffe:

> Since all identity is relational – even if the system of relations does not reach the point of being fixed as a stable system of differences – since, too, all discourse is subverted by a field of discursivity which overflows it, the transition from 'elements' to 'moments' can never be complete. The status of the 'elements' is that of floating signifiers, incapable of being wholly articulated to a discursive chain. (1985: 113)

This is, of course, not a new claim for the object as a thing-in-itself capable of being described accurately. This relation can be seen as like the relation suggested in Gadamer's (1975) terms, the demand of the subject matter over every determination of it (see Deetz, 1990). The assumption of fixed objects, i.e., naturalization or reification, is the move of control that tries to reduce the 'element' to its moment of articulation. Quoting Laclau and Mouffe further:

> This presence of the contingent in the necessary…manifests itself as symbolization, metaphorization, paradox, which deform and question the literal character of every necessity. Necessity, therefore, exists not under the form of an underlying principle, of a ground, but as an effort of literalization that fixes the differences of a relational system. The necessity of the social [historically defined] is the necessity proper to purely relational identities – as in the linguistic principle of value [Saussure's] – not natural 'necessity' or the necessity of an analytic judgment. (1985: 114)

The possibility of excess or difference presents the possibility of socially determinable antagonisms and a discourse of conflict. The political character and open formation of experience are left a space, a space experienced as conflict and fostered by appropriate analysis. The production of alternative social memories and counternarratives demonstrates the possibility of new articulations of the elements of experience and opens them to a new political understanding. The open formation of personal identity is dependent on recovered conflict processes.

The presence of a space for conflict does not assure its actualization. In fact, as shown there are active processes of closure often facilitated by HRM which protect current articulations against the possibility of competing ones (Deetz, 1992). Fundamentally we must reclaim a conception of the communicative process powerful enough to give liberatory guidance to communicative practice. A new understanding of HRM could aid in this process. If HRM could be freed from the focus on system integration and the psychological theories of people and human interaction, the space would be open for the development of HRM conceptions focused on the recovery of meaningful conflicts. The recovery of such conflicts allows for forms of human interaction and collaboration focused on new creative articulations of the elements rather than reproduction of past articulations. Central to this is a new understanding of human communication.

The contemporary everyday conceptions of interacting with others through effective communication is conceptually flawed as a basis for more open and democratic organizations. The everyday conception focused attention on the act of self-expression and the processes by which that is transferred to others. With such a view the self is held as fixed and knowable and language and information technologies are rendered invisible. The constitutive conditions of self-production cannot be seen as politically charged. In practice this gives a false sense of the individual as the originator of meaning and leads to self-expressionism and strategic control of others through expressive acts. The stage is set for control of self and control of others, but strategically positioned outside of the illusionary self. The growth, differentiation and progressive individualization of the self require giving up the unitary self and its control fostered by HRM. Only in the development of the 'other' (the outside as concretely different) can the self develop. Otherness can be discovered in seeing present conceptions as partial and incomplete, in recognizing alternative possible determination, and in recognizing complexity and contradictions.

With a new understanding, the point of communication as a social act is to overcome one's fixed subjectivity, one's conceptions, one's strategies, to be opened to the indeterminacy of people and the external environment. Communication in its democratic form is productive rather than reproductive. It produces what self and other can experience, rather than reproducing what either has. Self-expression is misleading not because people don't or should try to express their experiences, but because such expressions are the raw material for the production of something new rather than the product of self interests. The self cannot simply choose to be open for that would presume that it has already determined that which it is to be open to. Rather process subjectivity happens in the responsiveness to the pull from the outside. The recognition of 'the otherness of the other', and the resultant complexity of self in regard to the other, breaks a discursive stoppage by posing questions to any particular conception of self or other. The 'other' exceeds every possible conception of it and in so doing deconstructs any singularity of the self.

'Otherness' is a property of people, but also of things and events. The excess of the element over its articulation represents its pull of otherness. The fundamental otherness suggests that any possible label or conception of self, other, and world is capable of being questioned. Perception, as well as conception, is the end product of a conflict: a struggle between one's fixed identity and conceptual scheme and the excess of the 'other' over that. The remembrance of this struggle leaves each and every attempt to form an object potentially available to be questioned. Otherness in this sense is critical to the formation of self and other. Every interaction thus holds both the possibility of closure or new meaning, either a reproduction to the dominant socially produced subjectivity or responsiveness to the excess of external events over these conceptions. Developing a sense of *care*, as an appreciation of *otherness*, is central to reclaiming a form of democracy appropriate to the modern age. Greater democracy of this sort in organizations can aid organizational innovation and adaptation while enhancing employee and societal self-determination. The ability to reclaim contestation in place of reproducting past solutions enables redecisions based in conditions of the present and shows the possibility of choice even where that existing seems neutral and natural.

REFERENCES

Alvesson, M. (1987) *Organizational Theory and Technocratic Consciousness: Rationality, Ideology and Quality of Work*. New York: de Gruyter.

Alvesson, M. and Deetz, S. (1996) Postmodernism and critical approaches to organizations. In S. Clegg, C. Hardy and W. Nord (eds), *Handbook of Organization Studies*. London: Sage.

Alvesson, M. and Deetz, S. (2000) *Doing Critical Management Research*. London: Sage.

Baldamus, W. (1961) *Efficiency and Effort*. London: Tavistock.

Baudrillard, J. (1975) *The Mirror of Production*, trans. Michal Poster. St Louis: Telos Press.

Begin, J. (1997) *Dynamic Human Resource Systems: Cross National Comparisons*. New York: de Gruyter.

Bourdieu, P. (1977) *Outline of a Theory of Practice*. Cambridge: Cambridge University Press.

Burawoy, M. (1979) *Manufacturing Consent*. Berkeley: University of California Press.

Burrell, G. (1988) Modernism, Post Modernism and organizational analysis 2: The contribution of Michel Foucault. *Organization Studies*. 9: 221–35.

Constantin, J. and Lusch, R. (1994) *Understanding Resource Management*. Oxford, OH: The Planning Forum.

Deetz, S. (1990) Reclaiming the subject matter as a guide to mutual understanding: Effectiveness and ethics in interpersonal interaction. *Communication Quarterly*. 38: 226–43.

Deetz, S. (1992) *Democracy in an Age of Corporate Colonization: Developments in Communication and the Politics of Everyday Life*. Albany: State University of New York Press.

Deetz, S. (1995) *Transforming Communication, Transforming Business: Building Responsive and Responsible Workplaces*. Cresskill, NJ: Hampton Press.

Deetz, S. (1996) Describing differences in approaches to organizational science: Rethinking Burrell and Morgan and their legacy. *Organization Science*. 7: 191–207.

Deetz, S. (1998) Discursive formations, strategized subordination, and self-surveillance: An empirical case. In A. McKinlay and K. Starkey (eds), *Foucault, Management and Organization Theory*. London: Sage.

DuGay, P. (1997) *Production of Culture, Culture of Production*. London: Sage.

Edwards, R. (1979) *Contested Terrain: The Transformation of the Workplace in the Twentieth Century*. New York: Basic Books.

Foucault, M. (1977) *Discipline and Punish*, trans. A. Sheridan. New York: Random House.

Foucault, M. (1980a) *Power/Knowledge: Selected Interviews and Other Writings, 1972–77*, ed. C. Gordon. New York: Pantheon.

Foucault, M. (1980b) *The History of Sexuality*, trans. R. Hurley. New York: Vintage.

Gadamer, H.G. (1975) *Truth and Method*, ed. and trans. G. Barden and J. Cumming. New York: Seabury Press.

Giddens, A. (1991) *Modernity and Self-identity: Self and Society in the Late Modern Age*. Stanford, CA: Stanford University Press.

Gramsci, A. (1971) *Selections from the Prison Notebooks*, trans. Q. Hoare and G. Nowell Smith. New York: International.

Guest, D. (1987) Human resource management and industrial relations. *Journal of Management Studies*. 24: 503–21.

Guest, D. (1990) Human resource management and the American dream. *Journal of Management Studies*. 27: 377–97.

Hollway, W. (1984) Gender differences and the production of subjectivity. In J. Henriques, W. Hollway, C. Urwin, C. Venn, and V. Walkerdine (eds), *Changing the Subject*. New York: Methuen.

Hollway, W. (1991) *Work Psychology and Organizational Behaviour*. London: Sage.

Holmer-Nadesan, M. (1996) Organizational identity and space of action. *Organization Studies*. 17: 49–81.

Holmer-Nadesan, M. (1997) Constructing paper dolls: The discourse of personality testing in organizational practice. *Communication Theory*. 7: 189–218.

Jacques, R. (1996) *Manufacturing the Employee: Management Knowledge from the 19th to 21st centuries*. Thousand Oaks, CA: Sage.

Knights, D. and Willmott, H. (1985) Power and identity in theory and practice. *The Sociological Review*. 33: 22–46.

Knights, D. and Willmott, H. (1989) Power and subjectivity at work: From degradation to subjugation in social relations. *Sociology*. 23: 535–58.

Kochan, T., Katz, H. and McKersie, R. (1986) *The Transformation of American Industrial Relations*. New York: Basic Books.

Laclau, E. and Mouffe, C. (1985) *Hegemony and Socialist Strategy*, trans. W. Moore and P. Cammack. London: Verso.

Legge, K. (1995) *Human Resource Management*. London: Macmillan.

Legge, K. (1998) The morality of MRM. In C. Maber, D. Skinner and T. Clark (eds), *Experiencing Human Resource Management*. London: Sage.

Lewin, D., Mitchell, D. and Zaidi, M. (1997) *The Human Resource Management Handbook*. London: JAI Press.

Martin, J. (1990) Deconstructing organizational taboos: The suppression of gender conflict in organizations. *Organization Science*. 1: 339–59.

Miller, P. and Rose, N. (1995) Production, identity, democracy. *Theory and Society*. 24: 427–67.

Niven, M. (1967) *Personnel Management, 1913–1963*. London: IPM.

Przeworski, A. (1980) Material bases of consent: Economic and politics in a hegemonic system. *Political Power and Social Theory*. 1: 21–66.

Rose, N. (1990) *Governing the Soul: The Shaping of the Private Self*. London: Routledge.

Townley, B. (1993) Foucault, power/knowledge, and its relevance for human resource management. *Academy of Management Review*. 18: 518–45.

Weedon, C. (1987) *Feminist Practice and Poststructuralist Theory*. Oxford: Basil Blackwell.

Willis, P. (1977) *Learning to Labor*. New York: Columbia University Press.

Chapter 3

On Fieldwork in a Habermasian Way: Critical Ethnography and The Extra-ordinary Character of Ordinary Professional Work

John Forester

On the train to a Rotterdam conference on critical social theory, I'd been prepared to discuss Jürgen Habermas's *Theory of Communicative Action* (1984). I had read the relevant literatures, but I found the terribly abstract and often tortured commentaries on Habermas's work more frustrating and pointless than ever. These commentaries missed much of the real sociological and political promise of his work, I thought – but how could I show that? Here was work, I felt, that had enormous implications for the analysis of everyday practice and politics, especially an interactive micropolitics with which I was fascinated. But academic readers of Habermas's action theory hardly seemed to see its connections to ordinary practice and political life at all.

So I opened my briefcase and turned to several transcripts I'd made of meetings of city planning staff in a small New York municipality, and I wondered if I could put my prepared paper aside and do something altogether new: try really to *show*, not just to promise, that Habermas's work could illuminate the ordinary daily work of professional-political conversation and interaction.

As I scanned the meeting transcripts on the train, I found a twelve line passage that seemed self-contained enough to make sense to an audience who would not be familiar with the history of the municipality. Here was a brief, if frustrated, discussion of a new information system, a system which seemed destined like many other bureaucratic innovations to run aground soon enough. If Habermas's work was so promising, as I'd tried to argue in a string of publications (Forester, 1989, 1993), would it not surely illuminate this brief passage from the city hall staff meeting? This would be a test, then, to show rather than to claim, to *talk* a bit less about Habermas's theory and to *do* a bit more with it.

When the train arrived in Rotterdam, I found my way to the conference and asked the organizers for an overhead transparency so I could show the audience the transcript, line by line, speech act by speech act, statement by statement, question by question. Since Habermas's work argued that the crux of communicative action was performative *action* and not some mystical communication of meaning from soul to soul, my presentation explored the practical work the staff were actually doing in the performance captured by the transcript. Reading back from the transcript to the meeting, I asked what actions were reflected in the transcript. What were the staff doing? Could Habermas's work help us see not the foundations of ethics but the real practice of agents in an ordinary but quite political and institutionally structured setting?

My presentation went well enough so that several members of the audience sought me out to say they'd never seen such an appropriation of Habermas's work. I took that as enough encouragement to write up the talk – and to try to carry this line of analysis farther. Habermas's own recent work, unfortunately, has not been helpful here, if only because it largely treats another problem altogether, the principled character of moral theory, not the earlier problems of social interaction worked over in the *Theory of Communicative Action*.

The result of that Rotterdam talk and several subsequent drafts now takes the shape of this chapter. This analysis begins, rather than concludes, a research strategy. But it shows clearly, I hope, that the basic elements of the *Theory of Communicative Action* suggest a rich and productive approach to the analysis of actual flows of social and political interaction. This, and not only the clarification of moral theory, represents a contribution of Habermas's Critical Theory that we can ill afford to neglect.

CRITICAL ETHNOGRAPHY AND PROFESSIONAL PRACTICE

When we walk into a meeting in a city hall (or in a church basement, or in a Dean's office, and so on), we want to know typically who seeks which ends and has which purposes, interests, wants and intentions, but we want to know much more than that too. We want to know not only about other actors' likely decisions about costs, benefits and trade-offs – in general, about their utilities – but we want to know too about their allegiances and loyalties, their trustworthiness and integrity – in general about their political and social identities.

In Steven Lukes's terms, we want to know not just about their instrumental decision-making, but about their abilities to shape agendas and even others' senses of their own best interests (Lukes, 1974). We want to know how in shaping attention – and neglect – selectively, they will shape other people's senses of 'can' and 'can't', others' senses of what is and is not possible, and thus others' political senses of self, their political identities (Forester, 1989, 1999; Sager, 1994). As actors pursue ends, they refashion social and political relations as well. As decisions are made, relations of power are refashioned too. When we decide what to say and what not to say, when to challenge and when not, we often consider both our immediate purposes and our future relationships, today's goals and tomorrow's prospects of acting with others, our 'strategic position'.

James March and Johann Olsen put the point crisply, writing that

> choice situations are not simply occasions for making substantive decisions. They are also arenas in which important symbolic meanings are developed. People gain status and exhibit virtue. Problems are accorded significance. Novices are educated into the values of the society and organization. Participation rights are certification of social legitimacy; participation performances are critical presentations of self. (March and Olsen, 1976: 52)

But how does all this happen?

When we examine it, ordinary action turns out to be extraordinarily rich. What passes for 'ordinary work' in professional-bureaucratic settings is a thickly layered texture of political struggles concerning power and authority, cultural negotiations over identities, and social constructions of the 'problems' at hand.

As this chapter will illustrate by considering just a fragment of a professional staff meeting, the purpose of critical ethnographic work is to reveal the politics of this multilayered complexity. Such work is 'critical' insofar as it focuses on relations of power and hegemony and their contingencies – not because it provides any decision-rule or simple tool with which to 'measure' domination. Such work is ethnographic insofar as it is empirical and phenomenological: sensitive to socially constructed meanings, looking beyond distributions of utilities to the construction of identities (Fay, 1996; Sandercock, 1998).

Critical ethnographic work in general, then, and fieldwork done in a Habermasian way in particular, should show us practically how much more than instrumental action, deciding which means to use to get to which ends, takes place in ordinary practice, and what difference this makes for questions of power and powerlessness, community and autonomy (Alvesson, 1996; Flyvbjerg, 1998; Habermas, 1984, 1987; Mumby, 1988). Building on previous work, this chapter seeks to show, too, as very few others have done, how we can appropriate Habermas's work to promote insightful and politically acute, empirically rich social research (Forester, 1993).

We tell ourselves far too easily that ordinary action must be understood 'in its context', but the very context itself is not given but made, inherited and appropriated in subtle political ways (Fay, 1996; Heritage, 1984). Too easily too we assure ourselves that the 'micro' and the 'macro' must fit together, that any action occurs on a structured stage, that to understand any action we must understand the particular historical stage on which it takes place. But the same stage can support a bewildering variety of actions, judgements, deceits, strategies and expressions. We should certainly not put issues of context, stage and political structure aside, but look closely at practice, at careful action as it takes place. By looking closely, listening carefully, we can appreciate even the most apparently simple 'bureaucratic' interactions as entry points, as windows through which we might look to see the extraordinary political complexity of professional and organizational work (Fischler, 2000; Innes, 1995; Knorr-Cetina, 1981).

This chapter, accordingly, will argue that one small part of critical social theory – Habermas's sociological analysis of communicative action – has a vast and yet unrealized potential for concrete social and political research, for critical ethnographic analysis. Unfortunately, though, academic critics have often obscured the promise of such ethnographic research in favour of a flurry of narrow epistemological debates. We should not devalue those philosophical debates, but neither should we hold sociological and ethnographic inquiry hostage to their less than imminent resolutions (Alvesson and Deetz, 1999).

As a window to a field setting, we consider below a simple twelve-line fragment of a conversation taken from a staff meeting of a small city's Department of City Planning. The staff meeting provides an example of a professional setting – a relatively non-controversial, ordinary, even 'boring' setting – in which we can explore the ongoing 'micropolitics' of city planning practice. The conversational sequence we shall consider here followed some forty minutes of discussion of all the data the staff might want from a potentially new city-wide information system.

In this small city, as in many other small municipalities, the planners have found themselves attempting to balance development pressures with neighbourhood preservation and environmentalist pressures. The staff have been working on studies of low-income housing needs, downtown transportation patterns, the redesign of the city's most important public park, the location of a farmers' market, and ongoing economic development needs. Unemployment has been relatively low, compared with other municipalities in the state. Local politics have been largely controlled by the Democratic Party, with increasingly strong challenges being mounted recently from a 'green' and no-growth coalition – whose leaders have routinely attacked the planners for doing too little, too late in the face of 'new development'. Planning staff turnover has been fairly low, but the planning staff typically feel overwhelmed with the number of projects and issues for which they seem to be held responsible.

After 'brainstorming' a long, long list of desired information, a junior planner, Helena, finally asks, 'So now that we know everything that we want (data-wise), how do we get it?' and the stream of interactions presented in Figure 3.1 had begun.

1	Helena, Jr plnr:	So now that we know everything that we want (data-wise), how do we get it?
2	Director (facetiously):	Oh, Peter's gonna take care of that!
3	Peter, Asst Director:	Yeah, that's a minor detail...
4	Jack, Sr plnr:	Let John do it.
5	Kate, Sr plnr:	Is there any interest on the City Council to fund this sort of thing?
6	Director:	Well, we're going to ask them for money...
7	Peter:	And they're gonna give us a quarter of what we're going to ask for...
8	Director:	Then we won't do it.
9	Jack:	What kind of finance data would be appropriate for this?
10	Director:	I don't know.
11	Jack:	If we could interest people like Kano [another agency director], maybe we'd get a little more support for this.
12	Director:	That's an interesting idea. No, he's only interested in whether the numbers add up right...

FIGURE 3.1   *Field Data: Interaction in a City Planning Staff Meeting, City Hall, Northville*

What, then, do the staff do in this brief interaction? How do they refashion social and political relationships? What forms of rationality do the staff exhibit? And, finally, so what?

These questions reflect the theoretical agenda of this essay. We appropriate Habermas's account of the pragmatics of communicative action (Habermas, 1979; Sager, 1994) to examine how in practice the four pragmatic 'validity claims' Habermas discusses actually work. By developing work of John Austin and John Searle, Habermas suggests, roughly, that we can understand our actions by considering their practical-communicative, performative character. In particular, when we speak, we typically make four practical claims on listeners all at once:

1 we refer to 'outer' states of affairs, which a listener may explore as truly or falsely existing;

2 we invoke contextual norms that legitimate the action we're undertaking, norms to which listeners may consent or alternatively challenge as inappropriate to the situation at hand;

3 we express 'inner' states of self, emotions and dispositions such as seriousness, anger, impatience or frustration, which a listener may trust or alternatively challenge as feigned or inauthentic; and

4 we represent the issues before us in a selective language, terminology or framework, which a listener may accept or challenge as possibly incomprehensible (Habermas, 1979; Forester, 1985, 1989).

Listeners may challenge speakers or they may not, in a given setting, for no action is guaranteed. The point here is not to predict what listeners will do, but to understand how much is at stake when speakers speak and, more generally, whenever we act meaningfully, thus communicatively. Habermas's analysis of these performative claims can help us empirically to explore just how complex, how contingent, and how rich, social and political actions actually are.

We can also explore what happens when listeners accept and do not challenge these four pragmatic claims. As I have argued more politically, because much routine interaction enacts all four of these pragmatic claims simultaneously, such interaction (most of what we do!) refashions four subtle yet powerful relations of social belief, consent, status and attention to problems (Forester, 1989, 1993). Because social and political interactions have such a performative, pragmatic-communicative structure, this analysis can inform a far-reaching analysis of hegemony and discursive power (Alvesson, 1996; Benhabib, 1992; Forester, 1989; Throgmorton, 1996).

Let us return now to the meeting of our planners. What sort of pragmatic claims-making do they do? How can Habermas's attention to a claims-making structure of interaction help us? Once we have addressed those questions, we can turn to the issues of power and reproduction by asking what relations of belief, consent, trust and attention we see reproduced here.

What do the staff do here?

Notice that in the flow of the staff's interaction, whatever the role of 'communication' may be, any claims about 'what is true' are perhaps least important of all. In some frustration, Helena refers to 'everything we want', a list of information desired. The director responds by making a prediction – that Peter will accomplish the goal – which he and everyone else know to be patently false. The very untruth of his claim is central to its meaning and his action; taken literally, his words communicate nothing 'true'. The director's answer, 'Peter's gonna take care of that!' states a simple proposition, but it also enacts a far more complex performance. After all, everyone knows he's not trying to 'con' or lie to the assembled staff.

The same holds for Peter's response, 'Oh yeah; that's a minor detail.' This claim too is patently false, as everyone knows. 'Truth' is not the point of these communicative acts. Not conveying, describing or reporting facts here, the director and then Peter in turn instead rebuild their own working relationships – their moral order – in the face of a daunting and massive information gathering problem. So, Peter will be in charge, even if the staff will never really get all the information they'd like.

Similarly, Jack's claim that the summer intern, John, could do the job is quite obviously untrue too – but that, of course, is his point. Following Peter's reference to 'a minor detail', Jack identifies the least experienced member of the staff, the new student intern, as a (hardly) potential solution to the problem, and in doing so, he acknowledges ironically the immensity of the practical problem at hand.

So in the sequence of:

> 2 Director (facetiously): Oh, Peter's gonna take care of that!
> 3 Peter, Asst Dir.:   Yeah, that's a minor detail…
> 4 Jack, Senior plnr: Let John do it.

the obvious untruth of what's said is far more important than the 'facts' of any state of affairs. Practical communicative action, obviously, involves far more than the communication of true information.

Yet truth-claiming performances do matter. So Kate refers to a particular strategy of going to the City Council, and the staff predict the likely consequences of adopting that strategy. So too does Jack refer later to another strategy of involving another agency's director, Kano. The truth of the likely consequences of adopting these strategies – what's really likely to happen if the staff do one thing or another – does seem to matter. Knowing what's so and what isn't will help the staff gauge whose support they'll have, and what they can and can't effectively do.

But the staff do much more than gauge and predict the consequences of alternative strategies. They act politically and ethically: they assign responsibility, they reshape hierarchy, and they confer and challenge legitimacy too. Responding to Helena's call to action – essentially, 'Enough already! What're we going to do?' – the director says, in effect, 'As you all know, difficult projects like this are Peter's responsibility.'

Peter's facetious response then suggests a subtle political point: since the task is so intractable, the data that the planners will ultimately get will largely be a function neither of community need nor of the merit of cases at hand, but rather of the administrative difficulties of gathering good data. Information is not free, Peter is saying, and the quality of the public planning and decision-making process will be affected as a result. In discharging our responsibilities, Peter suggests, the staff will have to – and ought to – practically speaking, 'settle for less' than the 'everything we want' that Helena has referred to moments before.

When Jack suggests, 'Let John do it', he places John in a staff hierarchy as everyone's junior: for a job involving 'a minor detail', assign the least important, the most 'minor', member of the staff. John is new, relatively inexperienced, and free of prior commitments. Identified as powerless and subordinate, John's difference from the rest of the staff defines them as much as it characterizes him: the other staff have prior commitments, ongoing obligations, and obviously higher status. No other member of the staff could have been as casually invoked to deal with 'minor details'.

The ensuing discussion of 'what ought to be done' is revealing too. Just as Helena intervened to set a new agenda for the staff by saying, in effect,

'Enough talk! What are we going to do?!', Kate then intervenes by bringing her colleagues back to strategic issues. Her question identifies the City Council as the authority to be approached first, and she legitimates the council in that way. She tests staff support for the particular strategy of asking the City Council for its blessing. Yet as Peter predicts unhappy results, the staff explore the virtues of a second strategy: should they try to get support from Kano?

But the staff do more than evaluate, legitimate and recommend strategies. For they reconstitute themselves, too, in part as a community of frustration, in part as a community of strategists. Helena asks in frustration, what now? The director passes the burden of responding to Peter. Peter satirizes the massive problem as a minor detail. Jack echoes Peter's sentiment. As the City Council's response is predicted to be inadequate, the director backs off, 'Then we're not going to do it', if we don't have the necessary support.

The staff frame the issue at hand in terms of task assignments, City Council's or another agency director's support, and issues of personality too ('No, he's only interested in whether the numbers add up right.'). Surely this raises questions about other ways of addressing the issues: for example, addressing 'the merits' of gathering the needed information or organizing public, community support.

Consider too the three presumptive uses of 'we' in Helena's opening question, 'So now that we$_1$ know everything that we$_2$ want, how do we$_3$ get it?' The first use presumes the recognition of shared knowledge: we the staff know something together. The second use presumes a set of collectively shared goals and desires, just what it is that we the staff want here. The third use, in 'how do we get it?' refers to shared activity: we're a community of actors. These uses of 'we' appear as the quite ordinary expressions, or presumptions – altogether unchallenged here – of staff solidarity in the face of the practical problems at hand.

In these ordinary ways the staff accomplish extraordinary work: evaluating strategies, building solidarity, reinforcing hierarchy, legitimating courses of action, and adjusting their own expectations too. What we see here, then, is the many-layered practical significance of performative, communicative action.

As actors speak together, they act together. To explore this ordinary world of action, we must not just hear words, but listen to people. We must attend not only to what is said, but to what is being done in the saying – or in the gesture, or even in the silent refusal to speak. The same sentence can of course have multiple pragmatic meanings, as Habermas's delineation of the pragmatic 'validity claims' makes clear: each utterance can have significant referential, norm-invoking, feeling-expressing, and attention-framing aspects to it (Habermas, 1979; cf. Forester, 1999). So, observing and probing a wide range of interactions, we can assess how communicative actors, in their actual performances of speaking, simultaneously make each of the four practical claims upon one another that we have referred to above. We can study the actual and contingent ways that actors make practical claims that:

1   refer to states of affairs, and so shape their listener's beliefs;

2   invoke legitimate norms, and so appeal to their listener's consent;

3   express the speaker's disposition, and so appeal to their listener's trust; and

4   adopt a conventional way of representing issues, and so frame their listener's attention selectively.

Accordingly, our twelve line transcript can be explored as a series of four overlays so we can understand how, for example, a superficially factual claim ('Peter's gonna take care of that!') is at once (1) untrue; (2) responsibility-shifting; (3) distance-creating; and (4) problem-setting. As ordinary and natural listeners, of course, we are often able to interpret all four levels of such practical claims-making simultaneously and almost pre-reflectively.

Facing our transcript, then, we could ask after each utterance – if doing so were not so endless – a series of practical and ultimately political questions. First, what facts does the speaker refer to or seek to establish? Second, what norms of legitimacy does the speaker invoke? Third, what inner dispositions does the speaker express? Fourth, what categories are used by the speaker to frame attention to the issue at hand? In every communicative action, then, we might investigate issues of the control of information and belief, the management of legitimation and consent, the presentation of self and the construction of trust, and the selective organizing or disorganizing of others' attention (for the analysis of professional practice, see Alvesson, 1996; Forester, 1989; Innes 1995). Consider just two examples within our transcript: how the staff, first, make practical claims to legitimacy and so manage a moral order, and, second, make expressive claims and so shape both individual and collective senses of self.

Practical claims to legitimacy

Consider the performative claims to legitimacy made in just the first four lines:

- L1: Helena argues, in effect, we're planners, so wanting data isn't enough. We have to try to get that information so we can work with it. Shouldn't our wishes be tempered by what we can realistically do?

- L2: The director passes the ball: Peter, as the associate director, will be in charge of this project; it'll be his responsibility to figure out what we should do.

- L3: With his opening acknowledgement, 'Yeah', Peter says facetiously, in effect, 'I'm in total control', meaning, of course, that he is not. Further, with '*minor* detail', he implies that the data that will be available for planning purposes will be shaped by the *major* details of political-administrative considerations: the staff should appreciate the difficulties to be faced and so they should be prepared to accept a partial, limited, 'solution'.

- L4: Jack, as we have noted, suggests that John, the student intern, is subject to assignment. In echoing Peter's reference to the 'minor detail', Jack further legitimates Peter's and the director's professional judgements about the intractable character of the tasks at hand.

In four lines – four actions – we see, then, a call to action, the shifting of responsibility for that action, an argument about what the staff should settle for, and a supporting professional judgement. In the staff's ongoing work of making these claims, we see a subtle and ordinary micropolitics of practical argumentation. Questions and claims regarding what ought to be done, and what norms, obligations, rules and judgements are to be respected, are continually at issue here, in the most ordinary moments of professional practice.

Claims establishing the 'self'

In the same four lines we also find expressive claims that seek to establish identities:

- Helena begins in line one with a mixture of frustration and anticipation. She does not simply say, 'how do we get this information?' She begins, 'So…' to mark a turn, finally, in the conversation to an issue that she knows and feels needs attention: action. She also uses 'know everything we want' and not 'know what we want' – again marking the close of the prior topic, emphasizing its completeness, and expressing some irritation perhaps that that earlier conversation has not yet addressed how the staff will get the data they need.

- In the second line, then, the director deflects a potential criticism – should he have addressed the feasibility question earlier? – by humorously claiming that Peter (his thus esteemed associate director) would take care of everything. In so doing, he acknowledges the point of Helena's question, expresses a confidence in Peter, and at the same time distances himself from the responsibility and desire to solve the problem. Even so he manages the staff – pointing to Peter, hoping Peter will have a strategy of response, and indeed shifting responsibility to Peter to come up with something. In one quick response, the director expresses distance, confidence, acknowledgement and respect for Helena, and scepticism about success too.

- Peter follows in the third line by expressing both confidence and scepticism too. His acknowledgement, 'Yeah', reconstitutes or maintains his status as associate director: Of course I'll do it, whatever the task, that's who I am here. But of course he expresses his practical judgement too, by facetiously saying it's a 'minor detail' and meaning, of course, that it's a big deal! So he sympathizes with Helena and the director, acknowledges their concerns, shares them, and shows that he's the kind of person who's willing to take on projects and yet who's realistic and competent as a practical actor, too, one who shares the staff's concerns sympathetically while nevertheless being willing to laugh at their shared predicament. Notice that *both* the political difficulty, getting the desired information, and the substantive problem, lacking adequate data for public purposes, are internalized and then expressed in interpersonal humour, a building of solidarity among staff who face the same – collectively – exasperating conditions.

- In the fourth line, Jack does not literally mean, 'Let John do it', even though that's exactly what he's said, for that would be absurd on its face: the problem is enormous and complex, and John has just arrived. Instead, Jack welcomes John to the staff, acknowledging that he is there to perform productive (but possible!) work in the coming months. Yet he also seconds the sense of the director and Peter: he shares – he claims – their sentiments about the scale and difficulty of the task at hand. So he expresses a level of quite moderated, tongue-in-cheek, hope (his lowered expectations too), at the same time that he includes the new intern in the group while marking and defining as subordinate the intern's new status.

The line-by-line analysis illustrated here suggests the extraordinary richness of what the staff do with each quite ordinary utterance, with each action in speech. Of course, the virtues of such a method of close reading of social interaction also suggest its liabilities. How could we assess a two-hour meeting in this way, a meeting whose transcript would reveal many hundreds of pragmatic moves by the participants, *each of which might be referred to later in potentially political and practical ways by other participants, 'Well, you said…'*?

This threat of over-specificity reflects in part the challenge of articulating mid-level analyses devoted to the structure and change of organizations – a level of research relatively more aggregate and 'macro' than that focusing on interaction, and a level quite a bit more 'micro' than that focusing on political-economic structures (Forester, 1989; Healey, 1992, 1997). Yet the very plausibility of participants' later saying, 'Well, you did say…' suggests that participants in social interaction do already, routinely and quasi-naturally, ordinarily and tacitly, actually perform the intricate and detailed validity-claim analysis illustrated here. A critical ethnographic reading should do justice, then, both to participants' interpretations and to the ongoing production of hegemonic relations, a topic to which we turn in a moment.

Notice that the role of gender can be interpreted in quite different ways in this interaction (Mumby, 1996). What are we to make of Helena's opening and Kate's suggestion that follows? At least two interpretations are possible. First, the actions of these two women appear authoritative, agenda-setting, effectively initiative-taking. The men in our excerpt seem to act satirically; the women can be interpreted as exerting leadership, referring to collective challenges and strategies. On this interpretation, neither Helena nor Kate is a second-class citizen in this meeting or this staff. Yet another reading is possible too. Helena's intervention seems to be deflected and treated lightly by the director; Kate's suggestion is quickly superseded rather than discussed in any detail.

Which interpretation is correct? On the evidence before us, both might be right and actually far more compatible than they might first appear. It may well be that the staff is hierarchical, that Helena and Kate have neither the power nor status of the director or associate director, and that they are able nevertheless to exert leadership, bringing the staff and their 'superiors' back to the pressing tasks at hand. To pursue the issue, we need more evidence of the interactions of staff. We might then well be able to judge whether Kate's suggestions are deflected more than Jack's, whether Helena's participation is slighted or fully respected, and so on.

Now we could go beyond the first four lines of this one simple fragment to assess further norm-invoking and expressive claims, and we could, as well, probe the referential and attention-framing character of each utterance, each practical move in this meeting excerpt. But let us instead turn in the next section to consider how these same actions sustain and re-make the very institutional setting in which the staff work.

WHAT SOCIAL AND POLITICAL RELATIONS DO THE STAFF RESHAPE?

The staff not only act with purpose, seeking ends, but they also refashion the social and political order in which they work – learning about it, shaping it and changing it as they go. Habermas suggests that broad processes of social rationalization can actually be distinguished as learning processes in two dimensions, roughly instrumental and moral, which have systematic connections to the double structure of speech, to claims-making involving 'truth claims' on the one hand and 'legitimacy' and expressive claims on the other (1979: 142, 1984; cf. Forester, 1993). How do the staff in our meeting learn in such ways?

How, we can ask, do communicative interactions maintain or alter social structures – patterns of social action that make investments, recognize or discredit identities, establish or evade normative sanctions (e.g. regulations), and form or refute beliefs and world-views (Sayer and Storper, 1997)? To address this question, we must examine our transcript by focusing on the actors not only as speakers, but as listeners too. What, we should now ask, do the staff establish, contingently reorder or reshape, as they talk and listen – as they act together? Consider, then, how the staff reshape patterns of belief, consent, status and identity, and perceptions of 'the problem' at hand.

Shaping patterns of belief

How do the staff construct and reconstruct patterns of belief about the world? Helena makes the point that the issues of feasibility have to be faced: she has set out the topic, and as the following responses make clear, the staff recognize her problem as a serious one, one they share. The problem really is tough, the staff learn as they consider it together. Not only does Helena have the question, but the director, Peter, and Jack confirm the level of difficulty here. The desired information is not to be had. The information obtained will be a function of politics, not need, of funding levels, staff time, negotiations perhaps, but not 'the merits' – they now come jointly to believe.

The exchange about who's to fulfil the task establishes another common belief: getting the data will be quite difficult; the staff won't be able actually to get what they need. The subsequent two exchanges, one about approaching the City Council and one about approaching Kano, develop strategic beliefs as the staff explore possible lines of action and practice. The City Council will be approached, but they're not likely to be helpful. So other strategies are necessary. What about Kano? An interesting idea, but perhaps not a good one. As these beliefs are developed, so do the staff explore the world together and learn, factually speaking, about their common possibilities.

Shaping patterns of legitimacy: the management of consent

The opening exchange, before the City Council comes into the picture, also establishes the legitimacy of a quite modest, if not necessarily conservative, norm of action, a norm of politically bounded rationality (Alvesson, 1996, but cf. Flyvbjerg, 1998). The staff construct their common problem to be concretely practical, context-bound and limited. They have no illusions about acquiring perfect information. Instead, they prepare themselves not only to settle for less, to desire less, but to accept, condone, legitimate and judge as proper, obtaining far less information than they would like, and far less, too, than their professional knowledge suggests would be good and proper to have.

These planners acknowledge conflicting norms. Thus they propose as legitimate – and mutually consent to – what they take to be a reasonable and balanced way of proceeding. The city's problems – seen abstractly – warrant and deserve more information than the staff will be able to get, but the obligations of practical action, acting in a timely manner with limited resources, justify settling for less.

The staff's attention to an evolving political order, one they are actively seeking to fashion themselves, does not stop here. They legitimate the City Council as the authority of first resort, and then they quickly undercut its legitimacy ('Well, we're going to ask them…'; 'And they're gonna give us a quarter of what we ask for…'). Similarly, the staff legitimate a secondary strategy of possibly forming a coalition with agency director Kano. In so doing, these planners reconstruct their collective sense of political order – what authority is to be respected and what courses of action are appropriate or not.

So two problems arise: lacking likely council support, what should be done? The director knows as much about the City Council as Peter knows. Sharing Peter's scepticism about their support, he nevertheless authorizes the move to go to the Council ('we're going to ask them') – for perhaps they will learn about the issue and the planning needs of the city. This much surely is to be expected of the planning staff, it seems, for they are, after all, on the public payroll.

Yet the staff also consider as legitimate the strategy of coalition-building with Kano – and so they explore another political game too: the more support for the data-collection project they can organize from other agencies, the greater the pressure (if not the moral claim) upon the City Council for support. Surely it is acceptable to join forces with Kano, should Kano's agency too need some of the information being pursued. This deceptively simple logic enables the planners to defend as politically legitimate a strategy of bureaucratic organizing to shape the very sentiments and responses of the City Council. So a political norm legitimating the staff's turn to the City Council is first respected and then contested, resisted with the appeal to an additional norm which authorizes coalition-building with yet another agency responsive to a public constituency.

The director also protects the planning staff – claiming authoritatively that the staff will not take on work if they are not adequately funded. He authorizes basic norms of the staff meeting too. When he says, 'That's an interesting idea', he not only expresses his interest, he also authorizes and affirms the place of staff suggestions, ideas and proposals. In so doing, he characterizes his disposition, his willingness to listen, and so he re-creates his working self, his reputation, the kind of person he can be taken to be – as we discuss in the following section (Frug, 1988; Sandercock, 1998; White, 1985).

Shaping patterns of status and identity

As the staff joke about what to do, they also reproduce their own social order: the hierarchy of the director's and Peter's authority, Jack's seniority, and John's subordinate status. They also assess and project the practical identities of both the City Council and Kano, the agency director. The staff wonder, in effect, 'What can we expect of them?' Who do we really have here, with whom we can work? They suppose that the Council will not care sufficiently to support their work, and Kano may only be 'interested in whether the numbers add up right', not presumably in the broader public needs for the information that the planners want.

The staff refashion themselves, as well, for they moderate their own desires. Beginning with 'everything we want', the discussion takes a sober turn: expectations of administrative difficulties being what they truly are, desire is to be moderated, what the staff 'really want' must be cut back. So the staff formulate their own expectations and commitments, what they shall want, and thus they shape, in part, who – in some practical measure – they shall be.

Notice, too, that although the director speaks often, each time that he does he responds to a staff member's initiative: he does not propose new lines of action. His judgements appear to have authority, but he presents himself – practically constructs himself – as a manager, not as a commander. From twelve lines, of course, we can hardly 'type' the director, but notice that even from this conversational fragment, we might be led to 'see him as' more managerial than authoritarian, more cautious than bold. The point of course is not whether *these* inferences are correct, but that our imputations of another's identity, 'who they are', are likely to derive in large part from our observation of what they do, act by act – rather than from, for example, their official titles, their self-descriptions, or even others' descriptions of them. Learning about others, we observe not just their pursuit of instrumental ends, but their display of virtue and character, their ongoing construction of self. So too more generally, as staff members must articulate their judgements in diverse settings will they appear competent or not in front of the City Council, pushy or not with Kano and other officials, sensitive or insensitive to community groups and popular leaders, and so on.

Shaping patterns of attention: problem formulation

Consider finally how the staff attend to the problem before them in three distinct ways. First, they discuss who is to be responsible: how the job is to be done in terms of formal staff assignments. The obvious limits of that discussion lead to a second focus: financial support – for more staff – from the elected body, the City Council. The limits of that strategy, in turn, lead to a focus on bureaucratic politics, the strategy of 'coalition building with Kano'.

This all seems plain and obvious enough, but what's unsaid suggests the political framing of what seems otherwise all too plain. Notice that the staff have not posed the issue in terms of political goals, political needs, constituency organizations, powerful leaders, historically abiding problems, obligations owed by the City Council to campaign promises, and so on. Inevitably, any problem formulation will shape attention selectively and thus too neglect, in principle, an infinite number of alternative ways of posing the same 'problem'. The point is not just *that* such selective problem-framing occurs, but that our research and practice should be sensitive to *how*, culturally and politically, such selectivity operates.

The staff focus attention on bureaucratic rather than constituency politics, a concern for personality rather than group or class, a concern with available resources rather than with a network of social relationships which might be brought into play (Gusfield, 1981). Their focus upon bureaucratic politics, resources and individual actors is rooted no doubt in experience and training; it reflects, in part, the resources they bring to the situation. We say that people with hammers look for nails; people with pens and pencils look for paper. So perhaps we should not be surprised that actors in a city agency respond as this staff does in our example. But that background, that training, that representational and rhetorical capacity to frame attention selectively matters, for the staff are creating a future – their own in part – for others. These representational capacities were suggested in Habermas's earlier (e.g. 1979) account of ordinary speakers' pragmatic claims to 'comprehensibility', an account curiously missing from his *Theory of Communicative Action* (1984). With such pragmatic claims, nevertheless, we orient ourselves and our listeners in particular ways, shaping the ways we attend to issues at hand (Forester, 1989, 1999; Lukes, 1974).

The staff here, then, do not only act in complex ways, saying one thing and meaning another, interweaving practical arguments about strategies with expressions of distance, deference and respect. For they also re-elaborate their own social organization as they shape patterns of belief, consent, identity and problem-formulation (Willmott, 1994). In so doing, the staff reshape relations of power too.

Consider briefly, now, what sort of practical rationality the staff enact in this conversation.

Practical and politically bounded rationality

The staff have no access to full information. So we can neither understand their action as focused on any optimization nor can we blame them for failing to be 'rational' economic men and women. Acknowledging the constrained nature of their actions, we should expect to find them practising a 'bounded rationality', but we know too little about the forms such rationality can take in political contexts like City Hall.

In the face of necessarily limited information-processing abilities, Herbert Simon argued long ago, skilled actors do and ought to lower their aspirations – to 'satisfice' rather than optimize. But Simon's account was concerned neither with (1) the role social structures may play in a given case to bound rationality, nor with (2) those bounds which might be otherwise, bounds that are 'unnecessary', alterable and contingent, not arguably part of being human. These distinctions – identifying bounds that are structural or not, necessary or not – suggest that appropriate practical actions will vary with the particular nature of the boundedness in the action situation at hand (Forester, 1989: 27–64; 1993).

In the light of these distinctions, the transcript suggests that the staff respond to a variety of constraints and match their strategies and actions accordingly. They do, as Simon says, lower aspirations. But they do more too. Facing a bureaucratically differentiated world, they look to Kano for support in a possible coalition. Facing a shifting political constellation of interests and support, they consider a negotiating position with the City Council: getting a quarter of what we need will not do, so we must strengthen our hand. Even in this fragment of the meeting, the staff show us a bounded rationality that is more politically sophisticated than a more conventionally social-psychological model of 'satisficing' might lead us to expect.

WHAT'S DISTINCTIVE ABOUT SUCH FIELDWORK IN A HABERMASIAN WAY?

We have read our twelve-line transcript as a fragment of an ongoing flow of interaction. Our interpretation raises many more problems than it answers, but it is still instructive. By attending to the performative character of communicative action, we can explore a four-layered practical structure of social and political interactions that shape (more or less true) beliefs, (more or less appropriate) consent, (more or less deserved) trust, and (more or less aptly focused) attention. In so doing, we can identify subtle, yet powerfully pragmatic moves of social actors who both seek ends instrumentally *and* yet continually reshape social and political relations too. We can utilize but move beyond a strictly phenomenological analysis. We can move beyond a phenomenology of political frustration, and perhaps the political frustration of phenomenology too, to an analysis of discursive or communicative power – legitimation, the construction of selves, the framing of attention, and the resulting social and political refashioning of the social organization at hand – in its relationships to encompassing political structures of (in our case) the state (Alvesson, 1996; Benhabib, 1992).

Doing fieldwork in a Habermasian way enables us to explore the continuing performance and practical accomplishment of relations of power. By refining Habermas's attention to a 'double structure of speech', we come to examine specifically the micropolitics of speech and interaction (Allmendinger, 2001; Habermas, 1979). Quite contrary to prevailing misinterpretations of Habermas, we come not to expect any idealized truth-telling; instead we look closely at the ways in which appeals to truth (and quite differently, truthfulness) serve varied and significantly contingent, variable ends (Forester, 1985, 1991). We presume neither that truth always serves the powerful nor that truth necessarily shall set anyone free; instead we look at concrete communicative practices to see what differences they can and do make (Innes, 1995). Similarly, too, for the contingencies of consent, claims to legitimacy and cultural conventions, and the contingencies of trust and forms of attention.

We are given absolutely no a priori guarantees that anything approximating ideal discourse takes place empirically (Forester, 1991). Quite the contrary, fieldwork done in a Habermasian way leads us to look carefully and closely at the complex and largely uninvestigated ways that normative claims are actually made in practice – to shape obligation, senses of membership and self, consent and deference, patterns of future action. In such ways, a Habermasian fieldwork tells us and helps us to 'look and see', neither to assume determinate structures a priori nor to expect any idealized discourse, but rather to shift from abstract discussions of truth and power, discourse and Other, to assess actual flows of action that reshape our beliefs, consent, trust and even more subtle frameworks of attention.

In so doing, a strategy of Habermasian fieldwork is immediately practical, making us more attentive listeners as we come to realize, walking into meetings, that we will soon witness and perhaps take part in the reconstruction of political, perhaps professional, relationships in complex and multi-levelled ways. We learn quickly that we are not only listeners but speakers too, not only observers and readers or writers of texts, but actors as well. So we can appreciate the ways we must learn not only about interests but about character, not only about utilities but about identities, as these are expressed and articulated in everyday practice.

This chapter's analysis can only be illustrative and suggestive: illustrating an empirical appropriation of Habermas's theory of communicative action and suggesting dimensions of power to assess more closely. To explore further the fruits of doing fieldwork in a Habermasian way, we must assess 'larger' streams of interaction located in their contingently structural contexts, and of course, we must compare our reading to other accounts (Becker, 1998; Van Maanen, 1988). Yet here, our analysis reveals the play of power and action, convention and performance, in flows of conversation – with multiple voices presenting and contesting facts, norms, selves and representational styles too (Williams and Matheny, 1995).

But does this analysis threaten to lose us in a multiplicity of voices, distracting us from power and the possibilities of emancipatory response? Quite the contrary, for we can now examine intimately four interwoven threads of action and meaning, power and resistance, rationality and politics as they are played out in concrete cases (Fischler, 2000). No longer mistaking a Habermasian fieldwork to presume ideal conditions, we are freed to investigate the actual communicative practices shaping relationships of ever-contingent belief, consent, trust and attention (Forester, 1989, 1999; Innes, 1995).

Habermas's theory of communicative action has far too often been understood as predominantly – and typically, as necessarily – meta-theoretical, having little to do with empirical cases and having less to say about what we might explore in such cases. Yet this reading – sketchy and preliminary as it is – suggests that if we seek an empirically grounded, phenomenologically sensitive, and politically critical sociology, appropriating and building upon Habermas's theory of communicative action, then the rumours of the emptiness of this line of analysis are quite exaggerated. There's a good deal here to explore.

NOTE

Earlier versions of this chapter were presented at Cornell's College of Human Ecology and the University of Iowa's Project on the Rhetoric of Inquiry. Thanks for critical comments are due to Jennifer Greene, Paul Dillon, Ralph Cintron, Rich Horowitz, Mats Alvesson, Jim Throgmorton and John Jermier, none of whom is responsible for the flaws of the present account.

REFERENCES

Allmendinger, Philip (2001) *Planning in Postmodern Times*. London: Routledge.
Alvesson, Mats (1996) *Communication, Power, and Organization*. New York: de Gruyter.
Alvesson, Mats and Deetz, Stan (1999) *Doing Critical Management Research*. Beverly Hills, CA: Sage.
Becker, Howard (1998) *Tricks of the Trade*. Chicago, IL: University of Chicago Press.
Benhabib, Seyla (1992) *Situating the Self*. New York: Polity Press.
Fay, Brian (1996) *Contemporary Philosophy of Social Science*. New York: Routledge.
Fischler, Raphaël (2000) Case studies of planners at work. *Journal of Planning Literature*. 15(2): 184–95.
Flyvbjerg, Bent (1998) *Rationality and Power*. Chicago, IL: University of Chicago Press.
Forester, John (ed.) (1985) *Critical Theory and Public Life*. Cambridge, MA: MIT Press.
Forester, John (1989) *Planning in the Face of Power*. Berkeley, CA: University of California Press.
Forester, John (1991) Reply to reviewers of *Planning in the Face of Power*. *International planning Theory Newsletter*. Dipartimento Interatenceo Territorio, Viole Mattioli 39, 10125 Torino, Italia. Spring.
Forester, John (1993) *Critical Theory, Public Policy, and Planning Practice*. Albany, NY: State University of New York Press.
Forester, John (1999) *The Deliberative Practitioner*. Cambridge, MA: MIT Press.
Frug, Jerry (1988) Argument as character. *Stanford Law Review*. 40(4): April.
Gusfield, Joseph (1981) *The Culture of Public Problems*. Chicago, IL: University of Chicago Press.
Habermas, Jürgen (1979) What is Universal Pragmatics? *Communication and the Evolution of Society*. Boston, MA: Beacon Press.
Habermas, Jürgen (1984, 1987) *Theory of Communicative Action* (2 vols). Boston, MA: Beacon Press.
Healey, Patsy (1992) Planning through debate: the communicative turn in planning theory. *Town Planning Review*. 63(2): 143–62.
Healey, Patsy (1997) *Collaborative Planning: Shaping Places in Fragmented Societies*. London: Macmillan.
Heritage, John (1984) *Garfinkel and Ethnomethodology*. Cambridge: Polity Press.
Innes, Judith E. (1995) Planning theory's emerging paradigm: Communicative action and interactive practice. *Journal of Planning Education and Research*. 14(3): 183–9.
Knorr-Cetina, Karin (1981) Introduction: The micro-sociological challenge of macro-sociology: towards a reconstruction of social theory and methodology. In Karin Knorr-Cetina and Aaron Cicourel (eds), *Advances in Social Theory and Methodology*. London: Routledge & Kegan Paul.
Lukes, Steven (1974) *Power: A Radical View*. New York: Macmillan.
March, James and Olsen, Johann (1976) *Ambiguity and Choice in Organizations*. Oslo: Universitetsforlaget.

Mumby, Dennis K. (1988) *Communication and Power in Organizations: Discourse, Ideology, and Domination*. Norwood, NJ: Ablex.

Mumby, Dennis K. (1996) Feminism, postmodernism and organizational communication studies: A critical reading. *Management Communication*. 9(3): 259.

Sager, Tore (1994) *Communicative Planning Theory*. London: Avebury.

Sandercock, Leonie (1998) *Towards Cosmopolis: Planning for Multicultural Cities*. New York: Wiley.

Sayer, Andrew and Storper, Michael (1997) Ethics unbound: for a normative turn in social theory. *Environment and Planning* B. 15: 1–17.

Throgmorton, James (1996) *Planning as Persuasive Storytelling*. Chicago, IL: University of Chicago Press.

Van Maanen, John (1988) *Tales of the Field: On Writing Ethnography*. Chicago, IL: University of Chicago Press.

White, James Boyd (1985) Rhetoric and law: the arts of cultural and communal life. In J.B. White (ed.), *Heracle's Bow*. Madison, WI: University of Wisconsin Press.

Williams, Bruce and Matheny, A. (1995) *Democracy, Dialogue, and Environmental Disputes*. New Haven, CT: Yale University Press.

Willmott, Hugh (1994) Theorizing human agency: responding to the crises of (post)modernity. In J. Hassard and M. Parker (eds), *Towards a New Theory of Organizations*. London: Routledge.

Chapter 4

Feminist Theory and Critical Theory: Unexplored Synergies

Joanne Martin

Although there are many varieties of feminist theory, they share two objectives. The first is descriptive: to reveal obvious and subtle gender inequalities. The second is change-oriented: to reduce or eradicate those inequalities. Feminist scholars differ with regard to how they use the terms sex and gender, and how much change in gender relations, and what means of change, they advocate. Some feminists are liberal advocates of equal opportunity, while others endorse more radical alternatives. In other words, there are both critical and non-critical versions of feminist scholarship.

Readers of this volume are aware that there are also many varieties of critical theory. Some, like Fournier and Grey (2000), take a more inclusive approach, including Marxist and structural perspectives. Others, like the authors of this volume (see also Alvesson and Deetz, 1996), restrict their attention primarily to the critical theory that is based on concepts drawn from the Frankfurt School (including the work of Adorno, Horkheimer, Marcuse, Habermas and sometimes Foucault). This chapter refers to the former, more inclusive approach as *critical theory*, and the latter, Frankfurt-based view, as *Critical Theory*, with the latter being a subset of the former. Both critical theory and Critical Theory have objectives that echo those of feminist theory. To cite just one example, some critical theorists who focus on management rather than the labour process, define their objectives as follows: 'to be engaged in critical management studies means, at the most basic level, to say that there is something wrong with management, as a practice and a body of knowledge, and that it should be changed' (Fournier and Grey, 2000: 16).

Although both critical and feminist theory focus on social and economic inequalities and both have an agenda of promoting system change, these two traditions have developed largely independently, with little deep intellectual exchange. In part, this divergence has occurred because feminist theorists use sex and gender as the fulcrum of their analyses (usually, but not always, with secondary emphases on class, race and ethnicity). In contrast, critical theorists often place class at the crux of their analyses,[1] with sex, gender, race and ethnicity being less emphasized. In spite of this crucial difference in emphasis, this chapter makes the case for a closer relationship between these two traditions of inquiry. The commonalities between critical theory and the more critical versions of feminist theory are many and important. To the extent that there are differences between these two traditions, these differences carry the potential for each to enrich the other.

This chapter begins by exploring how the main concerns of critical theory (with an emphasis on Critical Theory) overlap with those of feminist theory. These commonalities give rise to common blindspots and shared weaknesses. One of those weaknesses, ironically, centres on the most important goal the two traditions share: working towards system change. Both are better at critiquing the status quo than changing it. Taking this shared weakness as a starting point for rapprochement, this chapter explores the variety of ways feminist theorists have approached the change process. These change strategies effectively distinguish among more and less critical versions of feminist theory, pinpointing those aspects of organizational feminist work most likely to be of interest to organizational critical theorists. Next, common criticisms of feminist theory from some critical theorists are evaluated, to determine which are justified. Those parts of feminist theory that do not fit these criticisms have the most obvious synergies with critical theory.

COMMONALITIES BETWEEN FEMINIST THEORY AND CRITICAL THEORY

Alvesson and Deetz (1996) list the major achievements of Critical Theory as including: the skewing of historical discourse through reification, the universalization of sectional interests, the domination of instrumental reasoning, and the critique of hegemony, including the study of how consent to domination is orchestrated and the ways the subjugated participate in their own subjugation. Feminist theory has addressed some of these concerns more thoroughly than others, suggesting overlapping areas of concern as well as ways these two traditions could learn from each other.

The skewing of historical discourse through reification

A primary concern of feminist theory has been the reification and dichotomization of such concepts as male and female, objectivity and subjectivity, competition and cooperation, and rationality and emotionality. Feminists tend to see these dichotomies as socially constructed, ambiguous and misleading. Poststructural feminists, in particular, have cogently deconstructed these concepts, and attributes associated with them, showing how dichotomies have gendered associations that devalue the one of these paired concepts that is generally associated with the feminine (Irigaray, 1985b; Kristeva, 1977). For example, the dichotomy between rationality (attributed to males) and emotionality (attributed to females) has led to a 'valorization' of rationality, a tendency to see rationality as quite separate from emotions, with a concomitant devaluing of emotions (J. Martin et al., 1998; Mumby and Putnam, 1992). Feminists have shown how such reifications are reflected in ostensibly gender-neutral organizational theories, such as the work of Weber, Mintzberg, and the leadership theorists (Acker and Van Houten, 1974; Calas, 1987, 1993; J. Martin and Knopoff, 1997).

The universalization of sectional interests

Whereas Critical Theorists have explored the ways managerial interests have been represented as the interests of all employees, feminist scholars have explored how the interests of men have been assumed or asserted to be universal, silencing the voices and ignoring the concerns of women (Bambara, 1970; De Beauvoir, 1972 [1949]). More recent feminist scholarship has traced the universalization of sectional interests in gendered job descriptions (Acker, 1990; Collinson et al., 1990[2]), gendered organizational cultures (Gherardi, 1995; Mills, 1988), and the results of ostensibly gender-neutral research (Acker and Van Houten, 1974; J. Martin, 1994). Feminist research has repeatedly and powerfully revealed gendered interests hidden in ostensibly gender-neutral language and practices. These are all ways of challenging attempts to universalize sectional interests.

The domination of instrumental reasoning

The domination of instrumental reasoning is evident in organizational theory broadly defined, where it usually surfaces as a concern with the financial well-being of an organization, or the productivity of employees. This same kind of instrumental focus is also evident in some organizational feminist work, particularly that which takes a liberal approach to change and/or focuses on women in management or individual career success. For example, when feminist theorists describe gender inequalities, the focus is often on instrumental factors, such as pay or promotions. Some feminists justify gender equity by claiming it would improve productivity and financial performance. It is important to distinguish between these kinds of instrumental factors and material concerns that are framed in terms of meeting people's economic needs for survival. Given the feminization of poverty on a global scale, for example, a focus on material issues is called for in some contexts. Nevertheless, Critical Theory is generally more attuned than feminist theory to the dangers inherent in accepting a primary focus on organizational performance or individual career advancement, particularly given Critical Theory's insightful work, for example, on the dangers of consumerism.

The critique of hegemony, including the study of how consent to domination is orchestrated and the ways the subjugated participate in their own subjugation

In one sense, all of feminist theory is a critique of patriarchal[3] forms of hegemony. In addition, Marxist/socialist feminists, poststructural feminists, and some feminists studying alternative organizational structures have put a critique of all forms of hierarchical hegemony at the forefront of their scholarship. Feminist critiques of hegemony focused on discourse, communication and textual analysis are also plentiful (Irigaray, 1985a, 1985b).

Feminists have done less extensive analysis of how women and men are complicit in their own gendered subjugation (Collinson et al., 1990; De Beauvoir, 1972 [1949]). There is relatively little feminist work explicitly focused on false consciousness or the microprocesses that engineer consent (Foucault, 1977) to gendered arrangements (J. Martin and Meyerson, 1998). Critical theorists (Jermier, 1985) have expressed some discomfort with the elitism of researchers speaking for the disadvantaged, as in false consciousness. Nevertheless, some critical theorists have found ways to explore rather than avoid these difficulties (Willis, 1981 [1977]), which could be useful for feminist scholarship.

CHANGE AS A WEAK POINT IN FEMINIST AND CRITICAL SCHOLARSHIP

There is another commonality that feminist theory and Critical Theory share. This commonality, however, is a shared weakness. Both traditions share a commitment to system change, and yet neither tradition offers a generally accepted solution to the problem of how to achieve system change. Both offer ideological critiques, and both – with some important exceptions – stop short of action plans and recommendations.

Feminist theory is, in some ways, surprisingly optimistic. It seeks ways to change gender relations, even though feminist scholarship has convincingly documented that in all societies historians and anthropologists have studied, men dominate women (Rosaldo and Lamphere, 1974). The division of labour between men and women may vary, the justifications given for that division may differ, but – no matter if women do the hunting or the housekeeping, no matter if women or men have primary responsibility for growing food or cooking it – men hold more power than women. In spite of this evidence of widespread gender-related inequality, feminist theorists continue to seek to change the gender order.

Given the conclusions of feminist anthropologists, it is not surprising that feminist scholarship has been more successful in exposing and critiquing gender inequalities than in finding effective, long-term ways of reducing or eradicating them. With the exception of socialist-feminists, and those who advocate the creation of separatist, egalitarian havens, few feminist scholars have offered radical, action-oriented recommendations for system change, preferring instead to rely on ideological critique (Ferguson, 1984: ix, x).

Most varieties of critical theory limit their approaches to system change in a similar manner, offering impressive critiques of existing inequalities and inequities, but comparatively modest and limited approaches to delineating the route to emancipatory change, including calling for a more enlightened form of practice or using Habermas's ideal speech situation to challenge ideas and attitudes. Alvesson and Willmott (1992: 18) argue that 'The intent of [critical theory] is not to indulge in the Utopian project of eliminating hierarchy, removing specialist divisions of labour or even abolishing the separation of management and other forms of work' (1992: 18). Fournier and Grey take the position that '[Critical Management Studies] is expressly "anti-management": its task is not to reform management towards some more humane or ethically minded activity, but to undermine it (and maybe ultimately, if naively, to dethrone it) *through critique*' (2000: 24; emphasis added). The work of Foucault can be similarly characterized; his critique of existing arrangements is devastating, but his treatment of resistance to change, or system change itself, is controversially rather minimal.

There are versions of critical theory that take a more radical and more action-oriented approach to system change. Work in the industrial relations tradition, for example, has explored work slowdowns, sabotage, strikes and other forms of collective action. Marxist and neo-Marxist versions of critical theory take a more structural approach to system change, focusing on material aspects of ownership and contradictions inherent in the capitalist system that have the possibility of generating massive, revolutionary change. These more radical, action-oriented versions of critical theory generate critiques from other critical theorists, disputes that are beyond the scope of this chapter. Given this debate within critical theory, it seems fair to conclude that the issue of change remains problematic for Critical Theory, critical theory and feminist theory, but that the critical theory work that is most radical and action-oriented might have useful reverberations with the similarly radical feminist work, particularly that of feminist separatists and socialist-feminists.

EVALUATING FEMINIST CHANGE STRATEGIES

In spite of this tendency for much of feminist work to focus on ideational approaches to system change, there are at least six well-established feminist research streams that take a more action-oriented approach to system change. This feminist change literature is reviewed below, exploring how these research streams are relevant to the concerns of critical theorists.

The first four of the six change strategies, and the analysis of their shortcomings, were developed by faculty researchers at the Simmons Center for Gender in Organizations (Coleman and Rippin, 2000; Ely and Meyerson, 2000a, 2000b; Meyerson and Kolb, 2000). The last two of the six strategies are added to represent more radical feminist approaches to change. These six strategies are (using a mixture of my labels and those of the Simmons group):

1   Fixing individual women;
2   Valuing the feminine;
3   Adding women and stirring (minimal structural change);
4   Making small, deep cultural changes;
5   Creating new organizational structures; and
6   Transforming gendered society.

Below, each strategy is summarized and then critiqued, based on the results of feminist research.

Fixing individual women

This strategy is the primary approach of many organizations that seek to hire and retain more women employees, especially in previously male-dominated positions. The 'Fixing the women' strategy relies heavily on group training and individual advising to help women address their 'weaknesses'. For example, if women don't feel they will be able to gain a promotion, or don't want the advance once they get it, they are given self-esteem, assertiveness, and/or leadership training. Women at all ranks are urged to, and sometimes helped to, build networks of relationships with others who might assist their individual career advancement. They are encouraged, and sometimes helped, to find mentors who can coach them in the informal norms and political byways of organizational life. With this assistance, women should gain a repertoire of skills, at least some of which are thought of, by some, as traditionally masculine.

The Simmons researchers referred to above, dissect the many limitations of the 'Fixing individual women' strategy. This strategy implicitly assumes that women are to blame for not fitting into a system that is portrayed as relatively gender neutral. However, many organizational policies and practices are not gender neutral. Part of the reason for this is structural. Organizations have been, to a large extent, designed by men, in a context where men hold most of the highest-ranking positions and many of the better-paid blue-collar positions. Women have generally held lower-ranking, lower-paid positions (such as clerical jobs), some of which have been in effect reserved exclusively or primarily for women (Reskin and Roos, 1990; Strober, 1984). In part because of this occupational sex segregation, gendered norms have emerged, and everyday policies and practices in organizations, particularly in male-dominated positions, are often more comfortable for men than for women (Gherardi, 1995; Mills, 1988).

'Fixing the women' assumes that if women aspire to male-dominated jobs, they must learn to act as the men in those jobs do. However, women who act like men are often disliked and disrespected ('What is considered assertive for a man is considered aggressive for a woman') (Kanter, 1977). In any case, most women will be less successful than most men, in acting like a man. Thus, women are more likely to fail if a 'Fixing the women' strategy is adopted. If they succeed, they do so by learning to act like men, assimilating to male norms. It is therefore not unexpected to find that such 'pioneer' women often do little to help the women who would follow in their wake (Ely, 1995), and are likely to see the system that fostered their own success as meritocratic and gender neutral. Furthermore, those few women who do manage to enter previously male-dominated positions often find that their triumph is temporary because they are subjected to extreme scrutiny and criticism, and – all too often – ultimately forced out in some disgrace (Kanter, 1977).

'Fixing the women' change strategies are often focused mainly on managerial women, in part because of the costs of providing special training and assistance. To the extent that a change strategy has a managerial focus, it is important to note that the beneficiaries will be predominantly white, middle-class women. Working-class women have fewer opportunities for promotion into managerial ranks, have fewer well-paid options elsewhere, may be more dependent on seniority and pensions, and are more likely to work in 'pink velvet ghettos', that is mostly female-dominated job categories (Reskin and Roos, 1990; Strober, 1984). In such female jobs, there is no pressure to conform to male norms, but there is also little opportunity to escape traditional feminine behavioural expectations and pay limitations (Young, 1991).

Women who are members of racial, religious or ethnic minorities suffer the double jeopardy of both sex and other forms of inequality, and for many minority women, gendered inequalities may be of secondary importance. In addition, the pernicious effects of gender inequities may surface with a different form and intensity for minority women (Collins, 1991; Lorde, 1983). For example, because white men may view minority women as unsuitable marriage prospects, sexual harassment of minority women often takes a more hostile, less ostensibly 'romantic', and more dehumanizing form (Hurtado, 1999). Efforts to 'fix women' are seldom tailored to take into account the specialized difficulties of minority women. For working-class and minority women, then, 'Fixing the women' may be a particularly unhelpful change strategy.

Stereotypical images of masculinity (be tough, don't show emotions other than anger, aggression, and competitiveness, etc.) (Kerfoot and

Knights, 1993) are also left unchanged by this strategy. As recent research on masculinities has shown, on the shop floor (Collinson, 1988) and in the managerial and professional ranks (Collinson and Knights, 1986; Collinson and Hearn, 1996), such images of masculinity are constraining for men as well as their female co-workers. In summary, both men and women remain trapped when 'Fixing the women' is the approach taken.

Valuing the feminine

The Simmons researchers define this strategy as focusing on characteristics that are traditionally seen as 'feminine', such as being empathetic, sympathetic, nurturing, non-competitive, deferential and having good listening skills. Noting that these characteristics have been often devalued, this change strategy seeks to revalue them as equal or even superior to traditionally masculine characteristics, such as competitiveness, aggressiveness and so on.

There are many limitations of this approach. It reinforces stereotypes that do not acknowledge the variations in the actual behaviours of men and women, underestimating the variance within a category and failing to acknowledge the ways categories overlap (Fondas, 1997). Furthermore, stereotypes of women vary. For example, African-American women often have to cope with the harmful limitations of stereotypes such as Jezebel, the temptress, and Mammy, the all-understanding, endlessly nurturing servant (Nkomo, 1992). White women cope with an array of stereotypes as well, including the cute pet, the iron maiden, the mother and the seductress (Kanter, 1977). Women who do not conform to stereotypical preconceptions are sometimes ignored, disparaged and misperceived.

Especially when women work in positions where the formal job requirements or informal norms create pressure to conform to feminine stereotypes, various demeaning interactions become expected. The work of secretaries and service workers includes sexualized rituals of deference and flirtation (Hall, 1993; Pringle, 1988).[4] Female faculty members who become administrators often feel tacitly or explicitly pressured to take the role of 'office wife', caring for neglected student concerns and making sure necessary administrative work gets done, freeing their male administrative colleagues for long-term strategy meetings and political alliance building (Huff, 1990). The 'Valuing the feminine' change strategy fosters little change, and to the extent it reinforces gendered stereotypes, it is severely constraining, providing excuses for the underpayment and subordination of women.

Adding women and stirring (minimal structural change)

This change strategy alters a few rules, practices and structures, so that women are allowed to enter positions previously closed to them, but, as the Simmons group observes, the basics of bureaucratic organizational structure (hierarchy, division of labour, gendered organizational norms, etc.) are left largely untouched. This strategy assumes that hiring women into previously male-dominated jobs is equivalent to giving them 'equal opportunity' to succeed. Recruitment, rather than retention and promotion, is the focus of this strategy.

This is a difficult strategy to enact, in part because it is difficult to get women to apply for jobs that have previously been held mostly by males. If women are responsible for most housework and dependent care – and most women, even in dual career partnerships, are (Hochschild, 1989) – they may be unwilling or unable to accept a job that has been previously held mostly by men, especially if that job requires long hours, weekend and evening work, or extensive travel. In addition, women may (sometimes realistically) fear that they will be subject to isolation, hostility, sexual harassment or unfair performance evaluations. They may not apply because job descriptions or interviews include code words ('competitive', 'aggressive leadership style') or pronouns ('We expect that he...') that signal that male applicants are preferred (Collinson et al., 1990; Marshall, 1984).

Some of these problems can be addressed (through 'Fixing the women' strategies or by small structural changes, such as rewording job descriptions to remove gendered 'code words'). However, even if women do apply for and enter male-dominated positions, they must operate at a disadvantage that is often invisible, to themselves and to others. For example, when a woman is a 'solo' (that is, the only female or one of a very few women in a male-dominated job), her performance will be much more carefully scrutinized and there is a strong probability that it will be evaluated in a biased fashion (Kanter, 1977; Taylor et al., 1978). She may find it difficult, if not impossible, to avoid being stereotyped. She may be excluded with, for example, boundary-heightening sexualized jokes, or a lack of invitations to informal gatherings.[5] For these reasons, 'adding women and stirring' is a strategy that has been shown, repeatedly, to fail. One cannot change hiring laws and procedures, alter little else, and expect efforts to reduce gender inequality to succeed in the long term (Bielby and Baron, 1987).[6]

Making small, deep cultural changes (with dual objectives of improving gender equity and organizational efficiency)

This fourth approach emerged from the Simmons researchers' gender equity intervention work with corporations (Coleman and Rippin, 2000; Ely and Meyerson, 2000a, 2000b; Meyerson and Kolb, 2000). Rather than changing formal policies or structures, this fourth change strategy focuses on changing relatively small aspects of an organization's culture, aspects that are selected because they have deeply embedded implications for gender relations. For example, in a manufacturing plant, teams of assembly line workers were strictly sex segregated. Leaders of these teams were men who used a rather authoritarian style of management. After some training that heightened awareness of gender equity issues, the Simmons researchers introduced mixed sex teams and rotating leadership, permitting some women to hold leadership positions for the first time. Productivity increased, thereby achieving the dual objectives of the Simmons group's fourth change strategy: greater gender equity and greater efficiency. When the Simmons researchers introduced a number of these 'small wins' experimental projects within the same corporation, they found that for most of the projects, gender equity goals faded in salience (were forgotten); reasons for continuing or aborting the projects revolved almost completely around efficiency and productivity issues (Coleman and Rippen, 2000).

In a second example of this strategy, Bailyn (1993) studied engineers building a complex software system. The engineers complained about the need to work long hours, put in 'face time' at the office, and deal with constant interruptions. Many female engineers, and to a lesser extent many of their male colleagues involved in dual career partnerships, found the long hours especially difficult, given their family responsibilities. Bailyn and her colleagues collaborated with employees in designing a remedy that was apparently gender neutral: to set aside mornings for uninterrupted work, asking all the engineers to save their questions and meetings for the afternoons. These new time management norms benefited all concerned. Long hours decreased because work was completed more efficiently, and demands for 'face time' decreased, to the relief, especially, of women with families and men in dual career partnerships. Although this change strategy was designed, in part, to improve gender equity, its rationale was described primarily in terms of efficiency and productivity goals, because it was thought by the researchers that this would increase its chances of being accepted.

Limitations of this gender equity change strategy include a lack of attention to men's gender-related difficulties, the small scale of the changes implemented, and the fact that instrumental objectives showed a tendency to take precedence over gender equity goals. Although the dual objective focus of this fourth change strategy is controversial, it is important to note that few organizations would be willing to contemplate such interventions unless some organizational performance improvement were likely. In addition, if a series of small wins is to have a cumulative effect on gender equity, long-term time investment is required.

Creating new organizational structures (including feminist separatism)

The global proliferation of bureaucratic structures has been accompanied by a widespread reification of hierarchy and division of labour, in the name of efficiency and organizational survival. Feminist theorists, like many critical theorists, have been quite critical of this development, given the centrality of egalitarian values in feminist ideology. Ferguson (1984) has been exceptionally articulate in her critique of bureaucracy and the ways it works to the disadvantage, especially, of women. This fifth change strategy is anti-bureaucratic. It involves the planned introduction of major structural changes that minimize inequalities of all forms, including gender inequities. In these feminist organizational structures, hierarchy and division of labour are dramatically reduced, for example, by rotating all jobs, including leadership positions, and by relying on consensual decision-making practices. Although such structural alterations are common in non-feminist collective organizations (Rothschild-Whitt, 1979), feminist organizations often add two distinctive characteristics: an explicit commitment to feminist ideology and an emphasis on personal and emotional openness, challenging attempts to separate the public and the private spheres (Ferree and P. Martin, 1995). In many such feminist organizations, there is an explicit commitment that feminist goals will take precedence over organizational performance objectives, such as efficiency or profitability.

Feminist organizations include public sector endeavours, such as battered women's shelters and political action collectives, as well as businesses, particularly those that market to feminist customers (Epstein et al., 1988; Ferree and P. Martin, 1995). There are relatively few such feminist organizations, and most are small. Many are largely or exclusively founded and staffed by women (Valentine and McIntosh, 1990), providing a safe haven where feminists and others can earn their living without having to cope with the problems described in previous strategy descriptions.

Given that this fifth strategy does not give priority to organizational performance objectives over other feminist concerns, it is not surprising that most of these organizations find it difficult to survive, financially, for the long term. The intense personal relationships that such organizations foster can, and often do, breed intense interpersonal conflicts, particularly around those individuals who play more of a leadership role or work harder and longer than others, making some of these feminist organizations seem to be unpleasant places to work (Farrell, 1995; Valentine and McIntosh, 1990). It is difficult to enact egalitarian values when some organizational members consistently offer greater time commitment and expertise. In spite of Acker's (1990) admonitions for feminists to keep their eyes on class issues at all times (see also Pollert, 1996), all too often, class differences among women prove to be the critical weakness of these feminist organizations because well-intentioned, white, middle-class feminists fail to anticipate, comprehend and deal effectively with the needs and values of their working-class female co-workers (Tom, 1995). When feminist organizations do survive, like non-feminist collectives, they do provide a haven for their members, but their small scale, limited focus and separatism tends to limit the amount of influence they have on surrounding people and institutions.

Transforming gendered society

This sixth feminist change strategy focuses on transforming the gendered aspects of society, rather than attempting to alter individuals or single organizational contexts, paying particular attention to class-based sources of inequality (Pollert, 1996). This ambitious change strategy crosses institutional boundaries (involving for example religious, government, educational and corporate entities), seeking the dual objectives of the fourth change strategy: (1) gender equity and (2) at least sufficient economic efficiency for people's needs to be met.

No large-scale, long-term, successful examples of this sixth strategy exist, although smaller-scale, partial successes have been recorded. In South Africa the federal government has created gender equity task forces. These task forces include both men and women, who have been empowered, to some extent, to ensure that the national transformation of race relations and economic power includes a transformation in gender relations, for both men and women. The scale of societal transformation in South Africa has opened the door, many think, to changes in gender relations that would, in a more stable society, be more difficult to implement. It may be that widespread social turmoil, affecting one of these dimensions of inequality, loosens interdependencies, so changes along other dimensions of inequality become possible.[7] Another example of strategy six is Cisco's funding of Networking Academies, to train women and men for technical careers (not just at Cisco) in over 42 countries in some of the least economically developed areas of the world. Such ambitious change interventions require governmental support and/or large amounts of funding, a resource constraint that makes examples of strategy six exceedingly rare and simultaneously important to study.

Relationships among these feminist change strategies

Relationships among these six strategies are worth noting. There is a big gap between the liberalism of the first three strategies (or the incrementalism of the first four strategies), and the more radical change sought in 'Creating new organizational structures' and 'Transforming gendered society'. The latter two strategies are relatively more congruent with critical theory, although the feminist research that points out the shortcomings of the first three strategies is also, in a different way, consistent with the spirit of critical thinking.

The strategies are also, in practice, hard to separate. Often, one leads directly to another. For example, when the third strategy, 'Adding women and stirring', is adopted, problems usually become evident rapidly, and 'Fixing the women' is often implemented shortly thereafter. The second strategy, 'Valuing the feminine', is in some ways a weaker version of the fifth strategy, 'Creating new organizational structures', especially when those

TABLE 4.1 *Outcomes of gender inequality change strategies**

1 Fix the women	A few individuals succeed
2 Value the feminine	Virtually no change
3 Add women and stir	Slow, partial change with reversions
4 Make small, deep cultural changes, dual objectives	Instrumental goals take precedence, gender goals lost
5 Create new organizational structures	Few survive long term
6 Transform gendered society	Rare, perhaps in South Africa?

*First four strategies adapted from Coleman and Rippin, 2000; Ely and Meyerson 2000a, 2000b; Meyerson and Kolb, 2000.

new structures have mostly female members. In some ways, it is the relationships among these strategies, rather than evaluations of their separable effectiveness, that is of most interest.[8] Once again, critical theory might well offer helpful insights into these issues.

Table 4.1 lists the six strategies and summarizes the evidence on their effectiveness. None of these six strategies has had, so far, an impressive record of success, as all encounter resistance. However, in accord with the fourth strategy's emphasis on the importance of small wins (see also Fournier and Grey, 2000: 21), the combination of these strategies, used in different contexts with differing levels of success, has created some progress. Cross-national comparisons, particularly in some sectors (like public sector work in Scandinavia and Australia) where women have made major advances, would be useful. It is clear that a study of a wider range of change processes, including collective action, work slowdowns, sabotage, protests, community organizing techniques, major structural changes, as well as aspects of more conventional models of organizational development techniques, would help feminist theorists achieve more of their change objectives. Some critical theorists have long been dealing with this wider scope of change processes, and so the synergies possible might well be useful and important to both traditions of inquiry.

THE SEPARATE DEVELOPMENT OF FEMINIST AND CRITICAL THEORIES

If feminist theory and critical theory share so many issues of concern, and if feminist change strategies can be usefully criticized and strengthened by drawing on critical research, it is hard to understand why the two traditions have developed so independently. Although critical theory is an older intellectual tradition, it seems reasonable to expect that contemporary critical theory and feminist theory would cite each other's work and build theoretical synergies between the two traditions. This has not happened to a substantial extent. An index in a critical theory book usually will include few names of female scholars, few mentions of the words 'sex' or 'gender', and few ideas taken from feminist work. When critical theory publications do offer an extended discussion of feminist ideas, it is often relegated to a footnote, a parenthetical aside, a list of 'also relevant' types of literature, or at best a separate chapter – forms of marginalization that can inadvertently serve as a justification for excluding gender issues from the rest of the text.

Unfortunately, feminist theorists are just as likely to fail to cite and integrate critical theory literature, even when that work is of central, explicit concern to feminist ideas (e.g. Alvesson and Billing, 1997: 186). Feminist theorists also tend to marginalize relevant critical theory in lists of related literature, parenthetical asides, and footnotes. Extended discussions of the relevance of critical work to feminist thinking are unfortunately rare, even in sections or chapters that are kept separate from the rest of a text.

Thus, feminist theorists generally treat critical theory, and critical theorists generally treat feminist theory, as separate and unequal. As race relations in the US have shown, separate-but-equal may sound desirable to some, but dichotomies that delineate difference tend to evolve into inequalities. When critical theorists integrate feminist work, and when feminist theorists do the same for critical work, more interesting synergies may emerge (Alvesson and Billing, 1997; Diamond and Quinby, 1988; Fraser, 1987; Pollert, 1996; Sawicki, 1991; Smircich and Calas, 1995). To move towards integration, however, we need to understand why this separation has occurred and why it has been perpetuated.

EVALUATING THE VALIDITY OF CRITIQUES OF FEMINIST THEORY

Some critical theorists offer reasons why feminist theory can be legitimately excluded from consideration. Some of these criticisms are well founded, at least for some kinds of feminist theory, and others are based on misconceptions. Table 4.2 and the remainder of this chapter summarize the orientation of each feminist change strategy with regard to these critiques. (Cell entries in this table summarize the results of research to date, rather than the ultimate potential of each strategy.)

Does feminist theory focus primarily on privileged women and therefore fail to critique hegemony?

Some critical theorists assert that feminist theory focuses on the concerns of middle-class white women who want more access to well-paid managerial and professional jobs. Because of this focus on the interests of women of privilege, these critical theorists argue, feminist theory does not challenge the hegemony of models of organization that assume the immutability and

TABLE 4.2 *Assumptions underlying gender inequality change strategies**

	Focus on privileged women?	Change system?	Change individual women?	Assimilate to male norms?	Primacy of instrumental goals?	Privilege women over men?
1 Fix the women	Usually	No	Yes	Yes	Yes	No
2 Value the feminine	No	No	No	No	No or dual goals	Superficially
3 Add women and stir	Yes	Minor changes	After entry, yes	Yes	Yes	Temporarily
4 Make small, deep cultural changes	No	Small wins	No?	No	Dual goals	No
5 Create new organizational structures	No	Yes	No?	No	No	Usually
6 Transform gendered society	No	Yes	No?	No	No	No

*First four strategies adapted from Coleman and Rippin, 2000; Ely and Meyerson, 2000a, 2000b; Meyerson and Kolb, 2000.

even desirability of hierarchy, division of labour, class differences and capitalism (Alvesson and Willmott, 1992: 6).

To assess the validity of this critique, let us turn first to the feminist change literature discussed above. As can be seen in Table 4.2, in agreement with this critique, much of the research on the first three strategies has tended to treat women as a homogeneous category, not acknowledging and exploring the effects of racial, ethnic and class differences on women's experiences. Also in accord with this critique, much of the research on the effectiveness of these three strategies has a tendency to focus on women with managerial or professional aspirations. However, contrary to this critique, the fourth, 'Making small, deep cultural changes', and the two more radical change strategies seldom have this narrow focus.

To address this important issue in more general terms, there are varieties of feminism for which this critique is merited. For example, there is a well-established liberal tradition of gender research (sometimes labelled the 'women in management' or 'dress for success' school of thought), that focuses on enabling women to gain success, defined usually as access to high-ranking managerial and professional positions, within existing organizational structures. Such women are usually white, middle class and otherwise privileged. This liberal tradition is relatively well represented in US business schools,[9] because its focus on 'breaking glass ceilings' and encouraging equal opportunity for women does not directly challenge assumptions about hierarchy, class-based divisions of labour, capitalism and so on.

However, this critique is not descriptive of all, or even most, of current feminist thinking. In a watershed book for feminist theory, Spelman (1989) outlined the devastating effects of assuming that all women are a category with homogeneous interests – a position often referred to as an 'essentialist' approach to feminist thinking. Most contemporary feminists would agree with Spelman; we cannot focus on privileged white women, then build theory presumed to apply to all women. Contemporary feminism, even that which does not embrace postmodernism, deconstructs the category 'woman' and the dichotomies of 'sex' and 'gender', examining the ways women's and men's identities are multiple, socially constructed, and reflective of class, race, ethnicity, and other cultural factors. The experiences of African-American women (Bell, 1990; Bell et al., 1993; Collins, 1990; hooks, 1981) and Hispanic women (Calas, 1992; Hurtado, 1999; Zavella, 1991), in particular, have been extensively explored.

Other feminist scholarship has explored the ways colonial and post-colonial histories have affected the material conditions and subjectivities of women, especially in less industrialized countries (Calas and Smircich, 1993; Minh-ha, 1989; Spivak, 1987). Of particular relevance, given the class focus of critical theory, a large, and long-standing feminist literature has focused on the experiences of working-class women holding clerical, manufacturing and service jobs (Hartmann, 1981; Kondo, 1990; Pringle, 1988; Young, 1991).

A branch of feminism has placed class issues at the forefront of feminist analysis (Acker, 1990), often with a socialist-feminist (class first) or feminist-socialist (gender first) orientation that challenges assumptions of capitalism by exploring its basis in class-based partriarchal systems (Eisenstein, 1983; Haraway, 1985; Hartmann, 1981; Young, 1980).

Some critical theorists have argued that feminist scholarship should not focus on helping women to gain access to existing hierarchies, by increasing their skills and competencies, because that individually focused change strategy does not seek to change existing hierarchical arrangements that perpetuate class, as well as gender and racial, inequalities. In accord with this critique, the first four change strategies do not attempt major structural change of hierarchical arrangements, although the fourth approach hopes to achieve major changes in gender equity for women of all classes, through small, incremental steps. However, this critique is not an apt criticism of the last two, more radical change strategies.

To explore this critique in more detail, feminist scholarship that fails to critique hegemony, and prefers instead to focus on preparing women of privilege to enter well-paid managerial and professional positions in male-dominated hierarchies, should exhibit several distinguishing characteristics. Several of these characteristics are assessed below.

Versions of feminist theory that fail to critique hegemony should focus on helping individual women to gain entry to hierarchies, rather than working to change the surrounding context. When individual shortcomings are blamed for observed inequalities, meritocratic assumptions remain unchallenged. Only the first strategy, 'Fixing the women', has this tendency to focus on changing individual women. However, when women encounter problems of adjustment to male-dominated systems, in strategy three, 'Adding women and stirring', their difficulties are often attributed to individual shortcomings. The remaining four change strategies attend more to altering the surrounding context, rather than blaming individual women for difficulties, although these change strategies vary in the extent to which they seek to alter that context.

Next, a feminist theory that does not seek major alterations in existing arrangements might well take the position that women should assimilate to the norms of male-dominated systems, rather than focusing on changing those gendered norms. Only 'Fixing the women' and 'Adding women and stirring' take an assimilationist position; the remaining strategies work on changing the context rather than asking individual women to conform to norms created by and for men.

Finally, approaches that do not seek to alter existing hegemonic arrangements generally give primacy to instrumental goals, such as maximizing organizational efficiency, effectiveness and profitability or seeking individual career success, as measured by pay and promotions. The first strategy, 'Fixing the women', does give priority to these kinds of instrumental goals.

The second strategy, 'Valuing the feminine', calls for revaluing traditionally feminine characteristics, such as caring for others' emotional well-being. Often, but not always, advocates of this strategy (and its variants) argue that these feminine characteristics may also serve instrumental functions for an organization, as when a warm, caring management style or improved inter-personal relations improve team productivity (Fletcher, 1999). The remaining strategies have dual objectives, one of which is instrumental, and the other, focused on gender equity. None of the feminist strategies reviewed here denies the importance of instrumental objectives, although strategies with dual objectives do not give instrumental goals unchallenged primacy. In the last two strategies, 'Creating new organizational structures' and 'Transforming gendered society', gender equity objectives are equal to or greater in importance than instrumental goals. In summary, to equate all of feminist thinking with work congruent with the first three change strategies is to exclude from consideration precisely those aspects of feminist work most relevant to critical theory.

Does feminist theory seek to reverse gender inequalities by privileging women over men?

Another critique, less frequently voiced, is that feminist theory seeks to reverse prior gender inequalities, leaving women (temporarily or permanently) in a privileged position. According to this critique, in an effort to create more equitable gender relations, the views and objectives of women are given, at least temporarily, a privileged status, thereby producing a new form of gender hegemony, one that reverses the priorities of patriarchy. This is an important critique to address, even though it is made relatively infrequently, because it bears directly on affirmative action policies that give temporary advantage to the historically disadvantaged, including in some contexts, women.

This critique involves a misunderstanding of feminist ideology. Most versions of feminism do not seek to reverse gender inequalities, putting women ahead of men, but rather seek to eradicate gender inequalities while, for some issues (such as pregnancy), acknowledging and preserving some differences. Nevertheless, in a limited sense, this critique is merited, especially with regard to two change strategies, 'Valuing the feminine' and 'Creating new organizational structures'. It is likely that these strategies would create organizational contexts where some men (and some women) would feel uncomfortable and would find it difficult to conform to some organizational norms, much like many women now react with discomfort to some male-dominated organizational contexts. The third strategy, 'Adding women and stirring', is sometimes interpreted as calling to give women a temporary advantage, at the entry level, so they will have equal opportunity to achieve. However, this third strategy is not usually formulated in terms of necessarily achieving equal outcomes (equal opportunity at entry is the focus), so no generalized, long-term domination by women is anticipated or achieved. The remaining four change strategies 'Fixing the women', 'Adding women and stirring', 'Making small, deep cultural changes', and 'Transforming gendered societies' are striving for forms of gender equality and equity, not seeking to put women in a position superior to men.

In more general terms, there are versions of feminist theory that privilege traditionally feminine practices (Fletcher, 1999; Rosener, 1995), for example, lauding women's distinctive 'ways of knowing' or 'feminine ways of leading'. Other feminists argue that because of their positions in patriarchal societies, women have a distinctively insightful vantage point from which to see and criticize traditional gender arrangements (Hartsock, 1983), an approach termed feminist 'standpoint' theory. However, in spite of these reasons for advocating temporary or more permanent pre-eminence for women's views, most feminist theorists refrain from advocating the domination of men by women. Most contemporary feminists are more likely to challenge dichotomous conceptualizations of sex and gender, and seek the abolition rather than the reversal, of systems of domination.

> Is feminist theory incomplete, or narrow, unless it includes study of men, the constraints of masculinities, and relations between genders? Is critical theory broader because it considers abstract topics, such as technocracy and ecological problems, that pertain to both genders?

A related critique is that feminist theory focuses primarily on the concerns of women, rather than exploring relations between the genders, and in particular, the ways masculinities constrain men. Some Critical Theorists have argued that feminism is too narrow unless it expands its focus to include men and masculinity, and becomes a study of gender relations rather than feminism (Alvesson and Billing, 1997: 180). First, let us address this critique with reference to the feminist change literature reviewed above. Four strategies, 'Fixing the women', 'Valuing the feminine', 'Adding women and stirring', and 'Creating new organizational structures' (when those structures are female-dominated) are indeed focused primarily on the concerns of women. The fourth strategy explicitly deals with the concerns of both men and women, although it focuses more on alleviating gender inequalities that work to the disadvantage of women. The sixth strategy, 'Transforming gendered society', is similarly concerned with both men and women.

In more general terms, relations between the genders is a tacit subtext or partial focus of much feminist thinking, particularly in work that examines processes of domination, the creation and perpetuation of gender inequalities, and the interdependence of ideas about masculinities and femininities. A focus on gender relations is particularly visible in the feminist work that deconstructs attempts to separate public and private spheres of influence (Hochschild, 1989; J. Martin, 1990; Rosenberg, 1982), showing how work and family concerns affect each other, for both men and women. Feminist scholars, particularly in the United Kingdom (Collinson, 1988; Collinson and Hearn, 1996; Collinson and Knights, 1986), have shown how stereotypes of masculinity constrain men, and women, in a variety of working settings, ranging from the shopfloor to the executive suite. Sexuality at work is another arena (Hearn and Parkin, 1987) where a focus on both men and women (primarily those who are heterosexual) is evident.

This kind of expansion of feminist thought is essential, but it is understandable that feminist scholars, after years of exclusion and marginalization, would want to focus primarily on the concerns of women. However, if feminist thought is to make greater progress achieving change in gender equity, women cannot do it by themselves, long term; even separatist havens need to find ways of surviving in environments where their ideology is not shared. Consideration of the constraining effects of men's roles and our ideas of masculinity must be part of any major, long-lasting change in relations between the genders. Gender relations at work, for example, are unlikely to change, unless gender relations at home are altered, and change in both arenas will involve men. In general terms, then, this critique is a point well taken. However, as long as the interests and practices of the 'other' gender are ignored or distorted, there will be a need for feminism to focus, disproportionately, on women and the constraints of assumptions about femininities.

A related critique of feminist theory also merits analysis: the idea that Critical Theory is broader than feminist theory. For example, Alvesson and Willmott state this critique explicitly and cogently:

> [Critical Theory] has the strength of being sufficiently broad to serve as a source of critical reflection on a large number of central issues in management studies: epistemological issues, notions of rationality and progress, technocracy and social engineering, autonomy and control, communicative action, power and ideology. In comparison, Marxist, Foucauldian and feminist perspectives are more specialized and restricted. (1992: 9)

In direct contradiction to the critique of narrowness, feminist theory is exceptionally broad in its focus, in part because it arose in an explicitly interdisciplinary context. In many universities, the 'one woman in each department' would meet in informal interdisciplinary gatherings. To illustrate the resulting breadth of feminist inquiry, reconsider each disciplinary or topic area mentioned in Alvesson and Willmott's critique. Feminist studies relevant to each of these issues have shown how these broad and apparently gender neutral phenomena are not gender neutral: epistemology

(Benhabib, 1984; Harding and Hintikka, 1983; Knights, 1992); rationality (Mumby and Putnam, 1992); progress (Brenner, 1987; Lorde, 1983; Minh-ha, 1989); technocracy and social engineering (De Laurentis, 1984; Haraway, 1985); autonomy and control (Calas, 1993; Fraad et al., 1989); communicative action (Hall, 1993; Kerfoot and Knights, 1993; Kristeva, 1977); power and ideology (Butler and Scott, 1992; Smith, 1990). Any domain of inquiry is by definition narrow if it excludes women's concerns.[10] Much of organizational theory, and much of critical theory (including Critical Theory), does just that – it claims to study all of an abstract noun, like bureaucracy or management, without exploring the ways that ostensibly gender-neutral ideas and practices reflect gendered assumptions about both masculinity and femininity. Only by combining the strengths of these traditions, and including assumptions about masculinity as well as femininity, will either of these traditions gain the breadth needed.

To summarize this analysis of critiques of feminist theory, it is clear that feminist theory no longer focuses exclusively or even primarily on privileged white women. The intersections of gender with, for example, race, ethnicity and class are all prominent features of contemporary feminist analysis. There are many varieties of feminist theory that do not focus on success within existing organizational hierarchies (seeking instrumental goals of individual career success, consumerism, etc.). These versions of feminist theory advocate system-wide change. The goal of most versions of feminist theory is not to reverse existing gender inequalities, as that would replace one system of domination with another. The goal, rather, is to challenge and hopefully change aspects of social relations that create the need for one group to dominate another. These are goals that many critical theorists, including some Critical Theorists, share.

THE TURN TOWARDS CRITIQUING THE STATUS QUO, RATHER THAN SEEKING SYSTEM CHANGE

Many contemporary critical theorists have turned away from seeking society-wide transformation, to focus on a critique of the status quo, 'refraining from directive statements about what people should do (revolt, liberate) but emphasizing the problematization of dominating values and beliefs' (Alvesson and Deetz, 1996: 202). Similarly, as indicated in the evaluation of the six feminist change strategies, feminist theory has generally focused more on critiquing the status quo, exposing gendered inequalities; it has not shown us how, effectively, to reduce or eradicate those inequalities. Perhaps if critical theorists and feminist theorists were to work together on problems of change, unexpected synergies would arise.

NOTES

I would like to thank the Scandinavian visitors to Stanford in the Spring of 2001, Mats Alvesson, Myra Strober, Dick Scott and Woody Powell for their comments on an earlier draft of this paper. Walter Nord, John Jermier, Paul Adler and David Knights have helped me find my way into the critical theory literature; my primary guides into organizational feminist theory have been Linda Smircich, Marta Calas and Deb Meyerson. Although all of these people have been helpful, in person and through their writing, none should be held responsible for the content of this paper.

1 Critical Theorists are less likely than critical theorists to focus on class issues.
2 Some are uncomfortable labelling male scholars feminists. Personally I am not.
3 Patriarchy is a form of hegemony where men dominate women, its opposite is matriarchy.
4 Gherardi (1995) argues that flirtation on the job eases male discomfort with women in professional roles, creating a more pleasurable atmosphere for women as well as men. In contrast, US feminists are more likely to consider the expectation of flirtation with male co-workers to be demeaning and a possible, tepid precursor to sexual harassment. It is possible that the meaning and behavioural expectations (of sexual interest) associated with flirtation differ internationally.
5 In contrast, when men are solos in a group of women, they are more likely to be fussed over, selected as leader, and generally made to feel welcome (Taylor et al., 1978).
6 Even if numbers of women do increase in selected, previously male-dominated job categories, such as bank tellers (Strober and Arnold, 1987), symphony orchestras (Allemendinger and Hackman, 1995), or college administrators (Pfeffer and Davis-Blake, 1987), the job usually 'tips', becoming all-female rather rapidly, with a concomitant decrease in pay and prestige. Professors of organizational behaviour, marketing, and psychology should beware, given the increasing numbers of female PhD students we are producing.
7 I am indebted to Professor Myra Strober for pointing this out.
8 Again, I am grateful to Professor Strober for raising these questions.
9 'Relatively', in part because women faculty are still rare in business schools (J. Martin, 1994).
10 This is not to say that in some domains, most women may have the same concerns as men. Furthermore, as Alvesson and Willmott contend, 'arguably, most if not all social phenomena involve a gender aspect, but it would be reductionist to capture most aspects of management, production, and consumption basically in feminist terms' (1992: 9).

REFERENCES

Acker, J. (1990) Hierarchies, jobs, bodies: A theory of gendered organizations. *Gender & Society*. 4: 139–58.

Acker, J. and Van Houten, D.R. (1974) Differential recruitment and control: The sex structuring of organizations. *Administrative Science Quarterly*. 19: 152–63.

Allmendinger, J. and Hackman, J.R. (1995) The more the better? A four-nation study of the inclusion of women in symphony orchestras. *Social Forces*. 74: 423–60.

Alvesson, M. and Billing, Y.D. (1997) *Understanding Gender and Organizations*. Thousand Oaks, CA: Sage.

Alvesson, M. and Deetz, S. (1996) Critical theory and postmodernism approaches to organizational studies. In S. Clegg, C. Hardy and W. Nord (eds), *Handbook of Organization Studies*. Thousand Oaks, CA: Sage. pp. 191–217.

Alvesson, M. and Willmott, H. (eds) (1992) *Critical Management Studies*. Newbury Park, CA: Sage.

Bailyn, L. (1993) *Breaking the Mold: Women, Men and Time in the New Corporate World*. New York: Free Press.

Bambara, T.C. (ed.) (1970) *The Black Woman: An Anthology*. New York: New American Library.

Bell, E.L. (1990) The bicultural life experience of career-oriented black women. *Journal of Organizational Behavior*. 11: 459–77.

Bell, E.L., Denton, T.C. and Nkomo, S. (1993) Women of color: Toward an inclusive analysis. In E.A. Fagenson (ed.), *Women in Management: Trends, Issues and Challenges in Managerial Diversity*. Newbury Park, CA: Sage. pp. 105–30.

Benhabib, S. (1984) Epistemologies of postmodernism: A rejoinder to Jean-François Lyotard. *New German Critique*. 33: 103–26.

Bielby, W.T. and Baron, J.N. (1987) Undoing discrimination: Job integration and comparable worth. In C. Bose and G. Spitze (eds), *Ingredients for Women's Employment Policy*. Albany, NY: State University of New York Press. pp. 211–29.

Brenner, J. (1987) Feminist political discourses: Radical vs. liberal approaches to the feminization of poverty and comparable worth. *Gender & Society*. 1: 447–65.

Butler, J. and Scott, J.W. (1992) *Feminists Theorize the Political*. New York: Routledge.

Calas, M. (1987) Organizational science/fiction: The postmodern in the management disciplines. PhD dissertation. University of Massachusetts, Amherst, MA.

Calas, M.B. (1992) An/other silent voice? Representing 'Hispanic woman' in organizational texts. In A.J. Mills and P. Tancred (eds), *Gendering Organizational Analysis*. Newbury Park, CA: Sage. pp. 201–21.

Calas, M.B. (1993) Deconstructing charismatic leadership: Re-reading Weber from the darker side. *Leadership Quarterly*. 4: 305–28.

Calas, M.B. and Smircich, L. (1993). Dangerous liaisons: The 'feminine-in-management' meets globalization. *Business Horizons*. March/April: 71–81.

Coleman, G. and Rippin, A. (2000) Putting feminist theory to work: Collaboration as a means toward organizational change. *Organization*. 7: 573–87.

Collins, P.H. (1990) *Black Feminist Thought*. New York: Routledge.

Collins, P.H. (1991) *Black Feminist Thought: Knowledge, Consciousness, and the Politics of Empowerment*. New York: Routledge.

Collinson, D. (1988) 'Engineering humour': Masculinity, joking, and conflict in shop floor relations. *Organization Studies*. 9: 181–99.

Collinson, D. and Hearn, J. (eds) (1996) *Men as Managers, Managers as Men: Critical Perspectives on Men, Masculinities and Managements*. London: Sage.

Collinson, D. and Knights, D. (1986) 'Men only': Theories and practices of job segregation in insurance. In D. Knights and H. Willmott (eds), *Gender and the Labour Process*. Aldershot: Gower. pp. 140–78.

Collinson, D., Knights, D. and Collinson, M. (1990) *Managing to Discriminate*. London: Routledge.

De Beauvoir, S. (1972 [1949]) *The Second Sex*. Harmondsworth, Middlesex: Penguin.

De Lauretis, T. (1984) *Alice Doesn't: Feminism, Semiotics, Cinema*. Bloomington, IN: Indiana University Press.

Diamond, I. and Quinby, L. (eds) (1988) *Feminism and Foucault*. Boston, MA: Northeastern University Press.

Eisenstein, H. (1983) *Contemporary Feminist Thought*. Boston, MA: G.K. Hall.

Ely, R.J. (1995) The power in demography: Women's social construction of gender identity at work. *Academy of Management Journal*. 38: 589–634.

Ely, R.J. and Meyerson, D. (2000a) Theories of gender in organizations: A new approach to organizational analysis and change. In B. Staw and R. Sutton (eds), *Research in Organizational Behavior*. Greenwich, CN: JAI Press. pp. 105–53.

Ely, R. J. and Meyerson, D. (2000b) Advancing gender equity in organizations: The challenge and importance of maintaining a gender narrative. *Organization*. 7: 589–608.

Epstein, S., Russell, G. and Silvern, L. (1988) Structure and ideology of shelters for battered women. *American Journal of Community Psychology*. 16: 345–67.

Ferguson, K.E. (1984) *The Feminist Case against Bureaucracy*. Philadelphia, PA: Temple University Press.

Ferree, M.M. and Martin, P.Y. (1995) Doing the work of the movement: Feminist organizations. In M.M. Ferree and P.Y. Martin (eds), *Feminist Organizations: Harvest of the New Women's Movement*. Philadelphia, PA: Temple University Press. pp. 3–23.

Fletcher, J.K. (1999) *Disappearing Acts: Gender, Power and Relational Practice at Work*. Cambridge, MA: MIT Press.

Fondas, N. (1997) Feminization unveiled: Management qualities in contemporary writings. *Academy of Management Review*. 22: 257–82.

Foucault, M. (1977) *Discipline and Punish*. London: Allen Lane.

Fournier, V. and Grey, C. (2000) At the critical moment: Conditions and prospects for critical management studies. *Human Relations*. 53: 7–32.

Fraad, H., Resnick, S. and Wolff, R. (1989) For every knight in shining armor, there's a castle waiting to be cleaned: A Marxist-feminist analysis of the household. *Rethinking Marxism*. 2: 9–69.

Fraser, N. (1987) What's critical about critical theory? The case of Habermas and gender. In S. Benhabib and D. Cornell (eds), *Feminism as Critique*. Cambridge: Polity Press. pp. 31–55.

Gherardi, S. (1995) *Gender, Symbolism and Organizational Cultures*. London: Sage.

Hall, E.J. (1993) Smiling, deferring, and flirting: Doing gender by giving 'good service'. *Work and Occupations*. 20: 452–71.

Haraway, D. (1985) A manifesto for cyborgs: science, technology, and socialist feminism in the 1980s. *Socialist Review*. 80: 65–107.

Harding, S. and Hintikka, M. (eds) (1983) *Discovering Reality: Feminist Perspectives on Epistemology, Metaphysics, Methodology, and Philosophy of Science*. Dordrecht, Holland: D. Reidel.

Hartmann, H. (1981) The unhappy marriage of Marxism and feminism: Towards a more progressive union. In L. Sargent (ed.), *Women and Revolution*. Boston: South End Press. pp. 1–41.

Hartsock, N. (1983) The feminist standpoint: developing the ground for a specifically feminist historical materialism. In S. Harding and M.B. Hintikka (eds), *Discovering Reality*. Dordrecht, Holland: D. Reidel. pp. 283–310.

Hearn, J. and Parkin, P.W. (1987) *'Sex' at Work*. New York: St Martins Press.

Hochschild, A. (1989) *The Second Shift: Working Parents and the Revolution at Home*. New York: John Wiley.

hooks, b. (1981) *Ain't I a Woman*. Boston, MA: South End Press.

Huff, A. (1990) *Wives of the Organization*. Paper presented at the Conference on Women and Work, Arlington, TX.

Hurtado, A. (1999) *Disappearing Dynamics of Women of Color*. Paper presented at the conference on Gender at Work: Beyond White, Western, Middle-class, Heterosexual, Professional Women, Center for Gender in Organizations, Simmons Graduate School of Management, Boston, MA.

Irigaray, L. (1985a) *Speculum of the Other Woman,* trans. G.C. Gil, Ithaca, NY: Cornell University Press.

Irigaray, L. (1985b) *This Sex Which is Not One,* trans. C. Porter, Ithaca, NY: Cornell University Press.

Jermier, J.M. (1985) 'When the sleeper wakes': A short story extending themes in radical organizational theory. *Journal of Management.* 11: 67–80.

Kanter, R.M. (1977) *Men and Women of the Corporation.* New York: Basic Books.

Kerfoot, D. and Knights, D. (1993) Management, masculinity and manipulation: From paternalism to corporate strategy in financial services in Britain. *Journal of Management Studies.* 30: 659–77.

Knights, D. (1992) Changing spaces: The disruptive impact of a new epistemological location or the study of management. *Academy of Management Review.* 17: 514–36.

Kondo, D.K. (1990) *Crafting Selves.* Chicago: University of Chicago Press.

Kristeva, J. (1977) *Desire in Language.* New York: Columbia University Press.

Lorde, A. (1983) The master's tools will never dismantle the master's house. In C. Moraga and G. Anzaldua (eds), *This Bridge Called My Back.* New York: Kitchen Table Press. pp. 98–101.

Marshall, J. (1984) *Women Managers: Travelers in a Male World.* London: Wiley.

Martin, J. (1990) Deconstructing organizational taboos: The suppression of gender conflict in organizations. *Organizational Science.* 1: 339–59.

Martin, J. (1994) The organization of exclusion: Institutionalization of sex inequality, gendered faculty jobs and gendered knowledge in organizational theory and research. *Organization.* 1: 401–31.

Martin, J. and Knopoff, K. (1997) The gendered implications of apparently gender-neutral organizational theory: Re-reading Weber. In A. Larson and E. Freeman (eds), *Ruffin Lecture Series: Business Ethics and Women's Studies* (Vol. III). Oxford: Oxford University Press. pp. 30–49.

Martin, J. and Meyerson, D. (1998) Women and power: Conformity, resistance and disorganized co-action. In R. Kramer and M. Neale (eds), *Power and Influence in Organizations.* Thousand Oaks, CA: Sage.

Martin, J., Knopoff, K. and Beckman, C. (1998) An alternative to bureaucratic impersonality and emotional labor: Bounded emotionality at The Body Shop. *Administrative Science Quarterly.* 43: 429–69.

Meyerson, D. and Kolb, D. (2000) Moving out of the armchair: Developing a framework to bridge the gap between feminist theory and practice. *Organization.* 7: 573–87.

Mills, A.J. (1988) Organization, gender and culture. *Organization Studies.* 9: 351–69.

Minh-ha, T.T. (1989) *Woman, Native, Other: Writing Postcoloniality and Feminism.* Bloomington, IN: Indiana University Press.

Mumby, D.K. and Putnam, L.L. (1992) The politics of emotion: A feminist reading of bounded rationality. *Academy of Management Review.* 17: 465–86.

Nkomo, S.M. (1992) The emperor has no clothes: Rewriting 'race in organizations'. *Academy of Management Review.* 17: 133–50.

Pfeffer, J. and Davis-Blake, A. (1987) The effect of the proportion of women on salaries: The case of college administrators. *Administrative Science Quarterly.* 32: 1–24.

Pollert, A. (1996) Gender and class revisited: Or, the poverty of 'Patriarchy'. *Sociology.* 30(4): 639–59.

Pringle, R. (1988) *Secretaries Talk.* London: Verso.

Reskin, B.F. and Roos, P.A. (1990) *Job Queues, Gender Queues.* Philadelphia, PA: Temple University Press.

Rosaldo, M. and Lamphere, L. (eds) (1974) *Woman, Culture and Society.* Stanford, CA: Stanford University Press.

Rosenberg, R. (1982) *Beyond Separate Spheres: Intellectual Roots of Modern Feminism.* New Haven, CT: Yale University Press.

Rosener, J.B. (1995) *America's Competitive Secret: Utilizing Women as a Management Strategy.* New York: Oxford University Press.

Rothschild-Whitt, J. (1979). The collectivist organization: An alternative to rational-bureaucratic models. *American Sociological Review.* 44: 509–27.

Sawicki, J. (1991) *Disciplining Foucault.* London: Routledge.

Smircich, L. and Calas, M. (eds) (1995) *Critical Perspectives on Organization and Management Theory.* Aldershot: Dartmouth.

Smith, D. (1990) *The Conceptual Practices of Power.* Boston, MA: Northeastern University Press.

Spelman, E.V. (1989) *Inessential Woman: Problems of Exclusion in Feminist Thought.* Boston: MA: Beacon Press.

Spivak, G.C. (1987) *In Other Worlds.* New York: Methuen.

Strober, M. (1984) Toward a general theory of occupational sex segregation: The case of public school teaching. In B.F. Reskin (ed.), *Sex Segregation in the Workplace.* Washington, DC: National Academy Press. pp. 144–56.

Strober, M. and Arnold, C.L. (1987) The dynamics of occupational segregation among bank tellers. In C. Brown and J.A. Pechman (eds), *Gender in the Workplace.* Washington, DC: Brookings Institution. pp. 107–57.

Taylor, S., Fiske, S., Etcoff, N. and Ruderman, A. (1978) Categorical and contextual person memory and stereotyping. *Journal of Personality and Social Psychology.* 36: 778–93.

Tom, A. (1995) Children of our culture? Class, power, and learning in a feminist bank. In M.M. Ferree and P.Y. Martin (eds), *Feminist Organizations.* Philadelphia, PA: Temple University Press. pp. 165–79.

Valentine, P. and Mcintosh, G. (1990) Food for thought: Realities of a women-dominated organization. *Alberta Journal of Educational Research.* XXXVI(V): 353–69.

Willis, P. (1981 [1977]) *Learning to Labour. How Working Class Kids Get Working Class Jobs.* London: Routledge & Kegan Paul.

Young, E. (1991) On the naming of the rose: Interests and multiple meanings as elements of organizational culture. In P. Frost, L. Moore, M. Louis, C. Lundberg and J. Martin (eds), *Reframing Organizational Culture.* Newbury Park, CA: Sage. pp. 90–103.

Young, I. (1980) Socialist feminism and the limits of dual systems theory. *Socialist Review.* 10(2–3): 169–88.

Zavella, P. (1991) Mujeres in factories: Race and class perspectives on women, work and family. In M.D. Leonardo (ed.), *Gender at the Crossroads of Knowledge.* Berkeley, CA: University of California Press. pp. 312–36.

Chapter 5

Critical Approaches to Strategic Management

*David L. Levy, Mats Alvesson
and Hugh Willmott*

It is only comparatively recently that 'strategic management' has been labelled, studied and privileged as a field of managerial practice and scholarly attention (Knights and Morgan, 1991). Many business schools have crowned their programmes with a 'capstone' course in strategic management, which is intended to provide a 'top-management perspective', in addition to fostering a familiarity with the key concepts in the field. As perhaps the most managerialist of the management specialties, 'strategy' largely takes for granted the historical and political conditions under which managerial priorities are determined and enacted. Moreover, as a technocratic mode of decision-making serving particular interests, strategy is not simply confined to the business world; rather, 'strategy' can be seen in the ever-widening circle of problems which are deemed suitable for its application – from public sector and non-profit management to regional economic development and business school accreditation.

This chapter contributes to the development of a critical understanding of strategic management that is less coloured by the preoccupations and sectional interests of top managers. Where a managerialist perspective employs an instrumental rationality to help managers improve organizational effectiveness and corporate profitability, a critical lens seeks to explore the nature of strategic management as an organizational process, one that has significant political ramifications within organizations and in the broader society. Strategy can, for example, be examined as discourse and practice in order to probe its historical roots and how it came to be constituted in its current form (Knights and Morgan, 1991). Some of the work in the processual school of strategy (Mintzberg, 1990) provides a sceptical perspective on established classical and rational perspectives. However, writings in this tradition do not explore broader issues of domination or scrutinize managerialist assumptions. Where the processual school examines power, for example, it tends to do so within an intra-organizational perspective that eschews consideration of broader social and political structures (Alvesson and Willmott, 1996).

When analysis draws from Critical Theory (see Introduction to this volume), management is viewed as a set of practices and discourses embedded within broader asymmetrical power relations, which systematically privilege the interests and viewpoints of some groups while silencing and marginalizing others (see also Alvesson and Willmott, 1996). Critical Theory (CT) has an emancipatory agenda, which seeks to probe taken-for-granted assumptions for their ideological underpinnings and restore meaningful participation in arenas subject to systematic distortion of communication. CT draws attention, moreover, to the dominance of a technical rationality obsessed with the ostensibly efficient pursuit of unquestioned objectives, and attempts instead to rekindle societal debate around goals and values. Drawing from this perspective, embryonic critical scholarship on strategic management has tended to emphasize the discursive and ideological dimensions of strategy, such as the constitution of certain problems as 'strategic' and the legitimation of specific groups of people as the 'strategic managers' capable of addressing them (see Thomas, 1998).

An alternative strand of critique offers an historical materialist perspective that has intellectual roots in the Marxism of Antonio Gramsci. It is useful to point out a number of points of commonality and difference between Gramsci and Critical Theory (CT). Gramsci anticipated theorists of the Frankfurt School in his critique of the neutrality of philosophy and science, and the economism and determinism of orthodox Marxism. Both approaches view organizational structures and managerial practices as inherently political. Another point of contact with CT is the importance attached to ideology as a force that stabilizes and reproduces social relations while masking and distorting these same structures and processes. Gramsci also prefigures CT's position that intellectuals can and should apply theory for emancipatory purposes.

Points of difference between Gramsci and CT indicate the potential contribution of extending our range of critical inquiry. Critical Theorists have focused on the power of discursive closure and distortion, both at the broader level of mass culture (Marcuse, 1964) and in communicative action (Habermas, 1984). They invite recurrent critical reflection on the presence of distorted communications in even the most ostensibly radical or emancipatory conceptions of strategy – a point to which we return in our concluding remarks. In their turn towards culture and ideology, however, Critical Theorists have tended to downplay the role of economic structure. For Gramsci, by contrast, social systems are shaped and stabilized in the interlocking realms of ideology, economics and politics. If firms and markets are embedded in broader ideological and political structures (Callon, 1998; Fligstein, 1996; Granovetter, 1985), then corporate strategies to enhance competitive and technological positioning are closely related to broader strategies to secure social legitimacy and influence policy; the content of strategy, not just its ideology, is political.

Gramsci's concept of emancipation is broader and more strategic than that offered by CT. For Gramsci, power lies in the ensemble of economic, ideological and organizational forces; the emancipatory project must therefore encompass this wider totality. Gramsci's conception of hegemony as a dynamic, unstable relation of forces informs a strategic notion of power. A hegemonic formation results from an historically specific alignment of ideological, economic and organizational forces, laying the foundation for a dominant alliance of social groups. A coordinated strategy across these three pillars of hegemony is required to build and sustain hegemony, or indeed to contest the dominance of a particular hegemonic bloc. Subordinate social groups would need to adopt a long-term strategy, or a 'war of position' in Gramsci's terms, to disrupt and shift the balance of forces in their favour. While Gramsci's analysis was primarily at the level of the state, others have applied Gramscian concepts to understand social contestation over particular issue arenas, such as the environment or race (Hall, 1986; Sassoon, 2000). The complex, fragmented nature of hegemonic formations suggests that subordinate groups can, given appropriate analysis and understanding, identify key points of instability and leverage, justifying Gramsci's 'optimism of the will'.

CONTEMPORARY APPROACHES TO STRATEGY

Contemporary approaches to strategy are hardly monotholic, though much current thinking is anchored by the work of Michael Porter and Henry Mintzberg. Mintzberg and colleagues (1998) discuss ten schools and five definitions of strategy. One of these, 'strategy as ploy', builds on the game theoretic and military heritage of strategy. It suggests that strategy can be about deceptive and unpredictable manoeuvres that confuse and outflank competitors. The concept of 'ploy' implies a certain deviousness that invites critical scrutiny of underlying goals and motives. It also suggests that social contestation is more a matter of superior manoeuvring than ideological or coercive domination (Abercrombie et al., 1980). This 'take' on strategy implies possibilities for effective challenges by subordinate groups.

Strategy as 'position' offers a predominant conceptual framework in the field. Porter's (1980) landmark *Competitive Strategy* reinterpreted the microeconomics of industrial organization in a managerial context. Close analysis of Porter's work and subsequent developments provides considerable fuel for Critical Theorists concerned with the reproduction of hierarchical economic relations, since it highlights the contradictions between idealized myths of 'perfect competition' and the more grounded concepts of market power explored by business school strategists. Porter's work uses economic analysis of market failures to suggest how firms might seek above-normal profits in less than competitive market segments. Porter's subsequent book, *Competitive Advantage* (1985), which resonates more with the 'resource based view' of the firm (Wernerfelt, 1984), attempts to explain how a firm might actively build market barriers and sustain monopolistic structures. It was not without some justification, perhaps, that Microsoft argued in its anti-trust suit defence that it was merely pursuing the precepts of good business strategy.

Some scholars firmly established within the strategy field have critiqued the prescriptive, technocratic approach to strategy, represented by the work of Porter (1980; 1985), Andrews (1971) and Chandler (1962), for its reliance on a rational, logical and linear model of analysis and planning. Sun Tzu's classic work on military strategy (1983), though often expressed as a series of maxims, advocates an approach that is non-linear, unpredictable and paradoxical, commending the title 'The Art of War' rather than The Science of War' (Luttwak, 1987; Quinn and Cameron, 1988). Mintzberg (1994; Mintzberg et al., 1998) has been particularly prominent in arguing that 'the actuality of strategy is better characterized as an emergent rather than planned organizational phenomenon. Mintzberg emphasizes the recursive processes of learning, negotiation and adaptation by which strategy is actually enacted, and suggests that the planning–implementation distinction is unsustainable (Mintzberg, 1990). Mintzberg argues that such processes are both inevitable *and* functional.

A greater attentiveness to strategy as process has been accompanied by increased appreciation of the cognitive models, or frames, which channel managers' perceptions of their environment (El Sawy and Pauchant, 1988; Whipp et al., 1989). Weick (1995) has argued that organizational members actively constitute and reify their environments, bringing sense and order to complex and confusing social worlds in which they are located. In turn, perceptions of the external environment shape and constitute managerial cognition and action (Daft and Weick, 1984). Institutional theory, which has become increasingly prominent in recent management thought, clearly displays a constructivist influence in its emphasis on cognitive and normative pressures in shaping field-level norms and practices (DiMaggio and Powell, 1983; Scott and Meyer, 1994). Despite an affinity of the constructivist perspective with an instrumental formulation of CT's historical hermeneutic epistemology (see Willmott, 2003), which seeks to uncover meaning rather than causation, few authors utilize a constructivist analysis of strategy to draw implications concerning broader structures of dominance and inequity. Quite the contrary, the perspective is routinely used to generate suggestions for how managers can improve the strategy process by actively changing corporate cultures and frames (Whittington, 1993). A few notable exceptions have argued that if strategy is rooted in the values and cognitive frames of senior managers, it is likely to reproduce their ideological frameworks and promote their sectional interests (Bourgeois and Brodwin, 1984; Smircich and Stubbart, 1985).

Understanding the strategy process is also a concern of those who view it as the outcome of political bargaining processes among managerial elites (Bower and Doz, 1979; Child, 1972; Cressey et al., 1985). However, most studies of the politics of strategy focus on internal struggles among managerial factions rather than with labour or external stakeholders, and tend to abstract from wider historical and social contexts. Managers are still viewed as the only organizational actors with legitimate access to the strategy process, a form of discursive closure that trivializes the politics of strategic management. Pettigrew's (1985) influential study of ICI, for example, makes direct reference to the way dominant groups are protected by the 'existing bias of the structures and cultures of an organization' (1985: 45), and how these groups actively mobilize this socioeconomic context to 'legitimize existing definitions of the core strategic concerns, to help justify new priorities, and to delegitimize other novel and threatening definitions of the organization's situation' (1985: 45). Nevertheless, Pettigrew neglects the historically distinctive, politico-economic organization and contradictions of the production and consumption processes that have shaped the development and direction of strategic management at ICI. As Whittington contends, 'the limits of feasible change within ICI were defined not simply by the personal competencies and organizational advantages of particular managers...but also by the evolving class structures of contemporary British society' (1992: 701). As with the constructivist approach, advocates of strategy-as-bargaining are also quick to jump to managerialist prescriptions. Whittington (1993), for example, proposes mechanisms to ensure that the strategy process remains objective rather than being captured by a particular management faction; moreover, he suggests that managers can draw from broader, less visible sources of power, such as 'the political resources of the state, the network resources of ethnicity, or, if male, the patriarchal resources of masculinity' (1993: 38). In such thinking, the extra-organizational conditions and forces neglected by Mintzberg and others are identified as potentially decisive weapons in the arsenal of strategic management.

Critical Theory: unmasking and deconstructing strategy

A basic limitation of much processual analysis is that little account is taken of how managers come to assume and maintain a monopoly of what has become institutionalized as 'strategic' decision-making responsibility. Nor, relatedly is there concern to explore how managers' practical reasoning about corporate strategy is conditioned by, and contributes to, the constitution of politico-economic structures that extend well beyond the boundaries of any particular organization. Yet mainstream strategy talk is not innocent.

It is a powerful rhetorical device that frames issues in particular ways and augments instrumental reason; it operates to bestow expertise and rewards upon those who are 'strategists'; and its military connotations reinforce a patriarchal orientation to the organization of work.

Shrivastava's (1986) landmark critique analysed the strategy field using five operational criteria, derived from Giddens (1979). These indicate its ideological nature: the factual underdetermination of action norms; universalization of sectional interests; denial of conflict and contradiction; normative idealization of sectional goals; and the naturalization of the status quo. Shrivastava concluded that strategic management was undeniably ideological, and that strategic discourse helped legitimize existing power structures and resource inequalities. Drawing from Habermas, Shrivastava sought emancipation in the 'acquisition of communicative competence by all subjects that allows them to participate in discourse aimed at liberation from constraints on interaction' (1986: 373). He also called on researchers 'to generate less ideologically value-laden and more universal knowledge about strategic management of organizations' (1986: 374).

While Shrivastava's faith in the possibility of universal, objective knowledge betrays his modernist leanings, more recent critical contributions display a more postmodern sensibility. Abandoning the search for objective truth or for autonomous subjects who could potentially recognize their 'real' interests, postmodern critiques are concerned with the constitutive power of strategic discourse. Knights and Morgan, for example, see 'corporate strategy as a set of discourses and practices which transform managers and employees alike into subjects who secure their sense of purpose and reality by formulating, evaluating and conducting strategy' (1991: 252). Managers cannot stand outside of ideology to impose their stratagems on unwitting workers. Rather, they too are entangled in discursive webs. Strategy constructs a myth of commonality of organizational purpose by positing lofty and unattainable aspirations (Harfield, 1998). The invocation of military metaphors, for example, brands competitors as 'enemies' to be defeated, and mobilizes maximum effort from the rank and file, who are exhorted to sacrifice individual needs to the greater glory of the corporation.

While projecting solidarity of purpose and the universality of the interests of senior managers and stockholders, the discourse of strategy legitimates organizational hierarchy with differential influence and rewards. The importance attached to strategy also implies that employees who work outside of what is identified as the strategic core of an organization make a lesser contribution and therefore cannot be expected to participate, even marginally, in decisions for which others are responsible. It also provides a rationale for differentiating the pay and conditions of 'core' and 'peripheral' employees. The need to assert the status of an elite group of 'strategic managers' is perhaps particularly acute in advanced economies where manual labour is declining and traditional divisions between task execution and conception are loosened up. According to Stoney:

> In the strategic management model, responsibility for corporate level decision-making rests with a core or strategic elite who are discharged from the day-to-day responsibilities of operational activities, these being devolved to the lowest possible level of control. Undistracted by operational matters and line responsibility, the elite, often an 'executive board', is left free to concentrate on strategic thinking and decision-making. (Stoney, 1998: 4)

The strong top-down model of strategic management draws upon the picture of the general drawing up a battle plan and then ordering the troops to carry it through. This image stands in a relation of (unresolved) tension to recent contributions to strategic management that have emphasized the core competence associated with employees. The literature on core competence and organizational learning acknowledges the significance of the skills and knowledge, much of it tacit, embodied and distributed throughout the organization on the one hand, yet assumes that top management can and should control it. As mentioned by Scarbrough (1998: 225), champions of a core competence approach treat the firm as the command and control mechanism beloved of the traditional planning school. The strategic management literature, focusing on the leadership role of top management, is typically oriented towards aspirant top managers. However, very few people are, or will ever become, top managers responsible for corporate strategies. Perhaps, then, the value and appeal of strategic management as a field of instruction lies elsewhere, in its ideological appeal to students and employees who are encouraged to adopt a top management perspective and engage in grandiose fantasies about sitting down with corporate elites to discuss strategy and direct the resources of major companies (see Knights and Morgan, 1991). It is far less gratifying to imagine oneself as a low-level manager working on mundane operational issues. Similar motives may guide academics interested in researching and teaching in the field.

The privileged status of 'strategy' is apparent in the promotional efforts of management consultants. One computer consultancy company claiming to integrate strategic and IT perspectives was, upon closer scrutiny, lacking competence in projects with any advanced strategic component. In retrospect, a senior manager described this talk of strategy as 'a sales trick', designed to keep customers and employees happy while the latter really were doing programming and 'getting the bucks in' (Alvesson, 2000). In a large R&D company, mid-level managers described themselves as 'occupied with the larger picture' and with 'strategies', even though they were far from the market, had no overall business responsibility, and were supposed to work strictly within a segment of an overall product development process (Alvesson and Sveningsson, 2003).

Strategic discourse constitutes not only strategists but also 'the problems for which it claims to be a solution' (Knights and Morgan, 1991: 255). In doing so, it contributes towards an instrumental, technocratic orientation in corporate life that emphasizes efficiency and competitiveness over consideration of environmental or social values. Moreover, problems worthy of strategic management are found in widening circles of social and economic life. Stoney (1998) has described the increasing pervasiveness of strategic management in the British public sector under the guise of concerns for efficiency and accountability. Although advocates of strategic management in the public sector claim that it professionalizes and depoliticizes government services, Stoney contends that 'it represents a deliberate attempt to change the very nature of local government in a manner which conformed to a specific set of interests: the interests of capital' (1998: 13). For local authorities competing to attract mobile capital, the language of strategy 'instills potential investors with confidence that "rational" economic strategy can be pursued locally without fear of political and bureaucratic hindrance and without the uncertainty and reversals in policy that used to accompany changes in the political complexion of the council' (1998: 19). Moreover, strategy in the public sector is seen to be complicit in promoting a market-based ideology in which citizens are transformed into consumers and state officials into a managerial elite: 'In this managerial transformation, the traditional public sector themes of collectivism, welfare and civic duty have become unfashionable' (1998: 19).

While Critical Theory offers considerable insight into the ideological and constitutive role of strategic discourse in reproducing organizational and societal relations of power, it is somewhat limited by the lack of concern with the 'truth of strategy' (Knights and Morgan, 1991: 252). Almost all the critical writing on strategy, including the three articles in the July 1998 special issue of the *Electronic Journal of Radical Organization Theory* (EJROT), draw primarily from Critical Theorists of the Frankfurt School and from postmodern scholars to critique strategy as ideology and discourse. While it is generally acknowledged that strategic discourse has effects in broader economic and power relations, making it difficult to disentangle the material and ideological dimensions (Smircich and Stubbart, 1985), much critical writing implies that 'it is not the *practices* of strategic management which require urgent investigation', as Booth (1998) puts it in the introduction to the aforementioned special issue of the EJROT.

It is tempting to be dismissive of the instrumental value of strategy, even on its own terms. Many maxims of strategy appear to be faddish aphorisms, which are likely to prove poor guides for action. We have seen trends towards conglomerate acquisitions in the 1970s followed by admonitions to 'stick to your knitting' in the 1980s (Peters and Waterman, 1982). Enthusiasm for elaborate and detailed strategic planning waned in the 1980s as General Electric led the way in dismantling its planning system. Mintzberg (1994) provides anecdotal evidence of the failure of planning, and reviews numerous empirical studies that failed to find a financial payoff from strategic planning. Many simple models, such as the growth-share matrix, have gone through cycles of popularity and disillusionment (Seeger, 1984). SWOT (Strengths, Weaknesses, Opportunities, and Threats) analysis, a cornerstone of the strategic planning process, is frequently undertaken but seemingly rarely carried through in the development of strategies (Hill and Westbrook, 1997). Pfeffer (1994) compared five highly successful US companies with Porter's framework for strategic positioning and found that none of the companies followed the prescribed recipe.

Nevertheless, the 'truth' of strategy does have import when we take seriously the agency of corporate and state actors in privileging and protecting economic and political advantage. An interest in the discourse of strategic management should not necessarily just focus on its ideological effects and the consequences for managers constituting themselves as 'strategists' but should also investigate the substantive effects of the subjects acting according to the strategic management precepts. Mintzberg (1990) criticizes the approach to strategic management taken by MBA education. He argues that it produces people with analytical skills and a great faith in running business from a distance, but with very limited knowledge of how companies actually work and create value. Their approach, Mintzberg argues, overemphasizes financial criteria and underplays productive corporate development, having harmful effects on the economy in the long run. Sveningsson (1999) has shown how strategic management knowledge 'colonized' the thinking and acting of senior managers in the Swedish newspaper industry and led to the transformation of newspapers into parts of conglomerates. A joint focus on managerial subjectivity and substantial effects is perhaps to be recommended (see Ezzamel and Willmott, 2002). A different form of strategic analysis could usefully inform appropriate action by progressive social forces concerned with social contests and emancipation, as well as assisting the development of more democratic organizational forms engaged in market competition such as co-ops and collectives. The following section explores the relevance of Gramsci's work to outline an approach to strategy that pays attention to the political economy of strategic practice and considers the hegemonic alignment of ideological, political and economic issues.

Strategy as power: a significance of hegemony

Gramsci's conception of hegemony provides a point of departure for a critical approach that emphasizes the interaction of material and discursive practices, structures and stratagems in establishing and sustaining corporate dominance and legitimacy in the face of challenges from social actors and economic rivals (Gramsci, 1971; Sassoon, 1987, 2000). This perspective refocuses attention on the content and goals of strategy as it draws attention to the political nature of strategic practice.

In corporations, 'strategy' is practised to improve market and technological positioning, sustain social legitimacy, discipline labour, influence government policy and, not least, we have suggested, aggrandize the architects and purveyors of strategy. In a broad sense, all strategy is political. Strategy-as-power operates through the dialectical interplay of 'structure' and 'agency'. Power inheres in the specific configurations of economic, ideological and organizational forces that regulate, stabilize and constitute social worlds and identities, and which form the terrain for strategic contestation; power is also exercised by agents attempting to shape – establish and resist – these configurations. Through this process, agency is attributed to actions to which strategic intent is ascribed.

Gramsci's perspective on power and ideology addresses some of the theoretical problems related to the treatment of agency and strategy in Critical Theory and poststructuralism. Critical Theorists explain consent to oppressive structures of capitalism in terms of ideological domination. Disadvantaged groups come to accept and reproduce their position of subordination as they uncritically accept ruling ideas. Abercrombie and colleagues (1980), among others, have criticized this 'dominant ideology thesis' on the grounds that it accords too little agency to the dominated 'dupes', and too much intent to the dominant class, as well as too little modesty to intellectuals who presume to know the 'real interests' of others. The CT concept of ideology is viewed as overly monolithic and functionalist. It also requires people seeking emancipation to turn to Critical Theory intellectuals who, along with ruling elites, ostensibly stand outside the dominant culture and ideology. From a Gramscian standpoint, poststructuralist conceptions of power embedded in pervasive discourse are also problematic when discursive disciplinary power is understood to pervade every societal nook and cranny. In such interpretations of poststructuralist analysis, agents are seen to have little room to resist or evade the constitutive power of discourses.

Hall (1986) argues that the Gramscian notion of hegemony finds some viable ground between the structural determination of ideas of crude Marxism and the fluid, endless slippage of meaning explored in some versions of poststructural analysis. Hegemony refers to a historically specific alignment of economic, political and ideological forces that coordinates major social groups into a dominant alliance. Hall argues that ideology can be understood as the articulation of meaning, temporarily fixed and loosely coupled to economic and political structures. Securing a relatively stable hegemonic bloc requires material payoffs, political compromises, and the projection of moral and intellectual leadership. Hegemony is never total and complete, however, and dissent persists: the persistence of plural, overlapping and interpenetrating social and cultural forms opens up theoretical space for agency and resistance. Processes of contestation and liberation are at once fuelled by the suffering and the frustration that the hegemonic bloc produces, and are enabled by the capability of people to question prevailing priorities and institutionalized norms of conduct. Crucially, consent in a hegemonic system does not rely principally on colonization by dominant ideologies. Instead, it is understood, at least in part, as a strategic, contingent compliance, based on a realistic assessment of the balance of forces. This formulation avoids some of the problems associated with ideology as 'false consciousness'.

It is the complex, dynamic and unstable nature of hegemonic formations that brings richness to Gramsci's strategic conception of power. Historical blocs rest on insecure foundations of fragmented, contradictory ideologies and uneasy alliances, providing the potential for instability, contestation and change. Gramsci asked of social structure: 'What is this effective reality? Is it something static and immobile, or is it not rather a relation of forces in continuous motion and shift of equilibrium?' (1971: 172). Understanding the dynamic relationships between the economic and ideological aspects of this complex system affords opportunities to uncover windows of opportunity and key points of leverage, but this requires careful analysis: 'It is the problem of the relations between structure and superstructure which must be accurately posed if the forces which are active in the history of a particular period are to be correctly analyzed and the relations between them determined' (Gramsci, 1971: 177). Gramsci outlined two particular forms of strategy commonly evinced in social conflicts. 'Passive revolution' describes a process of evolutionary, reformist change that, while preserving the essential aspects of social structure, entails extensive concessions by relatively weak hegemonic groups. One might formulate this form of strategy as depending heavily on the decline or disorganization of hegemonic groups, rather than the careful marshalling and application of resources by subordinate groups. The concept of 'war of position', in contrast, engages a military metaphor to suggest how subordinate groups might skilfully avoid a futile frontal assault against entrenched adversaries. The war of position constitutes a longer-term strategy, coordinated across multiple bases of power. Its intent is to gain influence in the cultural institutions of civil society, to develop organizational and economic capacity, and to exploit tensions in hegemonic coalitions in order to win new allies. As in a game of chess, power lies not just in possession of the playing pieces but in their configuration; each set of moves and counter-moves reconfigures the terrain and opens up new avenues for contestation.

This view of strategy is implicit in the literature that examines the conditions under which social movements emerge, analyse and pursue successful strategies for social change. By locating agents of change outside of dominant corporate organizational forms, social movement theory offers a potentially more radical approach to resistance and change than progressive forms of 'participative strategy', with their attendant dangers of being co-opted as pseudo-participation. As McAdam and colleagues (1996) argue, effective social movements exploit historically specific political opportunities, develop organizational and material resources, and frame issues discursively in ways that challenge hegemonic thinking yet resonate sufficiently with extant cultural forms to mobilize broad support. Ganz (2000), for example, claims that the UFW succeeded in organizing California farmworkers where the AFL-CIO failed due to strategic capacity, not just because of a favourable opportunity structure or the possession of adequate resources. Strategic capacity in this case study comprised a diverse, well-networked leadership, and an organizational form that encouraged accountability, diverse perspectives, and explicit strategy-making. Cress and Snow (2000), in a study of fifteen homeless social movement organizations, found that outcomes were influenced by organizational, tactical, political and framing variables. The coordination of strategy across multiple bases of power indicates a largely unacknowledged intellectual affinity with the Gramscian concept of hegemony.

Traditional market-oriented strategies also have political dimensions. As Porter's Five Forces analysis indicates, the primary goal of strategy is to increase a firm's bargaining leverage over its competitors, potential entrants, suppliers and customers. The result of successful strategic practice is the weakening of competition and the concentration of economic power, an outcome which is hardly possible to separate from political and ideological power. Of course, companies also pursue overtly political strategies in their efforts to influence the regulatory environment. Much of the limited literature that does exist on corporate political strategy, however, adopts a managerialist rather than a critical orientation (Hillman and Hitt, 1999; Mahon, 1989; Schuler, 1996). Pfeffer and Salancik (1978), for example, have examined corporate strategies to secure advantage and reduce external dependency through control over information flows, influence over external actors, and engagement in coalition politics. Uncovering the political dimensions of apparently neutral strategic practices is, of course, a key concern of Critical Theory. Here we push further, and argue that the traditional distinction between market and political strategy is untenable. It is not just that firms need to coordinate market and non-market strategies to achieve economic goals (Baron, 1997). More fundamentally, markets are embedded in broader social and political structures (Callon, 1998; Granovetter, 1985) and the articulation of markets with ideological and political structures and processes enact 'circuits of power', to use Clegg's (1989) formulation. Shrivastava describes the 'continuing political battles that proactively shape the structure of competition' (1986: 371), and emphasizes the need to analyse 'the social and material conditions within which industry production is organized, the linkages of economic production with the social and cultural elements of life, the political and regulatory context of economic production, and the influence of production and firm strategies on the industry's economic, ecological, and social environments' (1986: 371).

The Gramscian approach can find purchase at the level of strategic contests within specific issue arenas. Levy and Egan (1998), for example, have examined the response of the fossil fuel industry to the prospect of climate change. Mandatory restrictions on emissions of greenhouse gases, radical technological change, and renewed environmental activism threaten oil and automobile companies with a loss of markets, more stringent regulation, and a loss of autonomy and legitimacy. The case demonstrates how companies responded to these threats to their hegemonic position with coordinated strategies in the economic, organizational and discursive realms. US-based companies in the fossil fuel sector organized a strong issue-specific industry association, challenged the scientific need for action, pointed to the high economic costs of controls, and formed alliances with unions, minorities and groups of retired people. They donated substantial amounts in political campaign contributions and have invested in shoring up markets for their traditional products. The industry has not been entirely successful in deflecting demands for change, and has drifted towards a strategy of accommodation, or 'passive revolution', in Gramsci's terms. The industry has moved towards accepting the scientific basis for emission controls, is investing substantial amounts in low-emission technologies, and has engaged in widespread public relations to portray itself and its products as green. In return, it has won broad acceptance for a flexible, market-based implementation system that preserves corporate autonomy and legitimacy. Mainstream environmental organizations and government agencies have signed on to this accommodation, offering companies renewed credibility in shaping the emerging market-based climate regime.

In recent years, companies have been deploying the discourse of social responsibility, stewardship, stakeholder management and corporate citizenship in their efforts to restore legitimacy (Levy, 1997; Luke, 1995). While some Critical Theorists might view such discursive moves as ideological distortions designed to mask the real relations of power, the Gramscian perspective interprets them as compromises that shift the terrain of contestation and create new opportunities, for example, by building external expectations of concomitant practices, and by legitimating broader managerial consideration of social and environmental goals. The difference between succumbing to ideological co-optation and an emancipatory 'war of position' is, to repeat, one of long-term strategy.

CONCLUSIONS

Strategic management deserves critical investigation because it has assumed a dominance in managerial discourse and become a model for decision processes in a wide range of organizations beyond the private sector. Strategy is privileged as a field of management theory and managerial practice. Strategy pundits and makers make claims to expertise, insight and authority that reproduce and legitimate organizational inequalities. Strategy frames and legitimizes managers' practices as they strive to advance a company's market position, defend against regulatory or social threats, and secure control amidst challenges from labour, stockholders or other stake-holders. When management practitioners and scholars proclaim the primacy of strategy, Critical Theorists need to subject the field to close scrutiny.

Various processual perspectives have critiqued strategy for its overly rational and programmatic orientation. By aspiring to describe how strategy is actually developed in organizations, these approaches acknowledge, for example, the role of managerial cognitive frames and conflict among managerial elites. But they generally fail to address strategy as a political project, except in their recognition of contests and skirmishes between managers over their 'choice' of strategy and its means of implementation. Moreover, they then leap from avowed description to managerialist recommendation, blunting any critical edge the processual approach might provide.

Critical Theory holds out the promise of revealing the taken-for-granted assumptions and ideologies embedded in the discourse and practice of strategy as it challenges the latter's self-understanding as a politically neutral tool to improve the technical performance and effectiveness of organizations. Critical thinking pushes us to question the universality of managerial interests and to bring to the surface latent conflicts. It asks that we excavate below the apparent consensus on organizational 'ends', and pay more attention to means and values. Such analysis points, for example, to the role of military metaphors in legitimating organizational inequality, hierarchy, and the imperative of 'competitiveness'. To ameliorate the totalitarian tendencies of organizational structure and process, Critical Theory commends 'communicative rationality' (Habermas, 1984). In principle, such rationality fosters more participative decision-making, in which previously marginalized voices are included.

It can be allowed that grassroots strategic processes harbour some potential for challenging existing hierarchies and increasing participation (Bourgeois and Brodwin, 1984; Westley, 1991). But there is also a need for caution regarding the political neutrality of participatory processes and the celebration of autonomy under management's technocratic ground rules (Alvesson, 1996; Knights and Willmott, 2002). For example, advocates of decentralized, emergent strategy often argue for the promulgation of shared values and mission to provide a force for integration. Wrapped up in the discourse of empowerment and non-hierarchical networks, efforts to instil a strong common culture and vision can be interpreted as the promulgation of the particular interests of senior management (Willmott, 1993). Even if participants do perceive their interests to be in conflict with management, they may be silenced by organizational sanctions for expressing dissident views. Senge's concept of 'free dialogue', for example, resonates with Habermas's notion of undistorted communication, but lacks any critical analysis of systematic barriers to such dialogue. Participative approaches to strategic management share the same burden as Total Quality Management and other methods rooted in Human Relations, in that they need to demonstrate that they go beyond managerialist efforts to harness local knowledge and commitment (Alvesson, 1993; Boje and Winsor, 1993; McCabe et al., 1998).

Analysis inspired by the work of Gramsci shares the scepticism and hostility of Critical Theory towards diverse managerialist formulations of strategic management. But it is less negative and pessimistic while, at the same time, being more politically orientated and engaged. Instead of appealing to the abstraction of 'communicative rationality', such analysis strives to expose hegemonic weaknesses and highlights opportunities for mobilizing and improving the prospects of subordinated groups. Gramsci's analysis of contestation among social forces suggests that the strategic coordination of economic, organizational and discursive resources secures the hegemony of dominant groups, but also opens up space for resistance by labour, environmentalists, and other forces challenging the status quo. This contestation for influence takes place at multiple, interacting levels, including the firm, the industry, and specific social and environmental issues. And it is to the study of, and alliance with, counter-hegemonic forces and networks that Gramscian thinking invites our engagement.

Although the efficient political action of disadvantaged progressive groups and social movements are applauded by proponents of Critical Theory, some problems must be borne in mind. Strategic action means a certain emphasis on the instrumental, and a downplaying of the ongoing discussion and reconsideration of values and objectives. There is a trade-off between an emphasis on results and on communicatively grounded consensus or, more pragmatically, the ambitious discussions involving the questioning of ideas and beliefs (see Forester, in this volume). Thinking 'strategically' routinely invites a degree of top-down control, self-discipline and the freezing of goals. Inherent in such means–ends thinking is a restrictive or even an anti-communicative element. A particular problem concerns the questionable neutrality of knowledge of political strategy in relationship to different interests. Progressive groups, as well as authoritarian leftists, right-wing groups and religious fundamentalists may take on board ideas of political strategy. CT, with its emphasis on communicatively grounded positions and the need to prepare an openness for critical dialogue around beliefs and objectives, can offer an antidote to authoritarianism and the risk that a positive project loses its ethical commitment.

An engagement with Gramsci, we have suggested, allows both a retention and a reconstruction of the concept of strategy. No longer is strategy (commonsensically and hegemonically) conceived as the preserve of a managerial elite for whom academics are (self-evidently) stationed to provide more 'scientific' and/or 'effective' theories and recipes. Instead academics and practitioners are invited to abandon the illusion of spurious objectivity and associated technocratic conceptions of effectiveness in favour of a perspective that locates 'strategic management' – its discourses and its enactments – in the interaction of forces that establish and sustain, or challenge and remove, the socially divisive and ecologically destructive practices of corporations and their elites. This perspective suggests a conception of power relations in which the formation of alliances and the temporal and geographic deployment of discursive and material resources are key to challenging as well as sustaining forms of domination and exploitation. An emancipatory agenda requires that strategy be taken seriously as a method of analysis and action. At the same time, we have cautioned that a Gramscian conception of strategy risks an impetuous, overconfident, dogmatic identification of dominant and subordinate groups and their interests in ways that promote diversiveness and preclude critical reflection on societal goals and virtues. To reduce such risks, we have argued, it is relevant to temper a tendentially instrumentalist conception of strategy with one that is attentive to the communicative conditions of its formulation and pursuit.

REFERENCES

Abercrombie, N., Hill, S. and Turner, B.S. (1980) *The Dominant Ideology Thesis*. London: Allen & Unwin.

Alvesson, M. (1993) Participation and pseudo-participation in a professional service company. In W. Lafferty and E. Rosentein (eds), *International Handbook of Participation in Organizations* (Vol. 3). Oxford: Oxford University Press.

Alvesson, M. (1996) *Communication, Power and Organization*. Berlin: de Gruyter.

Alvesson, M. (2000) *Ledning av kunskapsföretag*, 3rd edn (Management of Knowledge-Intensive Companies). Stockholm: Norstedts.

Alvesson, M. and Sveningsson, S. (forthcoming) The good visions, bad micro-management and ugly ambiguity: Contradictions of (non)leadership in a knowledge intensive setting. *Organization Studies*.

Alvesson, M. and Willmott, H. (1996) *Making Sense of Management: A Critical Introduction*. London: Sage.

Andrews, K.R. (1971) *The Concept of Corporate Strategy*. Homewood, IL: Irwin.

Baron, D.P. (1997) Integrated strategy, trade policy and global competition. *Californian Management Review*, 39(2): 145–69.

Boje, D.M. and Winsor, R.D. (1993) The resurrection of Taylorism: Total quality management's hidden agenda. *Journal of Organizational Change Management*. 6(3): 57–70.

Booth, C. (1998) Critical approaches to strategy: an introduction to the special competition. *Electronic Journal of Radical Organization Theory*, 4(1).

Bourgeois, L. and Brodwin, D. (1984) Strategic implementation: Five approaches to an elusive phenomenon. *Strategic Management Journal*. 5: 241–64.

Bower, J.L. and Doz, Y. (1979) Strategy formulation: A social and political process. In D.E. Schendel and C.W. Hofer (eds), *Strategic Management*. Boston, MA: Little, Brown.

Callon, M. (1998) *The Laws of the Markets*. Oxford: Blackwell.

Chandler, A.D. (1962) *Strategy and Structure: Chapters in the History of the American Industrial Enterprise*. Cambridge, MA: MIT Press.

Child, J. (1972) Organizational structure, environment and performance: the role of strategic choice. *Sociology*. 6: 1–22.

Clegg, S. (1989) *Frameworks of Power*. London: Sage.

Cress, D.M. and Snow, D.A. (2000) The outcomes of homeless mobilization: The influence of organization, disruption, political mediation, and framing. *American Journal of Sociology*, 105: 1063–1104.

Cressey, P., Eldridge, J. and MacInnes, J. (1985) *Just Managing: Authority and Democracy in Industry*. Milton Keynes: Open University Press.

Daft, R.L. and Weick, K.E. (1984) Toward a model of organizations as interpretation systems. *Academy of Management Review*. 9(2): 284–95.

DiMaggio, P.J. and Powell, W.W. (1983) The iron cage revisited: institutional isomorphism and collective rationality in organizational fields. *American Sociological Review*. 48(2): 147–60.

El Sawy, O.A. and Pauchant, T.C. (1988) Triggers, templates, and twitches in the tracking of emerging strategic issues. *Strategic Management Journal*. 7(2): 455–74.

Ezzamel, M. and Willmott, H.C. (2002) Organizing as Discursive Practice: Beyond Rational and Processual Analyses of Strategic Management. Working Paper, Judge Institute of Management, Cambridge University, England.

Fligstein, N. (1996) Markets as politics: A political cultural approach to market institutions. *American Sociological Review*. 61(4): 656–73.

Ganz, M. (2000) Resources and resourcefulness: Strategic capacity in the unionization of California agriculture, 1959–1966. *American Journal of Sociology*.

Giddens, A. (1979) *Central Problems in Social Theory*. London: Macmillan.

Gramsci, A. (1971) *Selections from the Prison Notebooks* (ed. Quintin Hoare and trans. Geoffrey Nowell-Smith). New York: International Publishers.

Granovetter, M. (1985) Economic action and social structure: The problem of embeddedness. *American Journal of Sociology*. 91: 481–510.

Habermas, J. (1984) *The Theory of Communicative Action*. Cambridge: Polity Press.

Hall, S. (1986) Gramsci's relevance for the study of race and ethnicity. *Journal of Communication Inquiry*. 10(2): 5–27.

Harfield, T. (1998) Strategic Management and Michael Porter: a postmodern reading. *Electronic Journal of Radical Organization Theory*. 4(1).

Hill, T. and Westbrook, R. (1997) SWOT analysis: it's time for a product recall. *Long Range Planning*. 30(1): 46–52.

Hillman, A.J. and Hitt, M.A. (1999) Corporate political strategy formulation: a model of approach, participation, and strategy decisions. *Academy of Management Review*. 24(4): 825–42.

Knights, D. and Morgan, G. (1991) Corporate strategy, organizations, and subjectivity: A critique. *Organisation Studies*. 12(2): 251–73.

Knights, D. and Willmott, H.C. (2002) Autonomy as Utopia or Dystopia. In M. Parker (ed.), *Utopia and Organization*. Oxford: Blackwell.

Levy, D.L. (1997) Environmental management as political sustainability. *Organization and Environment*. 10(2): 126–47.

Levy, D.L. and Egan, D. (1998) Capital contests: National and transnational channels of corporate influence on the climate change negotiations. *Politics and Society*. 26(3): 337–61.

Luke, T.W. (1995) Between democratic populists and bureaucratic greens: The limits of liberal democratic responses to the environmental crisis. *Current Perspectives in Social Theory*. 15: 245–74.

Luttwak, E.N. (1987) *Strategy: the Logic of War and Peace*. Cambridge, MA: Harvard University Press.

Mahon, J.F. (1989) Corporate political strategy. *Business in the Contemporary World*. 21: 50–62.

Marcuse, H. (1964) *One-Dimensional Man: Studies in the Ideology of Advanced Industrial Society*. Boston, MA: Beacon Press.

McAdam, D., McCarthy, J. and Zald, M. (1996) *Comparative Perspectives on Social Movements*. New York: Cambridge University Press.

McCabe, D., Knights, D., Kerfoot, D., Morgan, G. and Willmott, H. (1998) Making sense of 'quality?' – toward a review and critique of quality initiatives in financial services. *Human Relations*. 51(3): 389–412.

Mintzberg, H. (1990) The design school: Reconsidering the basic premise of strategic management. *Strategic Management Journal*. 11: 171–95.

Mintzberg, H. (1994) *The Rise and Fall of Strategic Planning*. New York: Free Press.

Mintzberg, H., Ahlstrand, B. and Lampel, J. (1998) *Strategy Safari: A Guided Tour through the Wilds of Strategic Management*. New York: The Free Press.

Peters, T.H. and Waterman, R.H. (1982). *In Search of Excellence*. New York: Harper & Row.

Pettigrew, A. (1985) *The Awakening Giant: Continuity and Change in ICI*. Oxford: Blackwell.

Pfeffer, J. (1994) *Competitive Advantage Through People*. Boston, MA: Horvard Business School Press.

Pfeffer, J. and Salancik, G.R. (1978) *The External Control of Organizations: A Resource Dependence Perspective*. New York: Harper & Row.

Porter, M.E. (1980) *Competitive Strategy: Techniques for Analyzing Industries and Competitors*. New York: Free Press.

Porter, M.E. (1985) *Competitive Advantage: Creating and Sustaining Superior Performance*. New York: Free Press.

Quinn, R.E. and Cameron, K.S. (1988) *Paradox and Transformation: Toward a Theory of Change in Management and Organization*. Cambridge, MA: Ballinger.

Sassoon, A.S. (1987) *Gramsci's Politics*. London: Hutchinson.

Sassoon, A.S. (2000) *Gramsci and Contemporary Politics: Beyond Pessimism of the Intellect*. London: Routledge.

Scarbrough, H. (1998) Path(ological) dependency? Core competence from an organizational perspective. *British Journal of Management*. 9: 219–32.

Schuler, D. (1996) Corporate political strategy and foreign competition: The case of the steel industry. *Academy of Management Journal*. 39(3): 720–37.

Scott, W.R. and Meyer, J.W. (eds) (1994) *Institutional Environments and Organizations*. Thousand Oaks, CA: Sage.

Seeger, J.A. (1984) Reversing the images of BCG's growth share matrix. *Strategic Management Journal*. 5(1): 93–7.

Shrivastava, P. (1986) Is strategic management ideological? *Journal of Management*. 12: 363–77.

Smircich, L. and Stubbart, C. (1985) Strategic management in an enacted world. *Academy of Management Review*. 10(4): 724–36.

Stoney, C. (1998) Lifting the lid on strategic management: A sociological narrative. *Electronic Journal of Radical Organization Theory* 4(1).

Sun Tzu. (1983) *The Art of War* (trans. Lionel Giles). New York: Delacorte Press.

Sveningsson, S. (1999) *Strategic Change, Power and Knowledge*. On discipline and resistance in newspaper companies (in Swedish). Lund: Lund University Press.

Thomas, P. (1998) Ideology and the discourse of strategic management: A critical research framework. *Electronic Journal of Radical Organization Theory*. 4(1).

Weick, K. (1995) *Sensemaking in Organizations*. Thousand Oaks, CA: Sage.

Wernerfelt, B. (1984) A resource-based view of the firm. *Strategic Management Journal.* 5: 171–80.

Westley, F. (1991) Middle managers and strategy: Microdynamics of inclusion. *Strategic Management Journal.* 11: 337–51.

Whipp, R., Rosenfeld, R. and Pettigrew, A. (1989) Culture and competitiveness: evidence from two mature industries. *Journal of Management Studies.* 26(5): 561–89.

Whittington, R. (1992) Putting Giddens into action: Social systems and managerial agency. *Journal of Management Studies.* 29(6): 493–512.

Whittington, R. (1993) *What is Strategy – and Does it Matter?* London: Routledge.

Willmott, H.C. (1993) Strength is ignorance; slavery is freedom: Managing culture in modern organizations. *Journal of Management Studies.* 30(4): 515–52.

Willmott, H.C. (2003) Organization theory as critical science: The case of 'new organizational forms'. In C. Knudsen and H. Tsoukas (eds), *Organization Theory as Science: Prospects and Limitations.* Oxford: Oxford University Press.

Chapter 6

Marketing and Critique: Prospects and Problems

Glenn Morgan

In their introduction to the most comprehensive collection of critical articles on marketing recently published, Brownlie and his colleagues state that 'in many ways the 1990s have become the decade of marketing' (Brownlie et al., 1999b: 6). They relate this to the extensive use of marketing technologies outside the private sector, in relation to non-profit organizations, politics and the state sector as well as to the broader ideological and political context in which market capitalism became the single dominant mode of economic organization after the collapse of the Soviet system. These changes make the development of a critical approach to marketing increasingly important. This chapter builds on my arguments in the first version of this book (Morgan, 1992) to develop firstly a critique of existing orthodoxy and secondly to suggest the building blocks for critical approaches to marketing in the future.

In the first part of the chapter, I examine the dominant paradigm in marketing. I consider the nature of the 'marketing concept' and how marketing as a business school discipline has come to constitute firstly its own legitimacy and secondly its own epistemological and ontological basis. I examine in some detail how the marketing concept has evolved and constructed its legitimacy, in the process eschewing some of its earlier more radical origins and instead becoming a justification for markets per se. This legitimation process reproduces the underlying assumptions of a market-based society and thus constrains the development of a critical approach. This is reinforced by the dominant epistemological and ontological assumptions underlying the development of marketing as an academic discipline. By embracing positivism, marketing seeks to establish its legitimacy drawing on simplified models of how natural science works. These two features of marketing in the academic context create a significant bulwark against the emergence of a more critical approach to the discipline. In the second part of the chapter, I outline what I take to be the main sources of critique currently emerging in the area. I consider firstly the postmodern approach represented by Brown and his colleagues (Brown, 1995, 1998, 1999; Brown et al., 1996, 1998). I conclude that this approach is superficially attractive but as a social critique of marketing is considerably limited. I then return to a consideration of more overtly critical approaches and develop in particular the approach from Critical Theory. While this has particular strengths, I argue that it is necessary to supplement it with more specific examples of how marketing discourses and practices are developed. Therefore in the third part, I draw on some developing perspectives to point in possible directions for future research. I argue that this combination of forms of analysis offers the best hope for opening up a theoretically and empirically informed approach to the critical study of marketing.

MARKETING: THE DOMINANT PARADIGM

I consider the dominant paradigm from two points of view. Firstly, I examine its underpinning mechanisms of legitimation; in other words, why 'marketing' as a domain of knowledge about how the world of exchange works is a 'good thing'. The reason for doing this is that for all its positivistic methodology, marketing does not proclaim its virtue simply by an identification with the 'search for truth'. On the contrary, the 'virtue' of marketing resides in the perceived fact that it is doing something which is 'good' for people. In this sense, it can be argued that marketing has an ethical foundation, no matter how deeply it seeks to disguise it or how limited critics might perceive its definition of 'the good' and of 'ethics' to be. Secondly, however, there are key underlying epistemological and ontological suppositions which the dominant orthodoxy embraces and which need to be uncovered.

Marketing and legitimation

There is a story to be told about marketing as a discipline and a set of organizational practices. In this story, marketing is the handsome prince who rescues the captured princess (consumers) from the hands of the wicked witch (big business). This story links the radical origins of marketing in the Midwestern universities of the USA with its establishment as an orthodoxy in business schools and firms in the period from the 1960s through to the prominence of marketing in the 1990s across the public as well as the private sectors. This story begins in the USA in the late nineteenth century when the robber barons of the gilded age (Rockefeller, Morgan, Carnegie etc.) were establishing monopolistic positions in the key industries of railways, steel and oil through the use of ruthless pricing tactics against smaller competitors, thereby driving them out of business. Once a monopoly position was established, the dominant firms raised prices to consumers. The revolt against this system in the US was led by the populist and progressive movements which articulated the politics of the day in terms of a conflict between on the one hand, the forces of big business and corrupt politicians, and on the other hand, the 'people', composed of farmers, professionals, small businesses and workers. Free markets were being distorted by the power of oligopolistic businesses to set prices and keep out competitors; they were supported in this by corrupt politicians who resisted demands for reform. Marketing was established as an academic discipline in the state universities of the Midwest with a view to developing systematic analyses of how markets were being distorted by these powerful individuals and corporations. It was therefore closely linked to the institutionalist economics which during this period had some influence in the USA as elsewhere. In contrast to neoclassical economics, institutionalists had an interest in how markets could be shaped by forces such as large firms and the state. In academic terms, they were particularly influential in Midwest state universities such as Wisconsin (Desmond, 1998), where farmers felt themselves in conflict with the rail companies and the cartels in the wholesale markets for their products. The broader issue of monopoly power led to the passing of anti-trust laws and their application to the Standard Oil monopoly in the period 1910–13. Standard Oil was compulsorily broken up into a series of separate companies which were to compete with each other in the market for oil. Fligstein (1990) argues that the result of this was that US companies were no longer able to dominate industries simply by buying out or destroying all their competitors. They therefore began to turn inward and consider firstly how to improve the efficiency of their operations and secondly how to market their products more effectively. As a result, marketing began to find a place *within* the large corporations, this time as a guide to management practice rather than a critique of such practice as managers sought ways of influencing consumers' willingness to buy their products. Thus marketing as an academic discourse shifted from being a critical perspective that showed how companies were exploiting consumers through their control of the market to being imbued with a managerialist perspective, concerned to solve managers' problems.

However, although the handsome prince had gained entry to the stronghold of the wicked witch, this had marginal impact for the resulting era was characterized by a so-called 'productionist' mentality. Caricatured in Henry Ford's famous phrase that consumers could have any colour car they wanted 'so long as it was black', US firms were dominated by considerations of economies of scale and price. Standardization was the dominant feature of the Fordist era buttressed by the internal focus of managers on control of the labour process. It was production that ruled the wicked witch's castle and marketing had to be content to perform a subsidiary role. Although Sloan's General Motors introduced branding and annual model changes (which reflected a broader interest in creating brand identities through advertising in the press, posters and the emerging mass media industries), the focus was still on mass production and economies of scale as the drivers of firms. Thus marketing's role tended to be limited to areas such as advertising. During the 1950s and 1960s, however, this began to change. As competition became stronger, the focus on how to maintain and grow market share became more urgent for even the largest US companies. Economies of scale and resultant cheap prices were not in themselves enough to guarantee sales; nor indeed were more intensive sales efforts and advertising campaigns able to deliver markets for companies. It was into this context that the handsome prince Marketing began to emerge in all his glory. In this part of the story, the 'productionist' mentality was seen as at fault, since it ignored what customers really wanted in favour of producing what the firm could produce efficiently. In order to win market shares, therefore, it was advised that firms had to become more customer oriented. Firms had to listen to what customers wanted and then communicate with them more directly, producing goods and services according to what the customer required not what the production department thought could be made efficiently. The term 'marketing revolution' emerged to express the idea that the organization needed to be fundamentally changed. Big business was 'bad' because it had not listened to the consumers; it could become 'good' by listening to them. Developing a marketing orientation was legitimated by reference to serving customers. In political debates about 'big business', marketing appeared on the side of the 'angels'; it might be inside the firm but its goal was to listen to and serve those outside the firm. In this way, the sins of big business could be forgiven and the consumer could wholeheartedly embrace the corporation, capitalism and the market because it was possible to see that the interests of all could be equally met provided marketing was given a significant role within the firm. In this respect, marketing as a function within the firm and as a business school discipline legitimized big business and the market process itself.

Desmond argues that during the 1960s and 1970s, there was increasing scepticism about this, arising from authors such as J.K. Galbraith, Ralph Nader, Vance Packard and others who were beginning to argue that these legitimatory discourses concealed the way in which 'marketers worked in the interests of producers, not of consumers' (Desmond, 1998: 176). However, he also notes that this led in turn to a more sophisticated expression of the 'marketing concept' in which Kotler played a particularly important role. Kotler extended the marketing concept in ways that legitimized further its social role (Desmond, 1998: 177). For Kotler, 'marketing is specifically concerned with how transactions are created, stimulated and valued' (Kotler, 1985: 56). This in turn allows him to develop the 'generic concept of marketing' in which marketing can be viewed as a 'category of human action, indistinguishable from other categories of human action such as voting, loving, consuming; the marketer is a specialist at understanding human wants and value and knows what it takes for someone to act' (1985: 62). Marketing is a 'beneficent' technology that helps organizations to achieve what they wanted to do anyway and helps ensure that individuals' needs and wants are fulfilled.

Kotler therefore paved the way for an extension of the concept of marketing into non-business areas such as the public services, politics and voluntary organizations. While the 'hidden persuader' argument of Packard et al. never went away, marketing began to further enhance its respectability by turning all relationships into consumer relationships, whether these were with the state, with professionals, with voluntary organizations. This fitted very well with the ethos of Reagan and Thatcher in the 1980s who were intent on maximizing the role of markets and reducing the role of the state. Marketing with its discourse of consumerism and 'serving the needs of the consumer' became part of a wider critique about how organizations had ignored their 'consumers' and 'markets'. In the public sector, for example, the critique of bureaucracy was couched in very similar terms to the critique of a productionist ideology. Public bureaucracies, it was argued, had been run in the interests of the producers (the civil servants, the teachers, the doctors and nurses etc.) and not in the interests of the 'consumers'. They now needed to find out more clearly what people wanted and to deliver those services to them. Marketing played a crucial role in legitimating a change in public discourse towards concepts such as 'customers' and 'customer service', and away from traditional identifications such as governments and 'citizens', teachers and students, doctors and patients' (see Clarke and Newman, 1997; Sturdy et al., 2001). The discourse is seductive; it is closely tied to the language of choice and freedom which comes from market provision instead of provision which is administered by the state or by professionals. The elaboration of this discourse and its implementation in practice also enables a gradual transition to occur in public services from state provision to provision through quasi-markets to provision through deregulated private markets. The 'problem' for public sector organizations in this view is that they have failed to give their consumers choices. But how can public sector providers give consumers choice? The answer is that they have to be broken up into smaller units which constitute a quasi-market, a set of alternative providers among whom the consumer can choose. From marketing to markets is therefore a very small step often helped on its way by consultancies, gurus and other commentators eager to sell their expertise in transforming the public sector. As the high priest of free market economics entitles one of his books, this is about being 'Free to Choose' (Friedmann and Friedmann, 1979). Behind much of its technical puffery, the real legitimacy of marketing as an academic discipline and a set of professional practices lies in its claim to expertise and knowledge in these areas.

Marketing and science

The legitimation functions of the 'marketing concept' have provided marketing academics and practitioners with the time and space to develop their knowledge of consumers and their practices. Within this time and space, however, a particular set of assumptions about what marketing should be has become dominant. Firstly, this model is based on a positivistic view of the world, where the world is conceived of as independent of the observer and the perspective of the observer. The world has an objective existence which is predictable, stable and knowable. In terms of marketing as a business school discipline, therefore, the characteristics of consumers, their buyer behaviour, their responses to various features of products such as price and placement can be known. The issue is about the methodology which enables access to this reality and lies beneath the seemingly spontaneous actions of freely choosing individuals. The hypothetico-deductive model has become predominant in this respect, developing hypotheses and then testing them out on large populations (based on surveys or already existing databases) in order to identify statistically significant correlations. These then become the building blocks of positive knowledge about how consumers behave in markets. Positive knowledge implies that this can be then used to improve the performance of the firm; performativity is inherent in this vision of marketing. In his defence of this position, Hunt affirms that marketing can draw on the tradition of scientific realism in which:

> the world exists independently of its being perceived; the job of science is to develop genuine knowledge about the world, even though such knowledge will never be known with certainty; all knowledge claims must be critically evaluated and tested to determine the extent to which they do, or do not, truly represent, correspond or are in accordance with the world; the long-term success of any scientific theory gives us reason to believe that something like the entities and structure postulated by that theory actually exists. (Hunt, 1994: 24)

As a number of authors have pointed out (e.g. Wensley, 1995, 1999; Willmott, 1999), there is at least one major difficulty in Hunt's argument. Marketing practitioners continually express their dissatisfaction with the positive knowledge generated by the academic discipline. Because this knowledge has become so 'scientistic' (i.e. elaborated through complex statistical modelling based often on probability type inferences) and wrapped up in so many qualifications and abstractions, its implications for performativity are difficult to work out. Therefore, if one excludes the legitimating function described earlier, it is hard to know what the 'long-term success' which Hunt claims, consists of other than the maintenance of academic careers and journals in marketing.

BEYOND THE DOMINANT PARADIGM

Most outsiders would not have difficulty in agreeing that the marketing band-wagon rolls on down the route of positivism, performativity and scientism. In his use of Burrell and Morgan's paradigm approach (1979) in respect of marketing, Arndt (1985) argued that research in this area was dominated by what Burrell and Morgan labelled the structural-functionalist approach (in broad terms equivalent to what has been described as positivist here). He argued that it was possible to identify alternatives for marketing corresponding to Burrell and Morgan's interpretative, conflict and radical humanist approaches but that these were considerably underdeveloped. Arndt was optimistic that these alternatives might begin to emerge more strongly in future years. In the earlier version of this chapter, I followed a similar line, outlining a variety of perspectives that could emerge building on alternative theoretical positions (Morgan, 1992). In retrospect, there has been less diversity in terms of critique than both authors had suggested. In what follows, I identify two predominant strands which are critical of the dominant paradigm in marketing. The first strand which emerged strongly during the 1990s builds on particular strands of postmodernism. The second strand has deeper roots in the critique of marketing developed out of the Frankfurt School and Critical Theory.

POSTMODERNISM AND MARKETING

The rise of postmodernism in the social sciences has been reflected (if at a slightly delayed rate) by its rise in the sphere of marketing. In a series of books and articles, this approach has been most clearly articulated by Stephen Brown and his colleagues (Brown, 1995, 1998a; Brown et al., 1996, 1998). Brown claims that:

> marketing and postmodernism are already tightly interwoven. On reading the copious postmodern literature…one is struck not only by the sheer prevalence of marketing artefacts and institutions – shopping centres, department stores, advertising campaigns, package design, new product development and the entire consumption experience – but by the sheer originality and often dazzling acuity of these 'extra-marketing' marketing analyses. (Brown, 1999: 28)

Brown builds on those critiques of the dominant positivist paradigm which emerged during the 1980s out of ethnographic consumer research (discussed e.g. in Belk et al., 1988; 1989; Hirschmann, 1990; Holbrook, 1987; Lutz, 1989). However, unlike these authors, his reinterpretation of marketing is much more radical. He discusses a 'disciplinary apocalypse' which arises from taking the implications of postmodernism seriously for marketing:

> It regards as unattainable the modernist marketing vision of analysis,
> planning, implementation and control…It highlights the failure of man-
> ifold marketing generalizations…Disconcerting though it appears…
> This apocalyptic version of postmodernism should not be dismissed
> out of hand. With its 'anything goes' ethos; its assumption that nothing
> is excluded; its abandonment of stultifying orthodoxy; its determination
> to wipe the conceptual slate clean; and its preparedness to let a thou-
> sand methodological flowers bloom, the approach can be viewed as
> liberatory rather than threatening. (Brown, 1999: 50–1)

Brown's alternative to the orthodoxy is to seek to uncover the 'romance' of
the market; he refers to the 'essential enchantment of the marketplace' and
'the inherent romance of the marketplace' (Brown, 1998: 24). He states that
'everyone knows that marketing is inherently magical….Marketing is
irredeemably mystical' (Brown, 1998: 34, 35). 'Marketing, to put it in a
nutshell, is a bit raffish, a bit rambunctious, a bit of a loveable rogue' (Brown,
1998: 267–8).

Brown's approach raises in a very graphic way the question of what
sort of critical edge exists in this type of postmodernist analysis. Brown and
his colleagues clearly represent a challenge to the dominant orthodoxy by
their refusal to play the positivist game of hypothesis development and testing. Yet it is a limited sort of critique by virtue of its seeming unwillingness
to engage with anything about the economic organization of markets and
marketing or the social and ecological impacts of mass consumerism. Take,
for example, the sphere of shopping which is a frequent topic of these
authors. It is the shopping experience as 'magical' and 'carnivalesque' which
is their main interest. In this 'romance' literature, phenomena such as shopping malls are 'dematerialized' in the sense that they are given no positioning in the circuit of capital or in the role of finance in property speculation
and the building and development of such sites. How and why certain forms
of shopping space arise at particular times is not considered (cf. Harvey,
1989, 1990; Miller et al., 1998; Taylor et al., 1996). The consequent impact of
these forms on broader social relationships has also been ignored. For example, the enclosure of shopping space into private arenas policed and controlled by security forces defending 'private property' against the 'intrusion'
of 'undesirables' is barely considered. The way in which the public space of
cities is reconstituted by the power of mass consumption and the marketing
of products is a central issue in many societies. The struggle between the discourse of citizenship (and participation) and the discourse of the consumer
(and the rights to consumption) plays itself out in the very geography and
materiality of cityscapes and their suburban hinterlands. Privately owned
shopping malls, guarded by private security companies, located on the out-
skirts of big cities generate increased demands for public goods such as
roads while at the same time increasing the congestion on those already in

existence as shoppers climb into their cars in order to access the facilities of out of town malls (Hannigan, 1998; Marsden and Townley, 1999). Conversely cities become more complicated articulations of living, shopping and working areas constructed around the imperatives of consumption rather than citizenship. Grandiose public buildings such as post offices, customs houses and even churches get taken over for commercial development and turned into shopping developments, while former manufacturing or warehousing areas are converted into new developments of residential space for the wealthy. Meanwhile, the posters and neon lights advertising products and brands expand across the face of the city. These are not simply questions of style but involve a substantive reconstitution of social space as the site for consumer representations. This process leads into deeper questions of social division between the participants in the consumer process and those locked out by virtue of poverty. Privatizing shopping space allows security companies to avoid the glare of public accountability which periodically comes to rest on police forces struggling to deal with homelessness, criminality and all the other blights on the social space of cities. Private space can be subject to higher levels of surveillance and with less accountability than can be achieved in public space. The drive to protect and celebrate the consumer marginalizes those that cannot or will not play this game.

In conclusion, postmodern marketing in the guise of the 'romancers' seems to be happy in rejoicing in its ability to 'shock' the guardians of marketing orthodoxy by its rejection of standard modes of academic discourse. However, the result is critique that ultimately lacks any purpose beyond its own local struggle to broaden the discipline of marketing. Any critique of 'society' or the social consequences of markets, marketing and mass consumption is lost in the celebration of diversity and the 'magicality' of the experience undergone by the disembodied asocial selves who immerse themselves in the carnival of the market. The result is critique without substance that is all about style and very little about content.

MARKETING AS THE HIDDEN PERSUADER

In contrast, the second substantive strand of critique is more focused on the power of marketing as a way of manipulating individuals. In his 1957 book *The Hidden Persuaders*, Vance Packard argued that advertising and marketing are concerned primarily with shaping the needs of the consumer in ways that enable firms to make a profit. He rejected the idea that advertising and marketing were concerned with providing consumers with information on which they can make a choice between products and argued instead that advertising and marketing are about manipulating people into desiring things for which they have no real need. For Packard, big business is still seen as in charge of the market, 'rigging' it in ways that can enable firms to make the most profit. Packard's arguments have become common currency among critics of marketing and have fed what might be termed a reformist policy agenda. In such an agenda, the idea is that the manipulative capabilities of marketing and advertising need to be constrained either by government action or self-regulation. Thus, for example, governments have become increasingly involved in how and where cigarettes can be marketed or advertised. Advertisers and marketers develop professional bodies with codes of conduct about what is proper in these fields. The problem is seen as one of balancing the 'community' interest in fair information with the tendency of marketing and advertising to make exaggerated claims (see Desmond, 1998: 193 for a brief discussion of forms of regulation around the issue of consumer rights in the US context).

In recent years, this approach has been reinforced by the advent of the 'anti-globalization' movement, one of whose themes has been the 'tyranny of the brand'. In Naomi Klein's *No Logo* (2000), she argues that a number of corporations have 'made the bold claim that producing goods was only an incidental part of their operations…What these companies produced primarily were not things, they said, but *images* of their brands. Their real work lay not in manufacturing but in marketing' (Klein, 2000: 4). The brand, she says, is 'the core meaning of the corporation' (Klein, 2000: 5). The central concern of these corporations is therefore to build their brand, to market it to the world. Klein provides an entertaining and informative account of how companies get their brands into all sorts of superficially non-commercial arenas such as schools, universities, public urban space, sports events. Quite simply they use their political and economic power to force organizations to cooperate with them. There is an implicit threat that failure to cooperate leads to loss of revenue (compared to those who do co-operate) and a resultant spiral of decline. They also engage in 'brand bombing', saturating areas with their own stores and products until they drive out local providers and create a relentless uniformity of high streets and brands across entire countries. Klein refers to what she calls 'culture jamming' (Klein, 2000: ch. 12) as a form of opposition to this process which goes beyond legal regulation. The brand image can be punctured by the active consumers, using the images of the marketers to undermine the brand, e.g. through the use of ad-busting (i.e. putting graffiti onto advertising posters) or directly attacking companies for their bad labour or environmental practices by publicizing this through the internet as well as conventional journalistic sources. The active consumer uses market power to change corporate policy with the 'brand boomerang' (Klein, 2000: ch. 15).

As with the earlier 'hidden persuader' critique, however, Klein is ambivalent about the market itself. In some ways, she is reverting to aspects of the 'hidden persuader' model in its populist form, where it served as a weapon in the fight against 'big business'. If only the market could be made more transparent and consumers could see clearly how and where products were made, how wealth was distributed, then active consumers would make the market work in a fair way. Consumers are proactive and can become politically conscious in their buying choices if given the right information.

These approaches rely on the idea that the problem is the way in which the excessive power of large corporations and their marketing and advertising arms 'distorts' the market. They seem to cling to an ideal of the market as developed by Adam Smith – i.e. one in which consumers and producers meet in the marketplace as equals because nobody holds too much power. In such an ideal world, individuals' preferences reflect their underlying needs and the market provides an 'invisible hand' to sort out the price of goods and services in conditions of resource scarcity. So long as marketing itself is only about identifying these needs, communicating them to companies and then advertising them to consumers in order to inform them about their availability, this would be a positive outcome. It is only when power is used to distort communication (e.g. by making false claims for products) that the market 'fails'. Therefore, regulation and reform are limited to controlling the consequences of increasing concentrations of power.

The problem with the 'hidden persuader' approach (and its more recent adherents) is that it assumes that there are needs that exist at the individual level and which could be adequately 'satisfied by the market'. However, because large firms dominate the market and the means of information, these individual needs are frustrated. A countervailing power therefore must be constructed whether it is a statist solution (more control of large business), a voluntary code (e.g. for advertisers) or a mass movement of active consumers (what might be termed the 'Which? Solution' after the magazine produced for many years by the UK Consumers Association) or of adbusters and information guerillas (in line with Klein's anti-globalization arguments). However, another approach is to focus much more intensely on how the needs themselves are socially constructed.

This is the approach taken within the Critical Theory of the Frankfurt School. In this context, the needs which people think that they have for consumption goods reflect a society dominated by commodity fetishism. The problem is not simply that people are being persuaded to buy the 'wrong' product by the use of powerful advertising and marketing techniques. Rather the problem lies in the nature of a society where identity, status and subjectivity are intertwined with the purchase of goods and services on the market. Commodities are seen as things in themselves that can confer meaning and significance on people's lives. The fact that these commodities are produced by people in the first place is ignored and the commodity itself becomes worshipped and fetishized. Knights and Willmott describe this process as follows:

> As aspirations are raised and anxieties amplified by advertising, individuals are seduced and their energies directed narcissistically towards the acquisition of the symbols or attributes that signify a successful (self) image. In the context of an advanced capitalist society, the most compelling and legitimate means of relieving anxieties about social position and self-identity is through the individualistic pursuit of the material and symbolic indicators of success. (1999: 83)

(See also Alvesson, 1994; Alvesson and Willmott, 1996: 124.)

In his classic discussion of these processes, Marcuse stated that: 'The people recognize themselves in their commodities; they find their soul in their automobile, hi-fi set, split-level home, kitchen equipment…the products indoctrinate and manipulate; they promote a false consciousness which is immune against its falsehood' (1964: 24, 26). The problem for Marcuse is how to provide a foundation for his understanding that some needs are 'false' while others are by definition 'true'. His answer is unequivocal:

> We may distinguish both true and false needs. 'False' are those which are superimposed upon the individual by particular social interests in his repression…. No matter how much such needs may have become the individual's own, reproduced and fortified by the conditions of his own existence; no matter how much he identifies with them and finds himself in their satisfaction, they continue to be what they were from the beginning – products of a society whose dominant interest demands repression. (Marcuse, 1964: 22)

From this perspective, marketing is part of a wider problem with the nature of advanced capitalist societies where consumption has become the dominant mode of expression of self and identity. This is seen as false consciousness, a way of drawing the population's attention away from other phenomena, whether these are seen as existential angst and insecurities, inequalities of income and wealth, the repression of deep psychological needs or simply class struggle. The critique of marketing is a critique of false consciousness and the role of commodity fetishism in this process. The problem is that marketing and advertising seek to 'create needs, not to fulfil them; to generate new anxieties instead of allaying old ones' (C. Lasch, 1979, *The Culture of Narcissism*, quoted in Alvesson, 1994: 306).

In its rather puritanical rejection of consumption and its implied meta-narrative of true and false needs, this approach stands at odds particularly with postmodernist views of the world. As Desmond suggests, 'the whole creation of false needs quietly slipped off the critical agenda following "post-structuralist" questioning of the value of "ruling ideas" in perpetuating "false consciousness"' (1998: 176). Certainly, it was often the case that in some of the Frankfurt School (e.g. Adorno, 1973; Horkheimer and Adorno, 1947) this type of critique became locked into a discursive battle between 'popular culture' (which represented false needs generated by big business) and avant-garde culture (which was inaccessible to the masses and therefore free from commercial contamination). These sorts of judgements, delivered *ex cathedra* by (almost) dead white European men, seemed to fall exactly into the category of totalizing narratives which met with such a high degree of suspicion and scepticism among postmodern authors (e.g. Bauman, 1989; Burrell, 1997). As they also often involved a 'trashing' of popular culture (though not in the work of one member of the School, Walter Benjamin, 1992), which is the site par excellence of the postmodernists' forays into social analysis, it has become an increasingly difficult position to adopt in the current period. Nevertheless, particularly in the context of the marketing discipline, where the legitimacy of the activity is so easily assumed, this mode of critique justifiably re-emerges periodically to act as a powerful critique of marketing.

One way out of these tensions is to move away from overarching arguments about 'false' and 'true' needs towards more specific considerations of how 'needs' and markets are socially constructed and with what effects. Thus critique can be broken down into more specific and perhaps researchable questions, e.g. how is marketing discourse constructed? What is its impact on the subjectivity and identity of consumers? How can the historical preconditions and conditions of possibility of certain forms of marketing discourse be surfaced and used for purposes of critique? In the final section of the chapter, these issues are considered in more detail.

MARKETING DISCOURSE AND PRACTICE: DIRECTIONS FOR THE FUTURE

The fundamental problem for a critical study of marketing is in identifying the specific conditions of different forms of the discourse of marketing, how this becomes embedded into management practices and techniques, and finally how this impacts on the constitution of society, subjects, identities and objects of consumption. In turn, this implies that three levels of analysis could be usefully pursued in order to provide a deeper critique of marketing – firstly, more critical analysis of the construction of marketing as an academic discourse; secondly, a more sociologically informed account of the constitution of marketing as a set of management practices; thirdly, a more critical understanding of the consequences of marketing and its proliferation for the constitution of the self and society.

Marketing as an academic discourse

Earlier in this chapter, I marked out the origins of marketing in the academic world. Such an analysis is very preliminary and needs further development.

The key point is, however, that marketing, from being itself a weapon of critique of business (no matter how reformist in intention), became increasingly one of 'the servants of power' in Baritz's deadly phrase (Baritz, 1960). Part of this was the increasing colonization of marketing by two disciplinary groups. The first group consisted of neo-classical economists for whom the 'market' operates as an invisible hand to serve the interests of all. Institutionalist economics which had a critical element to it during the days of the American Depression and the New Deal was gradually driven out of the US academy in the 1950s and 1960s. The neo-classical model which replaced it was uninterested in the social constitution of markets. The second group were psychologists and their notion of 'human needs', again decontextualized and dehistoricized. Accessible through positivistic methods of survey research, consumers' needs, opinions and wants were supposed to drive the market. Putting these two together created a stock of knowledge which bracketed off issues concerned with the social construction of needs and wants. Finally, this was all wrapped into 'marketing management', a notion of the techniques available for identifying needs, defining products (their price, placement and distribution) and communicating information about them to consumers. As discussed earlier, once this was expanded to create a view not just about the distribution of commercially produced goods and services but also about how political and social messages could be communicated, marketing as an academic discipline was able to create powerful boundaries around itself even in the critical maelstrom of the 1980s when seemingly comparable disciplines such as Accounting were beginning to open up. In academic terms, the result means that there are strong barriers to social critique within the discipline of marketing itself. These barriers are reflected in the practices of journals and university appointment committees which act as the legitimating agents for the academic discipline of marketing. In a pluralistic society, such barriers are never likely to be perfect. Alternative journal (and conference) outlets exist for those in marketing wishing to go beyond the dominant paradigm. Academic orientations can change over the course of a career thus frustrating the gatekeepers' exclusionary tactics. Some institutions operate looser definitions of subject areas than others. Just such a combination of factors seems to have been the precondition for the entry of postmodernism into marketing (as well as the development of other critiques from within the discipline, e.g. Brownlie et al., 1999a; Desmond, 1998; Wensley, 1999). The challenge for critique is to find more ways of encouraging reflection on the construction of marketing knowledge not just from the epistemological and ontological point of view but as specific forms of knowledge implicated in distinctive settings.

One recent example of this has been the work of Miller and Rose on marketing consultancy projects conducted by the Tavistock Institute during the period from the 1950s to the 1970s. They identify three dominant conceptions of the consumer that draw upon different conceptions of the human being. They label these as 'psychoanalytical' (drawing on Freudian theory to understand attachment to products), 'social psychological' (a more general and open-ended view of 'psychological' needs, e.g. to demonstrate 'femininity' and their social manifestations in wants and desires for different types of products) and finally the 'rational consumer' making calculated choices. They argue that 'it was by no means "easy" to make up the consumer':

> What was entailed was an unprecedented and meticulous charting of the minutiae of the consuming passions by new techniques of group discussions, interviewing and testing. This charting does not merely uncover pre-existing desires or anxieties; it forces them into existence…it renders them thinkable by new techniques of calculation, classification and inscription…and hence makes them amenable to action and instrumentalization in the service of the sales of goods…This was not a matter of the unscrupulous manipulation of passive consumers; technologies of consumption depended upon fabricating delicate affiliations between the active choices of potential consumers and the qualities, pleasures and satisfactions represented in the product. (Miller and Rose, 1997: 31)

Miller and Rose indicate the complex way in which the development of academic forms of knowledge within marketing feeds into the construction of specific technologies of the self. Further research on this basis could provide a useful way of understanding the emergence of distinctive discourses of marketing knowledge and associated technologies.

Marketing as management practice

As a set of organizational practices, marketing has to be defined, implemented and applied in specific contexts where there are potentially competing groups. In the UK, this has led to many discussions about the 'need' to introduce marketing and the barriers to its introduction. This in turn has been related to different definitions of what is meant by marketing and why it is needed.

In studying the financial services sector, for example, Morgan and Sturdy reveal the debates which went on among managers in that industry about the role which marketing was to play and the implications which this would have for broader relations of power within firms. In particular, they emphasize the clear and knowledgeable clashes which occurred in banks and insurance companies between marketing as a discourse and an associated set of managers and professionals (with its emphasis on 'knowing the consumer') and sales, again as a discourse and set of associated managers and employees (with its emphasis on 'productivity'). Marketing academics and practitioners frequently brought out 'scare' stories, for example, revealing the lack of marketing research departments in financial institutions or the lack of sophistication of many marketing functions. Resistance to marketing was blamed on the 'productionist' ideology referred to earlier. Arguably the crucial factor in the 'victory' of marketing was the alliance which it was able to make with regulators and consumer advocacy bodies as a way of overcoming what were seen as 'old-fashioned' sales techniques which took little account of 'real consumer needs' (Morgan and Sturdy, 2000: ch. 6). Sales departments tended to lack any academic legitimators and found it hard in the long term to retain their independence from marketing.

This study reveals that we have much to learn about how marketing discourse and practice get incorporated into specific contexts. This is not a 'natural' process but one that emerges out of power, conflict and struggle. Two other examples could be considered here. One is the spread of marketing discourse into the public sector as explored, for example, in the UK context in the work of Clarke and Newman (1997) and Fairclough (1993, 2000) where, *contra* Kotler (1985), this change is seen in terms of struggles and conflicts between groups drawing on different sources of power. The second example relates to national differences. For example, it has often been suggested that German firms believe that their products should sell themselves – on the basis of their technical excellence – and therefore, marketing is not very well developed in Germany, or at least has not been until the recent challenges to German distinctiveness as a result of competition from other countries which have upgraded their technological capabilities. Similar comments could be made about Japanese firms, though here classic examples of Japanese market growth (e.g. Honda motorbikes in the USA) have become incorporated into the 'lessons' to be learnt by apprentice marketers. These cases raise the question of whether firms can 'succeed' without a culture of marketing or a set of academically legitimated marketing professionals. Obviously, there are huge interest groups only too keen to propound the importance of such knowledge and practices. As well as specialist firms in the marketing area, these range from professional associations through to IT companies keen to sell software for market analysis and on to consultants offering advice on marketing. Governments can also be instrumental in this process, e.g. not just the role which states have played in privatization processes but also the role which they play in providing funds for education and training for small businesses, a significant part of which usually goes on training in marketing. Finally it is clear that financial institutions increasingly see the existence of a credible marketing plan and strategy as a *sine qua non* of a successful firm, be it large or small. In conclusion, we have very little understanding of how marketing colonizes organizations – what are the national, sectoral and firm level features which enable this to happen and with what consequences?

Marketing technologies and the creation of the governable consumer

The third level of analysis concerns the interrelationship between marketing technologies of knowledge and the consumers. Rose, for example, states:

> The technologies of mass consumption, as they took shape over the course of the twentieth century, established a new relation between the sphere of the self and the world of goods. For the first time, this power of goods to shape identities was utilized in a calculated form, according to rationalities worked out and established not by politicians but by salesmen, market researchers, designers and advertisers who increasingly based their calculations upon psychological conceptions of humans and their desires. (Rose, 1998: 85; see also Rose, 1989)

In a joint paper with Miller, he has developed this argument in ways similar to their general approach to accounting and other disciplinary technologies. They state:

> We abstain from a mode of analysis which links the unholy alliance of psychology, advertising and capitalism with a manipulation of desires in the name of private profit, social anesthesia and commodity fetishism. We are concerned with what one might term the 'productive' features of these new techniques, the ways in which psychological knowledges have connected themselves up in complex ways with the technologies of advertising and marketing to make possible new kinds of relations that human beings can have with themselves and others through the medium of goods. (Miller and Rose, 1997: 3)

This argument returns to the idea of understanding the ways in which individuals have been taught to see their identity in terms of the consumption process and marketing. Actors begin to construct their knowledge of themselves in terms of being a particular type of consumer, even an example of a particular type of market segment, for example derived from the newspapers which they read, the cars which they drive, the houses in which they live, the supermarkets at which they shop. Marketing knowledge and its associated technologies constitute people as 'governable consumers' with characteristics that are stable and knowable. These characteristics enable companies to develop technologies that access consumers in distinctive ways. The needs and wants of the consumer become identified and constituted in increasingly complex ways drawing on the ever expanding range of psychological theories that are available. Advertising campaigns construct products, needs and wants in ways linked back to underlying conceptions of the governable person. Frequently these are accompanied and made more sophisticated by technologies that constitute individuals as members of particular sorts of groups with pre-defined needs, e.g. class, gender, age and so forth. These technologies of social segmentation become the basis for market segmentation. What is created is a landscape that is knowable, identifiable and calculable – the world of the 'governable consumer' capable of governance by those who hold the knowledge and through this the power.

By critically identifying these processes, it becomes possible to characterize some of the broader effects. One particularly important aspect is the interrelationship between discourses of marketing and the consumer and discourses of politics and citizenship. The political sphere itself has become transmuted into a sphere of consumption where individual preferences are articulated in focus groups and consumer surveys. Thus the tendency is for the aggregated preferences of consumers as individuals (for example for lower taxes or cheaper petrol prices) to become translated into political policies no matter what the broader consequences are. Marketing has provided a set of technological means to identify individual preferences and these are increasingly seen as the only way to legitimate political action. In this way, the struggle to create a civic society which represents the aspirations of the collectivity separate from though linked in to individual preferences is weakened. It finds no legitimate space in this context and shrinks to the margins of political debate as it cannot be justified on the basis of focus groups and surveys as the preference of individuals. However, this goes together with a recognition that only collective solutions that may involve the subjugation of personal individual preferences have a hope of resolving the ecological and social consequences of mass consumption. How is it possible to counteract the marketing logic which gives individuals rights to consume? The tendency seems to be to give up the struggle to create a collective sphere and reduce everything, even democracy, down to a choice for the individual between two or more consumer objects, Bush versus Gore, Blair versus Hague and so on. Politicians are marketed and constructed as products in a marketplace, their programmes determined by individualized preferences. Politics as a marketplace is not a new phenomenon but the power and tenacity of marketing technologies has reached such an extent that it makes it increasingly difficult to envisage an alternative of public discourse, civic society and collective decision-making.

CONCLUSION

In this chapter, I have tried to account for the power of marketing as a discourse and to suggest how critical approaches can begin to subvert that power. In historical terms, the crucial transition for marketing discourse is its move from a critical account of how markets work to a set of prescriptions and tools about how managers can market their products. While this switch can be explained in terms of the changing nature of the US economy in the early part of the twentieth century, what was particularly important was that marketing legitimated its role in terms of the beneficent effects which it had for both companies and consumers. In this respect, resistance to marketing inside companies by groups such as sales or production was useful. It enabled marketing to present itself as the champion of the consumer within the firm. Only when marketing was able to take on an important role could the interests of the consumer and the company be properly aligned, since only then would the company be really producing what the consumers 'needed'. Consumer needs were accessible through positivistic techniques as they were perceived as the fixed characteristics of individuals. Thus marketing discourse and practice presented itself as a friend to the consumer, a beneficent force in the struggle to get organizations to listen to their consumers rather than to allow internal interest groups to dictate the goals of the company. In the 1980s onwards, these ideas proved fertile ground for extending marketing's power into the public and the voluntary sectors; marketing could be used as a way of undermining the power of professional interests within these organizations to define their goals and products and instead presenting a new vision of how markets could be positively used even in these cases.

Efforts to undermine this hegemony are still limited. On the one side has been the growth of postmodernist deconstructions of marketing and markets. Such deconstructions have the merit of iconoclasm and the 'shock of the new' but seem ultimately devoid of any social critique. On the other side are those voices which raise the question of the false needs constructed by marketing as ultimately an outcome of capitalism and the commodity fetishism which is essential to its reproduction and expansion. It was argued in this chapter that the general critique of this approach could benefit from a closer engagement with specific social practices and contexts. The conception of marketing as a power-knowledge setting which produces 'the governable consumer' implies that there must be specific techniques and knowledges which open up what it is to be a consumer. Marketing constitutes specific technologies based on these discourses in order to learn what the consumer is and how the consumer can be approached and managed. These technologies (of advertising, segmentation, opinion and information gathering) have seldom been studied from this perspective, i.e. how they build the truth of the 'governable consumer' out of discourses concerned with the nature of the individual and thereby create a cycle of reproduction and reinforcement. The implications of this for the wider social context are huge. Rather than welcoming the penetration of marketing into the public sphere, it was argued that this leads to a diminution of collective life and its substitution by a marketing view of politics and collective social goals. The importation of focus groups and polling into politics is more than just a dumbing down of political debate; it also corresponds to the decline of the debate about public goods in favour of the idea that politics (like the market) can only legitimately and practically deliver on personal preferences. Collective problems that can only be solved at the expense of individual preferences are marginalized. This is due at least in part to the role which marketing as a set of discourses and practices has played in legitimating the idea that the only framework for markets and politics can be a context in which individual preferences and wants, revealed through the techniques of marketing, must be paramount. In response, therefore, the critique of marketing must be part of a wider attempt to reconstruct our understanding of the relationship between self and society in a context where global problems of insecurity, risk and inequality cannot be solved on the basis of individual preferences and are simultaneously outstripping the capacity of weakened collective institutions to tackle them.

REFERENCES

Adorno, T. (1973) *Negative Dialectics*. London: Heinemann.

Alvesson, M. (1994) Critical Theory and consumer marketing. *Scandinavian Journal of Management*. 10(2): 291–313.

Alvesson, M. and Willmott, H. (1996) *Making Sense of Management: A Critical Introduction*. London: Sage.

Arndt, J. (1985) The tyranny of paradigms: The case for paradigmatic pluralism in marketing. In N. Dhoklia and J. Arndt (eds), *Changing the Course of Marketing: Alternative Paradigms for Widening Marketing Theory*. Greenwich, CT: JAI Press.

Baritz, L. (1960) *The Servants of Power*. Middletown, CT: Wesleyan University Press.

Bauman, Z. (1989) *Modernity and the Holocaust*. Cambridge: Polity.

Benjamin, W. (1992) *Illuminations*. London: Fontana.

Brown, S. (1995) *Postmodern Marketing*. London: Routledge.

Brown, S. (1998) *Postmodern Marketing Two: Telling Tales*. London: ITBP.

Brown, S. (1999) Postmodernism: The end of marketing? In D. Brownlie, M. Saren, R. Wensley and R. Whittington (eds), *Rethinking Marketing: Towards Critical Marketing Accountings*. London: Sage.

Brown, S., Bell, J. and Carson, D. (eds) (1996) *Marketing Apocalypse*. London: Routledge.

Brown, S., Doherty, A.M. and Clarke, B. (eds) (1998) *Romancing the Market*. London: Routledge.

Brownlie, D., Saren, M., Wensley, R. and Whittington, R. (eds) (1999a) *Rethinking Marketing: Towards Critical Marketing Accountings*. London: Sage.

Brownlie, D., Saren, M., Wensley, R. and Whittington, R. (1999b) Marketing disequilibrium: On redress and restoration. In D. Brownlie, M. Saren, R. Wensley and R. Whittington (eds), *Rethinking Marketing: Towards Critical Marketing Accountings*. London: Sage.

Burrell, G. (1997) *Pandemonium: Towards a Retro-Organization Theory*. London: Sage.

Burrell, G. and Morgan, G. (1979) *Sociological Paradigms and Organizational Analysis*. London: Heinemann.

Clarke, J. and Newman, J. (1997) *The Managerial State*. London: Sage.

Desmond, J. (1998) Marketing and moral indifference. In M. Parker (ed.), *Ethics and Organizations*. London: Sage.

Fairclough, N. (1993) Critical discourse analysis and marketization of public discourse: the universities. *Discourse and Society*. 4 (2): 133–68.

Fairclough, N. (2000) *New Labour: New Language*. London: Routledge.

Fligstein, N. (1990) *The Transformation of Corporate Control*. Cambridge, MA: Harvard University Press.

Friedmann, M. and Friedmann, R. (1979) *Free to Choose*. London: Penguin.

Hannigan, J. (1998) *Fantasy City: Pleasure and Profit in the Postmodern Metropolis*. London: Routledge.

Harvey, D. (1989) *The Urban Experience*. Oxford: Basil Blackwell.

Harvey, D. (1990) *The Condition of Postmodernity*. Oxford: Basil Blackwell.

Horkheimer, M. and Adorno, T. (1997 [1947]) *Dialectic of Enlightenment*. London: Verso.

Hunt, S.D. (1994) On rethinking marketing: Our discipline, our practice, our methods. *European Journal of Marketing*. 28(3): 13–25.

Klein, N. (2000) *No Logo*. London: Flamingo.

Knights, D. and Willmott, H. (1999) *Management Lives: Power and Identity in Work Organizations*. London: Sage.

Kotler, P. (1985) A generic concept of marketing. In B. Enis and K. Cox (eds), *Marketing Clasics: A Selection of Influential Articles* (5th edn). Boston, MA: Allyn & Bacon.

Marcuse, H. (1964) *One-dimensional Man*. London: Sphere Books.

Marsden, R. and Townley, B. (1999) Power and postmodernity: Reflections on the pleasure dome. *Electronic Journal of Radical Organization Theory* (http://www.mngt.waikato.ac.nz/research/ejrot).

Miller, D., Jackson, P., Thrift, N., Holbrook, B. and Rowlands, M. (1998) *Shopping, Place and Identity*. London: Routledge.

Miller, P. and Rose, N. (1997) Mobilizing the consumer: Assembling the subject of consumption. *Theory, Culture and Society*. 14(1): 1–36.

Morgan, G. (1992) Marketing discourse and practice: Towards a critical analysis. In M. Alvesson and H. Willmott (eds), *Critical Management Studies*. London: Sage.

Morgan, G. and Sturdy, A. (2000) *Beyond Organizational Change*. London: Macmillan.

Rose, N. (1989) *Governing the Soul: The Shaping of the Private Self*. London: Routledge.

Rose, N. (1998) *Powers of Freedom*. Cambridge: Cambridge University Press.

Sturdy, A., Grugulis, I. and Willmott, H. (2001) *Customer Service*. London: Palgrave.

Taylor, I., Evans, K. and Fraser, P. (1996) *A Tale of Two Cities: A Study in Manchester and Sheffield*. London: Routledge.

Wensley, R. (1995) A critical review of research in marketing. *British Journal of Management*. 6: 63–82.

Wensley, R. (1999) Commentary. In D. Brownlie, M. Saren, R. Wensley and R. Whittington (eds), *Rethinking Marketing: Towards Critical Marketing Accountings*. London: Sage.

Willmott, H. (1999) On the idolization of markets and the denigration of marketers: Some critical reflections on a professional paradox. In D. Brownlie, M. Saren, R. Wensley and R. Whittington (eds), *Rethinking Marketing: Towards Critical Marketing Accountings*. London: Sage.

Chapter 7

Accounting and Critical Theory

Michael Power, Richard Laughlin
and David J. Cooper

Accounting has become a pervasive force in modern society. Its practitioners provide legitimate, credible and often influential advice to organizations, including governments, about issues as diverse as organizational reform, contracting out, accountability and governance arrangements, innovation, performance appraisal and risk management. Accounting information is said to influence the pricing of shares and other financial instruments, and, through systems of cost determination, affect what goods and services are produced, where production takes place and how goods are distributed. It is not surprising that accounting is seen as strongly connected to pressures for globalization and economic rationalization. From this perspective, the value of accounting information lies in its capacity to influence and mobilize, to fundamentally affect decision-making.

There is also a representational view of accounting, making claims to 'true costs' and 'the bottom line'. There are even attempts to represent the environment, intellectual capital, brands and human assets on the balance sheet. In the name of such representations, firms are closed as uneconomic, hospitals are closed as too costly, products and services are launched as low-cost alternatives, and training programmes are initiated as improving well-being. Yet, is accounting a system of pseudo information? Are its claims to represent reality hollow?

In this chapter we respond to these questions in the light of Habermas's Critical Theory and, in particular, his theory of communication (Habermas, 1984, 1987). If accounting is a practice which increasingly 'sounds true', it is also a powerful force in economic reasoning. Notwithstanding crises and scandals in which the failings of accounting are briefly evident, it retains its credibility as a whole (Power, 1997). Indeed, when accounting 'fails', the solution' invariably involves an investment in new or better accounting; such is its irresistible logic. If we are to control complex modern societies, then we seem to require ever more elaborate forms of economic calculation, of which accounting is a dominant instance.

This chapter introduces Critical Theory and its implications for accounting. While our treatment is by no means exhaustive, we have tried to capture the essential elements of Habermas's work in order to explore a powerful conception of the role and function of accounting. In the next section we begin with a broadly critical analysis of the view that accounting somehow represents economic reality. In the third section we articulate a perspective based upon Critical Theory within a field of different theories of accounting and its informational characteristics. This prepares the ground for the reception of some of Habermas's ideas in the fourth section. In the fifth section we consider the position of accounting as a 'steering medium' in Habermas's sense and in the sixth section we consider the role of accounting and its potential as a medium for enabling or distorting communication.

Overall, the arguments are suggestive of a conception of accounting in which there is a need both to recover the public dimension of its legitimacy and also to comprehend its possible effects on human subjects. This requires a richer theoretical perspective than that provided by dominant instrumental conceptions of accounting.

CONTESTING THE NATURE OF ACCOUNTING

What counts as accounting? This question tends not to be asked, for at least two reasons. First, there is an overwhelming presumption that the answer is obvious. Secondly, if it gets asked at all, it is usually in the context of some crisis in our understanding of accounting. Clearly there is a tension between these two reasons for a lack of fundamental questioning about accounting. If the occasions of crisis and/or scandal multiply, it becomes increasingly difficult to sustain the obviousness of accounting, analogous perhaps to the 'discovery' of epicycles which were used to sustain an increasingly suspect Ptolemaic cosmology. But the durability of the belief in the utility of existing forms of accounting also suggests a more appropriate analogy with the poison oracle of the Azande (Winch, 1964). Reality itself is constructed to bring it into line with the tribal practice.

Traditionally, accounting is regarded as a technique of quantification or calculation which is an important prerequisite for the smooth functioning of modern businesses. Accounting would therefore be understood largely as 'work' rather than 'interaction' (Habermas, 1971: ch. 6). Work practices such as accounting are commonly regarded as being merely technical, 'working' well or badly in a given context. Our criteria of appraisal are thereby limited to the instrumental success or otherwise of the technical attributes in achieving some pre-given end, for example supplying useful information. In other words, we can say that accounting is traditionally subsumed under a model of purposive rationality, '*Zweckrationalitaet*' in Weber's (1978: 24–6) sense. It functions as a merely formal set of procedures whose techniques are neutral and incontestable. On this view, accounting may supply guidance on appropriate means and methods to achieve given informational ends, but it cannot determine those ends themselves. This image of accounting as technique also supports a conception of accounting as an extension of common sense. It is an image of accounting as something that we can take for granted and that does not merit theoretical elaboration.[1]

The contemporary version of this slightly caricatured image of accounting relates to the goal of aiding decision-making. The American Accounting Association stated that 'accounting information must be useful to people accounting in various capacities both inside and outside of the entity concerned' (1966: 8). Despite widespread criticism, this conception of accounting has remained durable and has informed subsequent thinking (for example, Accounting Standards Steering Committee, 1975; Financial Accounting Standards Board, 1978). Accounting students learn very quickly to distinguish between accounting for internal decision-making purposes, i.e. management accounting, and accounting for external decision-making purposes, i.e. financial accounting. But although there are very different technical elaborations appropriate to each form of accounting (e.g. budgeting, variance analysis and costing for management accounting; recognition, valuation and disclosure conventions for financial accounting) there is a single common vision: accounting provides information that is *useful* to users of that information.

This textbook image of accounting as information for economic decision-making is promoted as sensible and robust. What else could accounting be for? While there has been a renewed focus on accounting as facilitating the development and enforcement of contracts, typically as part of calls for stewardship and accountability, this 'contracting' view typically still emphasizes economic decision-making (Watts and Zimmerman, 1986) rather than, for example, legal or social justice. Corresponding to the image of the accountant as a supplier of information, as a worthy under-labourer, a 'worker' for the lofty decision-maker, there is a perception of the accountant as an expert in technical niceties but with no pretence to pass value judgements on the goals of decision-making. His or her role is neutrally facilitative and, in a sense made popular by the media, rather dull (Beard, 1994; Friedman and Lyne, 2001).

If this is an exaggerated image of accounting, it is not wildly so. However, it is an image which has increasingly been subject to critical scrutiny and redefinition as the commonsense view that accounting simply 'represents' economic reality in an unbiased fashion has been questioned from a number of directions. In what follows we shall look briefly at the problem of accounting as a representational practice and explore some of the ways in which accounting theorists have voiced doubts about it. These approaches share a broad critical purpose in that they refuse to take for granted accounting concepts and practices on their own terms. However, they are also profoundly different from each other in many respects.

Information supposedly tells us something new ('supposedly' because, as we shall see, information is often used in practice for a variety of purposes, such as to reassure or confirm expectations and preconceptions). It is assumed to (re)present in some way events which are relatively independent of the representational system. In the case of accounting we might wish to call these independent events 'economic reality'. So here we have two crucial elements of accounting as information: novelty and representation. On the question of newness we shall have little to say.[2] As far as representation is concerned, criticism has come from many different sources. At a very simple level, the very possibility of 'creative' accounting practices suggests that the image of accounting as a simple mapping of an independent reality is naïve, although it is worth adding that the idea of creativity presupposes the existence of some 'objective' benchmark against which it can be evaluated. Hence a more radical critique of the representationalist credentials of accounting would see it as a practice that is 'creative' in a much deeper sense, i.e. not as a deviation from an objective standard but as a practice *without* objectivity.

In the context of financial accounting there is much more at stake than double-entry bookkeeping. Group accounting and the setting of provisions are examples of areas which are constantly open to judgement and negotiation. Accounting authorities such as the Financial Accounting Standards Board (FASB) in the USA, and the Accounting Standards Board (ASB) in the UK have attempted to stem the tide of creativity by reducing areas of judgement and negotiation (a move which effectively involves institutionalizing and privileging certain 'official' judgements over others). One example is 'Off Balance Sheet Finance', which is concerned about defining the boundaries of the firm. Attempts to police organizational boundaries run the risk of buying the virtue of consistency at the expense of being arbitrary. More significantly, these bodies have in addition been subject to considerable pressure and lobbying by parties who believe that the particular representational convention chosen will have important economic consequences for them (Solomons, 1986; Zeff, 1978). Classic complaints arise from high-tech firms (most recently the dotcoms) who complain that representing research as an expense leads to their undervaluation and hence susceptibility to takeovers.

The position is similar in management accounting. The determination of 'true' cost in some representational sense is a myth that the questions of overhead allocation or transfer pricing have done much to explode. Activity based costing was introduced in many regulated industries (including organizations working under systems of cost reimbursement pricing, such as defence contractors, hospitals, telecommunications and utilities) to produce 'true costs', where these costs would include all sorts of overheads and activities that had not traditionally be defined as related to the cost of producing products and services (such as administration, marketing, research and customer support and relations). In the case of transfer pricing, most textbooks attempt to determine optimal costs and prices through various forms of economic analysis, but in the end acknowledge that the appropriate price to charge for internal services is an issue of organizational power and politics (Armstrong, 1998; Swieringa and Waterhouse, 1982). Historically, accounting, like many social practices and disciplines, has aspired to an objectivity both grounded in common sense and theoretical justification. The search for 'true' income and 'true' cost indicate a representational ideal of accounting as a purely formal or procedural activity which has not been entirely expunged. The hope seems to be that if only we can refine or improve our set of accounting techniques then 'cost' and 'income' will be revealed.

Elsewhere, the very measurement convention on which accounting has been based has also been an important focus for the question of representation. The apparent objectivity of historic cost accounting has, in times of inflation, looked obviously suspect. Alternative systems of accounting for changing prices have effectively multiplied the possibilities for the unit of economic measurement, thus undermining this objectivity further. Yet, as we noted above, the traditional image of accounting and its allegiance to the historic cost convention have proved remarkably durable.

Given these internal tensions and contradictions in the idea of accounting as a representational practice, it should come as little surprise to encounter bolder critiques, which break with the notion of representation entirely. They hold that there is no independent economic reality. Rather, accounting is implicated in *creating* that reality. Hopwood (1987) has argued that management accounting systems provide a medium through which the organization becomes 'visible' to itself. That which is newly 'visible' is not a representation of an independent reality but the creation of a new domain of economic facts. Accounting therefore creates the economic facts that it purports to represent. Hines (1988) has argued in a similar fashion – the communication of economic 'facts' in financial statements is simultaneously their construction as facts. No doubt these are strange ideas and they seem to violate our deepest 'objectivist' and 'realist' intuitions. But we must take seriously the possibility that these intuitions in the context of accounting are simply mistaken.

ACCOUNTING INFORMATION AND DECISION-MAKING

The problem of representation suggests that there is no single way to account for economic reality, despite a continuing rhetoric to the contrary. There has been a variety of theoretical responses to this indeterminacy or subjectivity. These can be differentiated both according to their respective perceptions of the role and nature of accounting information for decision-making (whether accounting is fundamentally functional or dysfunctional and distorting) and also according to the explanatory level at which these perceptions are articulated (ranging from generalizable to context-specific explanations). Laughlin and Lowe (1990) and Power and Laughlin (1992) thereby 'position' various approaches to accounting relative to an understanding of Critical Theory.

Such classifications raise important questions. Close to the level of professional and industrial interests are functional concerns about the quality of the decision-making purpose. Are we making optimal decisions? Do we have sufficient information for this purpose? For example, Kaplan (1983) argues that traditional accounting culture has inhibited strategic decision-making in firms. There has developed a concern with strategic management accounting (Johnson, 1994; Johnson and Kaplan, 1987; Shank and Govindarajan, 1989), a concern that continues to accept the decision-making framework as somehow functionally unproblematic: accounting as an enabling practice is merely in need of improvement.

The idea of accounting for decision-making purposes seems so obvious that it is almost inconceivable that it could have any other role. But do we have a clear conception of what decision-making involves and how it takes place? What is a decision, what is it about, and what is the link to information? Studies have questioned the very nature of decision-making itself by confronting this ideal role for accounting with its actual functioning in organizational settings. The study by Burchell and colleagues (1980) attempts to enrich our conception of the role of information systems. Decision-making will only correspond to the enabling ideal where there is *high* certainty of the objectives or ends to which the decision is orientated together with *high* certainty concerning the causal relation between decision and action. However, this is only one possible (and rare) instance. In contrast, accounting information can also serve to rationalize and justify decisions ex post or can be used as 'ammunition' in organizational politics. These context-dependent roles are equally significant as the enabling ideal and, it is claimed, much more prevalent in practice. Following this critical initiative, numerous studies in the management accounting area have sought to analyse accounting in action and its consequences, not all of which, in contrast to the ideal, will be intended.

For example, studies of accounting innovation in organizational contexts have documented the sense in which accounting meets resistance to, and possible transformations of, its original purpose. Berry and colleagues (1985) document the resistance of one organization in the UK to the introduction of new financial controls. Ansari and Euske (1987) provide a similar study in the context of a US military enterprise. The ideal of improved decision-making, the official rationale for accounting innovation, encounters numerous pressures in organizational contexts. This suggests that accounting is less important as a functional resource for decision-making than as a symbolic resource for the organization as a whole (March, 1987).

An important extension of this contextualist research goes further and claims that whether accounting serves the decision-enabling role or not, it nevertheless has profound effects on human subjects, who are constructed as 'calculable' and 'calculating' individuals within the organization (Miller and O'Leary, 1987). Accounting distorts to the extent that individuals are subsumed within accounting regimes with important behavioural consequences in local organizational contexts (Knights and Collinson, 1987; Roberts and Scapens, 1990). Miller and O'Leary (1994a, 1994b) go on to argue that workers and production units are constructed as 'economic citizens', responsible to customers, and for their own performance. In an interesting debate on the role of theory in guiding empirical work, Arnold (1998) and Froud and colleagues (1998) challenge Miller and O'Leary's analysis that the 'reorganisation of a particular factory as a point where economic demands intersect with political ideals and expertises of work and identity' (1998: 710). They argue that Miller and O'Leary fail to acknowledge structural features which are so central to critical thinking. In short, this debate raises important questions of how 'context' should be conceived.

Radically orientated studies such as those by Tinker and Neimark (1987), Armstrong (1987) and Cooper and Sherer (1984) offer a contextualization around the concept of capitalism and articulate the sense in which accounting is a fundamentally distorting practice in so far as it represents and promulgates the interests of capital. Hence accounting is one important dimension of an economic system considered as a repressive totality. Such neo-Marxist perspectives attempt to express the complicity of traditional accounting with modes of exploitation in general by treating labour simply as one cost 'above the line' among others. From this point of view, even if accounting does fulfil its functional mission for management, it is nevertheless profoundly dysfunctional for labour.

Overall, Critical Theory recognizes that the enabling or distorting status of a practice such as accounting is an open empirical question, which is nevertheless guided by a distinctive theoretical model. This is the mode of analysis implicit in studies such as those by Laughlin (1987), Arrington and Puxty (1991), Puxty (1997), Townley, Cooper and Oakes (forthcoming). We need to consider this framework in more detail.

ACCOUNTING AND THE RATIONALIZATION OF THE LIFEWORLD

Weber (1978) argued that purposive rationality is at the heart of the modernization process. Indeed, bookkeeping seemed to represent and symbolize rationality itself (Weber, 1978: 92–3). In contrast, Habermas (1984, 1987) argues that rationalization is in substance a process of differentiation in which traditional forms of society develop relatively autonomous spheres of culture. The emergence of instrumental reason is just one possible sphere of development, and Habermas is concerned to render this visible. He identifies three cultural spheres or worlds, each with its distinctive style of learning, cognition and institutional practice. Thus the objective world, the intersubjective world and the subjective world correspond broadly to the practices of science, politics and art. Habermas is attempting to construct a model of the rationalization process as the release of specialized experience in these three domains, which represent distinctive rationality complexes: instrumental-reason, practical reason and affective reason respectively.[3] Habermas's model leads him to argue that it is this differentiation in general, rather than instrumental reason in particular, which characterizes modernity. It also opens the way for a critique of modernity in which one particular form of reason, the instrumental, has dominated at the expense of others. Hence we must distinguish Habermas's brand of Critical Theory from romanticist critiques of capitalism for which rehumanization is only possible through a rejection of technology itself (Marcuse, 1986).[4] Against the pessimism of his Frankfurt School predecessors, Habermas attempts to articulate a basis for reconstituting social life and institutional action as the recovery of a balance between the three fundamental spheres of social development. Modernization is therefore not rejected but reappraised. The theoretical contours of this reconstruction depend on the concepts of 'lifeworld', 'system' and 'steering media', which we shall now consider.

The concept of the 'lifeworld' is intended to provide a relatively unproblematic characterization of the domain of everyday experience (although from some Marxist perspectives, such as that of Althusser, it is profoundly problematic and ideological). The concept expresses a level of pre-theoretical practical experience in which social integration is effected by a largely unreflective cultural tradition. According to Habermas, the lifeworld exists both logically and historically prior to those processes of rationalization and differentiation which characterize modern societies. One of Habermas's deepest themes concerns the extent to which we have forgotten the collective symbolic structures of the lifeworld which actually enable and inform those predominant but narrow and specialized systems of action, such as accounting.

Habermas's concept of 'system' is that of a functionally definable arena of action such as the economy or, on a smaller scale, an organization. Systems emerge from the lifeworld as a consequence of processes of functional and cognitive differentiation. According to Habermas, systems rapidly develop an autonomous developmental logic of their own. Weber's (1978) analysis of domestic production provides an illustration of the point: traditional patterns of motivation and work are gradually replaced by more explicitly economic forms of organization and behaviour. Gorz (1989) has described this as the 'economic rationalization of labour' whereby the (lifeworld) contexts of an integrated relation between work and life give way to an autonomous economic domain of work. In an accounting context, Tinker and colleagues (1982) show that economic and accounting concepts of value are related historically to specific forms of social organization, or lifeworld, and Hopwood (1987) has argued for the historical role of accounting in installing a new realm of microeconomic facts in place of more traditional patterns of organizational control.

Habermas's Critical Theory is largely an attempt to recover and articulate the dependence of the system on the lifeworld. But he is no backward-looking romantic. For him, the emergence of autonomous systems is a potentially positive force which is not necessarily distorting; he shares this legacy with traditional Marxism which also regards social change (e.g. from feudalism to capitalism) as potentially progressive. To this extent, Habermas can be regarded as a systems theorist with a difference. The systems framework is premised upon a broadly functional view of social organization: societies consist of systems and subsystems which are governed principally by survival imperatives and react and adapt to their environments to this end. Habermas, however, has always questioned the analogy between social and biological systems which, he believes, sustains the many versions of systems theory. Thus Habermas is critical of Luhmann (1982) and others because their functionalist orientation fails to reflect upon the historical origins of the problems that systems theory addresses. For Habermas the problem of social 'survival' is not a quasi-biological matter but concerns the guiding symbolic structures of the lifeworld and their capacity to steer subsystems, such as the economy and firms, rather than be colonized by them.

The concept of 'steering' plays a pivotal role in this theoretical structure by providing the link between lifeworld and system. Habermas's model of balanced social development posits the possibility that systems receive 'symbolic guidance' from the lifeworld via mechanisms of steering which are grounded in, and controlled at, the level of the lifeworld. However, according to Habermas, this order of dependence of system on lifeworld has in fact become 'distorted' and effectively reversed. Systems and subsystems of increasing complexity have emerged which threaten to colonize the lifeworld itself. Guided by the steering media of 'money' and 'power', the domain of instrumental reason has come to smother and eclipse both the lifeworld and other possible orders of reasoning, e.g. politics and subjectivity. This results in what Habermas calls the 'inner colonization of the lifeworld' (though he is ultimately more optimistic than Weber concerning the possibilities for intervening in this process): 'The thesis of internal colonization states that the subsystems of the economy and the state become more and more complex as a consequence of capitalist growth and penetrate ever deeper into the symbolic reproduction of the lifeworld' (Habermas, 1987: 367).

This theory of social development must be understood in the context of Habermas's broader theory of communicative action. Borrowing from speech act theory, Habermas does not draw a sharp distinction between language and action. Language is itself a form of action and establishes relations of interaction in the process of communication. The categories of language and action are therefore not analytically distinct (Oakes and colleagues (1998) illustrate this argument in their analysis of the way the language of business planning alters the identity of cultural organizations, and shifts the orientations and actions of managers; following Bourdieu, they refer to this process as 'pedagogy'). Habermas has argued that in all speech 'acts' there are implicit claims raised with varying degrees of emphasis. These are 'validity' claims to truth, normative rightness (or justice), truthfulness (or sincerity) and comprehensibility. These claims are rarely made explicit in everyday life, notwithstanding that they lie at the heart of the communicative process. So when the waiter offers more coffee, one normally assumes that there is coffee available, i.e. that an implicit truth claim or *warrant* can be accepted. However, there are occasions in ordinary social interaction when such implicit claims may be explicitly questioned. Specialized practices such as science seek to institutionalize this form of critical questioning but, according to Habermas, they nevertheless presuppose truth claims as a basis for sustainable communication.

According to Habermas, communication always anticipates the possibility that implicit truth claims may be questioned and justified in an ideal speech situation. This philosophical structure is a 'necessary counterfactual' (Power, 1996). By this Habermas means that even though it cannot be realized in an empirical sense, the idea of such an ideal speech situation plays a deeply constitutive role in communication because it expresses an underlying ideal, goal, or direction to discourse. Indeed it provides a basis for a theory of communicative action to illuminate pathological or 'distorted' forms of communication which violate the conditions of this ideal. In general, such distortion consists in severing the institutional link to the possibility of discursive justification of implicit validity claims, a loss of reflection in which the communicative foundation of all forms of action is obscured from view.

In this sense the process of the colonization of the lifeworld by narrowly instrumental system imperatives is also a process of 'systematically distorted' communication. The lifeworld is a primary communicative resource which has become colonized by the functional dictates of system and subsystem. An example might be an economic system in which profitability, not necessarily maximized, is the predominant goal. Such a goal tends to negate and inhibit institutional possibilities for questioning and justifying itself. This means that the lifeworld is no longer capable of communicatively steering a complex economic system which has generated its own functional goals. The current concern with the alarming environmental effects of economically 'rational' action provides a dramatic illustration of the thesis. The rationalization of the lifeworld as a process of differentiation is not inherently distorting. But the discursive demarcation of specialized contexts of individual and collective action also brings the risk that such complex systems advance their own limited operational imperatives at the expense of others, with urgent consequences for social and global welfare.

There have been a number of attempts in accounting to spell out the implications of Habermas's theories of communication action. Shapiro (1998, 2002) incorporates pragmatist concerns and criteria with Habermas's model to develop a process for reasoned arguments in accounting standard setting. While Shapiro's approach may pay too little attention to the lifeworld, it is an ambitious attempt to apply Habermas to arguments about how to account for contentious issues (e.g. accounting for pensions, executive stock options and post-retirement benefits). Wright (1994) pays more attention to issues of power and competing interests in his analysis of the financial statements and arguments by management and auditors concerning the failure of a Canadian bank, but he rather narrowly focuses on the validity claims of comprehensibility, truth, truthfulness and rightness.

Having sketched the contours of Habermas's theory of communication, we need now to consider the position of accounting in relation to it. First we need to consider the role of accounting as a steering medium in Habermas's sense. Following this, we consider the conditions under which accounting is a form of 'distorted communication' or an 'enabling' practice.

ACCOUNTING AS A STEERING MEDIUM

The concept of 'steering' has its origins and meaning in systems theory. To the extent that Habermas is attempting to restore the legitimate steering function of the lifeworld, he can be regarded as a 'critical' systems theorist. Steering media in this ideal sense provide communicative mechanisms to facilitate system maintenance and/or adaptability.

In order to comprehend the phenomenon of accounting, we must elaborate Habermas's account a little further in directions that he does not pursue. It makes sense to distinguish initially between steering media that may be *internal* to particular systems or organizations (such as management accounting) and those that are *external* to such systems (such as financial regulation). However, this distinction between internal and external steering media is by no means absolute. Indeed one version of the colonization thesis focuses on the increasing internalization of external steering media. On the one hand we might call this 'regulatory capture', whereby systems increasingly internalize the capability for their own regulation. But, on the other hand, external regulatory initiatives may have important internal effects on an organization. Preston (1989) has provided an interesting analysis of the colonizing effects within a firm of the UK tax regime. Hence steering media such as accounting and the law do not have a fixed position in the lifeworld-system complex and may be increasingly subsumed and internalized within systemic imperatives. Colonization can go both ways.

Can this notion of steering illuminate accounting? First we need to recall the image of accounting as information for decision-making. We can now see that, in Habermas's terms, this concerns accounting and its function in steering economic activity. Accounting has often been called the language of business; and economic calculation presupposes a basis in accounting through which those calculations are effected. Management accounting 'steers' the economic decision-making of managers; and financial accounting 'steers' the economic decision-making of those external to the organization, typically reduced to investors.

But we saw above that steering in this ideal sense of decision facilitation is a special case in a complex process. Therefore steering in Habermas's sense is much messier and more problematic than the functionalist account would lead us to believe. Yet the thesis of the internal colonization of the lifeworld remains relevant to the accounting context. One way of demonstrating this is to develop some of Habermas's remarks on the law and his concept of 'juridification'. Here we shall find a richer theoretical model for understanding a transformation in the steering potential of practices such as law and accounting which corresponds to the colonization of the lifeworld (Power and Laughlin, 1996).

The concept of juridification describes the tendency to an increasing complexity and formality in the legal process. Juridification expresses not merely the expansion of the volume of law but also, and more crucially, the *expansion of its domain*. Legal process increasingly filters into new domains of social life and this is paralleled by a fragmentation of that process into specialisms that can control the definition of the problems that they purport to address. This conception is at the heart of Habermas's criticisms of the 'violent abstraction' of the juridification process:

> In the end the *generality of* legal situation-definitions is tailored to *bureaucratic implementation,* that is, to administration that deals with the social problems as presented by the legal entitlement. The situation to be regulated is embedded in the context of a life history and of a concrete form of life; it has to be subjected to violent abstraction, not merely because it has to be subsumed under the law, but so that it can be dealt with administratively. (Habermas, 1987: 362–3; emphasis in original)

There are strong parallels here with some of the suggestions made above concerning the manner in which accounting creates new visibilities and factualities within an organization. Accounting, like law, is much more than its technical elaborations, and its formal rationality is illusory. Weber (1978: 215) talks of the rational-legal authority of the law, the sense in which the law is at the very heart of the bureaucratic process. Accounting is also a potential mode of juridification. In order to pursue this idea further we need to consider Habermas's distinction between the 'regulative' and 'constitutive' functions of the law:

> From this standpoint we can distinguish processes of juridification according to whether they are linked to antecedent institutions of the lifeworld and juridically superimposed on socially integrated areas of action or whether they merely increase the density of legal relationships that are constitutive of systematically integrated areas of action. (Habermas, 1987: 366)

Building on this, Habermas distinguishes between two possible senses of steering for, in his case, law. First it may steer in a 'regulative' sense as a *supplement* to both lifeworld and system contexts. Second, following processes of juridification, the law 'steers' in a more 'constitutive' and colonizing sense. With increasing complexity, accounting also comes to provide the very definitions of the areas that it regulates (Hines, 1988). Steering in the regulative sense corresponds by analogy to the ideal model of information for decisions, an ideal that Habermas wishes to preserve while recognizing the risk that it may transform itself into steering in the second, constitutive, sense. Figure 7.1 represents potential dynamics of this model. The transformation from regulative to constitutive steering functions represents the process of the inner colonization of the lifeworld in which 'sub-systems of the economy and the state become more and more complex and penetrate ever deeper into the symbolic reproduction of the lifeworld' (Habermas, 1987: 367).

Although this is an abstract analysis, support for it is strongly suggested by a number of accounting studies in organizational contexts. Dent (1991) documents processes of financial and accounting colonization within railway and engineering industries. Despite initial resistance to change, accounting emerges as a new organizational language which displaces a previously dominant culture. Although this study is not informed by the lifeworld/system structure, it provides a good illustration of the colonization thesis. While the pattern of resistance and acceptance is reversed in Townley and colleagues (forthcoming), the colonization process is fundamentally similar. The colonizing power of accounting consists less in its manifest claims to information-based rationality than in its capacity to capture organizational self-understanding and to reframe it in accounting terms. Accounting becomes in this sense a 'disciplinary power' (Roberts and Scapens, 1990), which colonizes by virtue of its capability for creating a new ontology of economic facts. Gorz (1989) has rather clumsily called this 'economicization' but the point is the same: the rendering of increasing areas of social life within an economic language.

Processes of colonization have been widely studied in the public sector in general, and public systems of health care in particular. Hopwood (1984) has drawn attention to the significance of organizational transformations made in the name of 'efficiency', which have served to intensify internal investments in accounting in the public sector. However, studies by Chua

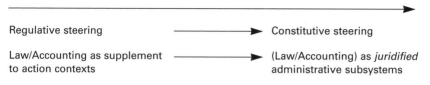

FIGURE 7.1   *The internal colonization of the lifeworld*

and Degeling (1993), Bourn and Ezzamel (1987) and Laughlin (1988) indicate that accounting in hospitals, universities and the Church can be subsumed under a dominant culture of the 'sacred', expressed respectively in terms of clinical, academic and spiritual freedom. Whether accounting can be restricted to a facilitating role in these contexts is an empirical matter, but there is evidence to suggest that in the area of health care the sacred domain of clinical action is becoming influenced, although not yet comprehensively transformed, by accounting initiatives, despite complex forms of resistance (Preston et al., 1992, 1997). As the accounting language of budgeting attempts to occupy clinical discourse, it has the potential to control significant definitions of the hospital environment. However, despite the colonizing intent of changes in the public sector (Laughlin and Broadbent, 1993), subtle forms of resistance through 'absorption' to prevent fundamental change have been observed in education (Broadbent and Laughlin, 1998; Laughlin et al., 1994).

Much more could be said in detail about the colonizing role of accounting but, in the context of Habermas's claims, it is necessary to return to a question of fundamental importance. We saw above that Habermas conceives, albeit ideally, of a *balanced* process of rationalization and differentiation. Colonization represents the process by which a steering function changes from being 'regulative' to 'constitutive', and therefore in some sense dysfunctional or distorting for the particular action-sphere, such as an organization.[5] Thus, as Habermas conceives of it, the 'critical' mission emerges as the need to:

> protect areas of life that are functionally dependent on social integration through values, norms and consensus formation, to preserve them from falling prey to the systemic imperatives of economic and administrative subsystems growing with dynamics of their own, and to defend them from becoming converted over, through the steering medium of the law, to a principle of sociation that is, for them, dysfunctional. (Habermas, 1987: 372–3)

How then can we limit the systemic imperatives of a subsystem such as accounting? As accounting is the medium which enables economic calculation, this is also a question about how we can limit economic thinking, or at least particular versions of it. Is there a sense in which we can retrieve a non-colonizing, non-distorting role for accounting? Can accounting be authentically, if modestly, communicative? It is to these questions that we turn in conclusion.

ACCOUNTING, USERS AND COMMUNICATION

According to Habermas, communicative processes may be 'systematically distorted' when they either strategically ignore or repress contexts of possible validity claim redemption such as spheres of public discourse (see Forester, Chapter 3 in this volume). It is not our intention to give a detailed elaboration of Habermas's theory of communication beyond what has already been said. But it is important to note the sense in which it provides a model of *procedural* rationality embodied in the possibility of discourse. Thus, when we come to think about what an 'undistorted' or 'new' accounting would look like, Habermas's theory provides little of substance. An 'undistorted' form of accounting will be whatever emerges from consensually based discursive procedures at the heart of a revitalized public domain of discussion (see Deetz, Chapter 2 in this volume). It is from this public domain, as the expression of the lifeworld, that accounting systems and regimes will emerge and to which they will be accountable. Hence those looking for a substantive blueprint for, for example, a new environmentally conscious accounting may find Habermas's procedural conception anaemic. However, we shall attempt to identify a number of possible issues. Before this, we reconsider the sense in which accounting is a colonizing and hence distorted form of communication.

Managerial and financial accounting can both be seen in terms of processes of juridification. This is not surprising given the close, if variable, relations between accounting and the law (Miller and Power, 1992). Professional accountants and lawyers have contested not only who should perform tax work, provide transfer pricing advice, dominate financial regulation, work on corporate reorganizations such as mergers and acquisitions, and corporate start-ups and insolvencies, but, perhaps more importantly in terms of juridification, what the appropriate logic for such work might be (Dezaley and Sugarman, 1995; Flood and Skordaki, 1993; Halliday and Carruthers, 1996; Radcliffe et al., 1994). Increasing refinements of costing and budgeting systems, developments in performance measurement systems both internal and external to the organization, the proliferation of detailed pronouncements on financial accounting practice, and the emergence of specialisms within the accounting profession, all testify to a growing density and complexity of accounting knowledge. It is no wonder that the largest accounting firms in the world no longer present themselves as 'accounting' organizations, and that there are increasing moves towards multidisciplinary practices, where accountants, lawyers, engineers and actuaries operate within one professional 'business advisory' firm.

Thus, the decision-making model is increasingly refined and specialized in its aspirations. With this density and complexity, the capacity of accounting to question its own mission and purpose is increasingly eroded, since questions of means and technique multiply at the expense of these ends. Although there is some evidence of attention to fundamentals at the level of standard setting, such as the conceptual framework project by the FASB in the USA, in general the articulation of detailed technical practices has proceeded in such a way that their ultimate legitimation remains a matter for an expert culture or profession, and not a broader public. Hence the process of juridification is intimately bound up with the expert culture of accounting. This fragments the possibility for public discourse by expert capture of a range of policy issues.

One example of this expert capture concerns conceptions of 'users' of accounting information. In raising questions about the nature of accounting as information for decision-making, we are necessarily led to question the constituency of claimed users of accounting data. We can distinguish two levels of critical inquiry about users. First there is the level which retains a broad commitment to the logic of economic decision-making and seeks to extend the range of users entitled to accounting information within this framework. Secondly there is the level which more radically departs from the framework of economic reason, concerning itself with different possibilities for accountability relations. On this second approach the idea of the 'user' and the strictly instrumentalist conception of its relation to accounting information give way to richer conceptions of human agency (Arrington and Puxty, 1991). This enables consideration of the moral and political dimensions of accountability, and this theme has been developed by a number of writers who distinguish between formal accountability systems, governed by experts and susceptible to individualization and juridification, and social accountability, which is relational, contingent and more personal (Arrington and Schweiker, 1992; Roberts, 1996).

It is not always easy to distinguish between these critiques. For example, the corporate social reporting literature tends to occupy a grey area between the two (Gray et al., 1987) – asserting the need to include users, such as environmentally concerned citizens and investors, and recognizing that corporate accountability may include non-economic issues. The very idea of users of accounting information for decision-making is in any event a relatively recent one. Historically, accounting has tended to serve a stewardship purpose, which is certainly a use value, but not one that is concerned with the assessment of something like economic performance. The rise of the user is closely tied to the rise of a corporate culture and capital markets with an interest in performance assessment; hence the priority of investor and creditor user populations over other groups. Indeed, citing other users of accounting information, such as employees or the public, only superficially extends the constituency. In the absence of richer models of what these groups might want from accounting information and the basis of their entitlement, this extension in fact requires that they be assimilated into the economic decision-making model. Other possible users of accounting information must, to count as users, be constructed as economic agents with economic interests and decision potential (for example, the idea that labour can only be a user for wage-bargaining or job security purposes).

The idea of a user is therefore relative to the model of accounting for decision-making. Raising doubts about this model automatically implies a need to rethink the status of the agents for whom accounting data may have, in some broad sense, consequences. Indeed, following Habermas, we need to consider those dimensions of accounting as a social practice with consequences for subjects that remain invisible to the decision-making model. Broadbent (1998) begins to build on feminist critiques of Habermas to explore a gendered conception of accounting logic (see also Hammond and Oakes, 1992; Hines, 1992). There is clearly much to be done in developing a feminist accounting, but Broadbent offers some useful suggestions about the development of Habermas's ideal speech situation. Further concerns about 'voice' (e.g., who is visible and over what domains) have begun to be examined in discussing the consequences of accounting – most notably over race, aboriginal and colonized peoples (e.g., Chew and Greer, 1997).

Arrington and Puxty's (1991) arguments parallel the concerns of this chapter and follow Habermas's theory of communicative action. They argue that accounting has three domains of contestability: the domains of instrumental reason, of public norms, and of subjective experience. Notwithstanding the ambiguity of accounting's instrumental aspirations, which was noted above, the domain of economic reasoning has eclipsed the possibility of contesting the normative context of accounting and its possible consequences for a subjectivity when humans cannot be conceived merely as an end user.

Increasing accounting-based specialization engenders a control of information which is much more than the appropriation of knowledge; it is more generally the monopolization of modes of reason. The expert culture of accounting, in its various elaborations, propagates an economically based discourse which can control the public definitions of social and organizational reality and hence the 'problems' and 'needs' of those domains (Power, 1997). According to Habermas, the rise of such an *'Expertenkultur'* transforms citizens into clients and is responsible for 'socially structured silences'. It is in the nature of an economically grounded concept such as 'efficiency' that no one can be against it; it exhausts the space of possible discourse. Not only can one not be against efficiency, accounting expertise is seen to be needed to provide advice, and to *materialize* that efficiency (Radcliffe, 1999, shows how auditing operationalizes general concerns to be efficient in government).

Colonization via the agency of expanding expert cultures involves the generation of new forms of dependency on lawyers, accountants and others as an administrative elite: 'specialists without vision', as Weber called them. Within such a context, regulatory structures of accountability, such as auditing, provide only pseudo-legitimation of corporate activity, providing mere conformity to accounting rules and practices. Auditing and other forms of inspection and control provide legitimation, but fail to offer a more substantive justification for the activities of organizations and the corporate sector. Similarly, financial accounting as information for the investing public can be regarded as a form of pseudo communication and legitimation for at least two reasons. First, the investing public cannot be identified with the public at large (notwithstanding attempts to create a 'share-owning' democracy) and secondly because accounting-based communications cannot convey many aspects of corporate activity.

This second point is worth elaborating further. Financial statements represent the pinnacle of accounting colonization by providing a dominant representation of an organization which eclipses other possibilities – the veritable 'bottom line'. There has been a variety of well-intentioned attempts to expand measures of organizational performance, to put a variety of assets on the corporate balance sheet and to encourage their active and responsible management. Examples include intellectual capital, human assets, innovation, customer satisfaction and environmental sustainability. The examples proliferate in the not-for-profit and government sectors. The quest is for new accountings which could reverse the colonizing tendencies of the dominant representation of an organization, its performance and accountability.

Considerable care is needed in such a quest. The external consequences of organizational activity have been acknowledged for many years and programmes for cost-benefit analysis have sought to quantify the effects of these externalities in economic terms. In effect this requires an extension of the accounting calculus into ever wider domains beyond the organization. In other words, one possible outcome of a programme for environmental accounting or measuring knowledge assets could be an *intensification* of the juridification process. The question of the environment could be captured by expert accountants who have merely extended their existing expertise in new directions involving new frontiers of 'asset' recognition, such as fresh air (Cooper, 1992).

In the context of current environmental awareness, this is a possibility that should cause considerable unease. In a broad sense, individualistic forms of economic rationality supported by accounting have been responsible for *creating* the newly perceived crisis. As every game theorist knows, individually rational actions may have, and have had, damaging collective consequences (see Hollis, 1987). To take an extreme example, organizational emphasis on profit obscures the effects of environmental damage because the latter does not appear as a cost to the organization. To internalize such external costs, for example via 'green' taxes, misses the point that it is not sufficient simply for accounting to co-opt the relevant environmental variables and formalize them within a new calculus. What is needed is a *change* of corporate practice, and for this a more substantive rather than a formal regulatory practice is necessary, a crucial point made by Tinker and colleagues (1991) in their critique of most proposals for social and environmental accounting. This critique is all the more disturbing in the light of the introduction of trading pollution allowances – compare, for example, the optimistic and technocratic suggestions of the US Federal Energy Regulatory Commission and Wambsganss and Sanford (1996) with the warnings of Lehman (1996) and Gibson (1996). More thorough and deep conceptions of corporate accountability are required. What may be needed is therefore less accounting in its traditional sense and a recovery of the social and subjective dimensions of accountability that Arrington and Puxty (1991) have articulated.

The ecological question is used here for illustrative purposes only, but it shows the potential ambiguity of programmes for a 'new' accounting which is non-colonizing and non-distorting. Habermas's Critical Theory effectively abstains from these substantive first-order issues in favour of a procedural conception of undistorted communication. Although we cannot specify ex ante what a 'truly' communicative and enabling accounting would look like, some useful suggestions have been made (e.g., Broadbent, 1998; Broadbent et al., 1997) and we can certainly identify the risks of colonization. In other words, public forms of discourse are the ultimate form of steering medium and these must subsume others such as accounting. Accounting threatens to 'delinguistify' the public realm (Arrington and Puxty, 1991) and to absorb and transform public discourse in its own image. Habermas's theory of communication suggests that a juridical intensification of accounting is a distortion and that the traditional functional claims for accounting in facilitating decision-making systematically ignore the prior formation of the key concepts of economic reason at the level of public norms embedded in the lifeworld.

CONCLUSION

In this chapter we have explored the potential contribution of Habermas's ideas on systems, lifeworld and steering to a Critical Theory of accounting. We suggest that the technical neutrality of accounting practice is illusory and that accounting is a potentially colonizing force which threatens to 'delinguistify' the public realm. The promotion and institutionalization of methods of economic calculation may have powerful and distorting effects where such methods control the definitions of organizational reality. Whether this occurs is, of course an empirical question and we have drawn attention to a number of suggestive studies.

It should be clear from what has been said that accounting is a powerful, practical vehicle for economic reason. Hence a Critical Theory of accounting cannot be disentangled from that of economic reason in general (see Gorz, 1989). Economic thinking plays such a dominant role in our lives that it becomes difficult to think and act non-economically. The growth of accounting has undoubtedly promoted the capability for economic understandings of ever greater areas of our social world. Recently it appears that other concerns – such as social justice, gender sensitivity, consumer, worker, third world and environmental protection – may provide a respite from our reverence for economic thinking. We therefore stand on the threshold of a number of possibilities for questioning the colonizing effects of economic reason. Habermas's Critical Theory provides one basis for articulating this. It is a programme of much more than theoretical interest and concerns nothing less than the very basis on which we organize our private and public lives; indeed it concerns the constructed nature of this split between the private and the public domains. 'Accountingization' is perhaps an ugly word, but it expresses the sense in which accounting as method may eclipse broader questions of accountability. Critical Theory posits not simply a rejection of accounting practice as such, but a limitation of its aspirations and a reflective awareness of the need for a regulative and therefore facilitating practice. We are only likely to achieve this with the help of broader-based transformations of economic reason and calculation.

This leads to questions about the role of theory, theorists and academics. How might we intervene in the world to question the colonization of accounting and economic reason, and those that promote technocratic solutions, whether they be fellow academics, consultants or bodies of professional expertise? In an apparently fragmented and risky world, we suggest that a start would be for academics to 'talk truth to power' (Neu et al., 2001; Sikka and Willmott, 1997) and point out the role of accounting firms (Mitchell et al., 1998), accounting bodies (Robson et al., 1994), educational practices (Cooper and Taylor, 2000) and ideas (Cooper, 1997; Okcabol and Tinker, 1993) in facilitating 'accountingization'.

NOTES

A version of the original chapter was presented at the Critical Theory and Management Studies Conference in Shrewsbury, UK in April 1990. The authors are grateful to the participants for their many suggestions. Particular thanks are extended to Mats Alvesson, Ed Arrington, Anthony Hopwood, Kalle Lyytinen, Peter Miller, John Mingers, Tony Puxty and Hugh Willmott.

1   An important by-product of this image is that it entitles us to make *prima facie* comparisons between accounting systems and regimes of different organizations and different countries. The image suggests that we know in advance what will count as accounting in these different settings and only minor technical differences

will emerge from such a study. In other words, if accounting is mere technique, then context is irrelevant to our understanding of it. This decontextualized image of accounting has dominated international and comparative accounting, and has been extensively criticized by Burchell et al. (1980).

2 The academic literature in this area is concerned with the efficiency or otherwise of capital markets, and various theories exist and compete (see Watts and Zimmerman, 1986). In brief, accounting information is 'novel' if its release has an impact on the share price of the company in question. Extensive empirical research has been undertaken to gauge the information value of accounting in this way. If anything, this literature suggests that the 'official' release of accounting information in financial statements has much less impact than might be imagined. A relatively 'efficient' capital market has already acquired the information – before financial accounts are published. It is also worth noting that this question of the 'newness' of information is entirely relative to the analyst population of sophisticated capital markets. However, concentrating on this narrow group of users of public information is unlikely to result in socially valuable information, and ignores other possible constituencies such as unions, consumers, suppliers and local communities.

3 In the management literature, Townley et al. (forthcoming) examine reactions to the implementation of performance measurement systems in government in terms of the interplay between instrumental and practical reason (or what they call communicative rationality).

4 Dillard and Bricker (1992) seem to follow such a romanticized critique in their examination of computer-based audit techniques.

5 It must be remembered that an organization, such as a company, is already a 'juridically' constituted entity. It is in this sense a legal fiction.

REFERENCES

Accounting Standards Steering Committee (1975) *The Corporate Report*. London: ASSC.

American Accounting Association (1966) *A Statement of Basic Accounting Theory*. Sarasota, FL: AAA.

Ansari, S. and Euske, K.J. (1987) Rational, rationalising and reifying uses of accounting data in organizations. *Accounting, Organizations and Society*. 12(6): 549–70.

Armstrong, M. (1998) The political economy of international transfer pricing, 1945–1994: State, capital and the decomposition of class. *Critical Perspectives on Accounting*. 9(4): 391–432.

Armstrong, P. (1987) The rise of accounting controls in British capitalist enterprises. *Accounting, Organizations and Society*. 12(5): 415–36.

Arnold, P.J. (1998) The limits of postmodernism in accounting history: The Decatur experience. *Accounting, Organizations and Society*. 23(7): 665–84.

Arrington, C.E. and Puxty, A.E. (1991) Accounting, interests and rationality: A communicative relation. *Critical Perspectives on Accounting*. 2(1): 31–58.

Arrington, C.E. and Schweiker, W. (1992) The rhetoric and reality of accounting research. *Accounting, Organizations, and Society*. 17(6): 511–33.

Beard, V. (1994) Popular culture and professional identity: accountants in the movies. *Accounting, Organizations and Society*. 19(3): 303–18.

Berry, A.J., Capps, T., Cooper, D.J., Ferguson, P., Hopper, T. and Lowe, E.A. (1985) Management control in an area of the National Coal Board: Rationales of accounting practices in a public enterprise. *Accounting, Organizations and Society*. 10(1): 3–28.

Bourn, M. and Ezzamel, M. (1987) Budgetary devolution in the National Health Service and universities in the United Kingdom. *Financial Accountability and Management*. 3(1): 29–45.

Broadbent, J. (1998) The gendered nature of 'accounting logic': Pointers to an accounting that encompasses multiple values. *Critical Perspectives on Accounting*. 9(3): 267–97.

Broadbent, J. and Laughlin, R.C. (1998) Resisting the 'new public management': Absorption and absorbing groups in schools and GP practices in the UK. *Accounting, Auditing and Accountability Journal*. 11(4): 403–35.

Broadbent, J., Ciancanelli, P., Gallhofer, S. and Haslam, J. (1997) Editorial: Enabling accounting: The way forward? *Accounting, Auditing and Accountability Journal*. 10(3): 265–75.

Burchell, S., Clubb, C., Hopwood, A.G., Hughes, H. and Naphapiet, J. (1980) The role of accounting in organizations and society. *Accounting, Organizations and Society*. 5(1): 5–27.

Chew, A. and Greer, S. (1997) Contrasting world views on accounting: Accountability and aboriginal culture. *Accounting, Auditing and Accountability Journal*. 10(3): 276–98.

Chua, W.F. and Degeling, P., (1993) Interrogating an accounting based intervention on three axes: Instrumental, moral and aesthetic. *Accounting, Organizations and Society*. 18(4): 291–318.

Cooper, C. (1992) The non and nom of accounting for (m)other nature. *Accounting, Auditing and Accountability Journal*. 5(3): 16–39.

Cooper, C. (1997) Against postmodernism: Class oriented questions for critical accounting. *Critical Perspectives on Accounting*. 8(1/2): 15–41.

Cooper, C. and Taylor, P. (2000) From Taylorism to Mrs Taylor: The transformation of the accounting craft. *Accounting, Organizations and Society*. 25(6): 555–78.

Cooper, D.J. and Sherer, M. (1984) The value of corporate accounting reports arguments for a political economy of accounting. *Accounting, Organizations and Society*. 9(3/4): 207–32.

Dent, J. (1991) Accounting and organisational cultures: A field study of the emergence of a new organisational reality. *Accounting, Organizations and Society*. 18: 705–32.

Dezaley, Y. and Sugarman, D. (1995) *Professional Competition and Professional Power: Lawyers, Accountants and the Social Construction of Markets*. London: Routledge.

Dillard, J.F. and Bricker, R. (1992) A critique of knowledge-based systems in auditing: The systemic encroachment of technical consciousness. *Critical Perspectives on Accounting*. 3(3): 205–24.

Financial Accounting Standards Board (1978) *Statement of Financial Accounting Concepts No. I – Objectives of Financial Reporting by Business Enterprises*. Stamford, CT: FASB.

Flood, J. and Skordaki, E. (1993) *Corporate Failure and the World of Insolvency Practitioners: Professional Jurisdiction and Big Corporate Insolvencies*. London: Association of Certified and Corporate Accountants.

Friedman, A.L. and Lyne, S.R. (2001) The beancounter stereotype: Towards a general model of stereotype generation. *Critical Perspectives on Accounting*. 12(3): 423–52.

Froud, J., Williams, K., Haslam, C., Johal, S. and Williams, J. (1998) Caterpillar: Two stories and an argument. *Accounting, Organizations and Society*. 23(7): 685–708.

Gibson, K. (1996) The problem with reporting pollution allowances: Reporting is not the problem. *Critical Perspectives on Accounting*. 7(6): 655–65.

Gorz, A. (1989) *Critique of Economic Reason*. London: Verso.

Gray, R., Owen, D. and Maunders, K. (1987) *Corporate Social Reporting: Accounting and Accountability*. Englewood Cliffs, NJ: Prentice-Hall.

Habermas, J. (1971) *Towards a Rational Society: Student Protest, Science and Politics*, trans. J.J. Shapiro. London: Heinemann.

Habermas, J. (1984) *The Theory of Communicative Action, Vol. 1: Reason and the Rationalization of Society*, trans. T. McCarthy. Cambridge: Polity Press.

Habermas, J. (1987) *The Theory of Communicative Action. Vol. 2*, trans. T. McCarthy. Cambridge: Polity Press.

Halliday, T.C. and Carruthers, B. (1996) The moral regulation of markets: Professions, privatizations and the English Insolvency Act, 1986. *Accounting, Organizations, and Society*. 21(4): 371–413.

Hammond, T. and Oakes, L. (1992) Some feminisms and their implications for accounting practice. *Accounting, Auditing and Accountability Journal*. 3(3): 52–70.

Hines, R. (1988) Financial accounting: In communicating reality we construct reality. *Accounting, Organizations and Society*. 13(3): 251–61.

Hines, R. (1992) Accounting: Filing the negative space. *Accounting, Organizations and Society*. 17(3/4): 313–41.

Hollis, M. (1987) *The Cunning of Reason*. Cambridge: Cambridge University Press.

Hopwood, A.G. (1984) Accounting and the pursuit of efficiency. In A.G. Hopwood and C.R. Tomkins (eds), *Issues in Public Sector Accounting*. London: Phillip Allen.

Hopwood, A.G. (1987) The archaeology of accounting systems. *Accounting, Organizations and Society*. 12(3): 207–34.

Johnson, H.T. (1994) Relevance regained: Total quality management and the role of management accounting. *Critical Perspectives on Accounting*. 5(3): 259–67.

Johnson, H.T. and Kaplan, R.S. (1987) *Relevance Lost: The Rise and Fall of Management Accounting*. Boston, MA: Harvard Business School Press.

Kaplan, R.S. (1983) Measuring manufacturing performance: A new challenge for managerial accounting research. *The Accounting Review*. 58(4): 686–705.

Knights, D. and Collinson, D. (1987) Disciplining the shop floor: A comparison of the disciplinary effects of managerial psychology and financial accounting. *Accounting Organizations and Society*. 12(5): 457–77.

Laughlin, R.C. (1987) Accounting systems in organisational contexts: A case for critical theory. *Accounting, Organizations and Society*. 12(5): 479–502.

Laughlin, R.C. (1988) Accounting in its social context: An analysis of the accounting systems of the Church of England. *Accounting, Auditing and Accountability Journal*. 1(2): 19–42.

Laughlin, R.C. and Broadbent, J. (1993) Accounting and law: Partners in the juridification of the public sector in the UK? *Critical Perspectives on Accounting*. 4(4): 337–68.

Laughlin, R.C. and Lowe, T. (1990) A critical analysis of accounting thought: Prognosis and prospects for understanding and accounting system design. In D.J. Cooper and T.M. Hopper (eds), *Critical Accounts*. London: Macmillan.

Laughlin, R.C., Broadbent, J., Shearn, D. and Willig-Atherton, H. (1994) Absorbing LMS: The coping mechanism of a small group. *Accounting, Auditing and Accountability Journal*. 7(1): 59–85.

Lehman, G. (1996) Environmental accounting: Pollution permits or selling the environment? *Critical Perspectives on Accounting*. 7(6): 667–76.

Luhmann, N. (1982) *The Differentiation of Society*. New York: Columbia University Press.

March, J.G. (1987) Ambiguity and accounting: The elusive link between information and decision making. *Accounting, Organizations and Society*. 12(2): 153–68.

Marcuse, H. (1986) *One-dimensional Man*. London: Ark.

Miller, P. and O'Leary, T. (1987) Accounting and the construction of the governable person. *Accounting, Organizations and Society*. 12(3): 235–66.

Miller, P. and O'Leary, T. (1994a) Accounting, economic citizenship and the spatial re-ordering of manufacture. *Accounting, Organizations and Society.* 19(3): 15–43.

Miller, P. and O'Leary, T. (1994b) The factory as laboratory. In M. Power (ed.), *Accounting and Science.* Cambridge: Cambridge University Press.

Miller, P. and O'Leary, T. (1998) Finding things out. *Accounting, Organizations and Society.* 23(7): 709–14.

Miller, P. and Power, M. (1992) Accounting, law and economic calculation. In M. Bromwich and A.G. Hopwood (eds), *Accounting and the Law.* London: Prentice Hall/ICAEW.

Mitchell, A., Sikka, P. and Willmott, H. (1998) Sweeping it under the carpet: the role of accountancy firms in money laundering. *Accounting, Organizations and Society.* 23(5/6): 589–607.

Neu, D., Cooper, D.J. and Everett, J. (2001) Critical accounting interventions. *Critical Perspectives on Accounting.* 12(6): 735–62.

Oakes, L., Townley, B. and Cooper, D.J. (1998) Business planning as pedagogy: language and control in a changing institutional field. *Administrative Science Quarterly.* 43: 257–92.

Okcabol, F. and Tinker, T. (1993) Dismantling financial disclosure regulations: Testing the Stigler–Benston hypothesis. *Accounting, Auditing and Accountability Journal.* 6(1): 10–38.

Power, M. (1996) Habermas and the counterfactual imagination. *Cardozo Law Review.* 17(4): 1005–25.

Power, M. (1997) *The Audit Society: Rituals of Verification.* Oxford: Oxford University Press.

Power, M. and Laughlin, R.C. (1992) Critical theory and accounting. In M. Alvesson and H. Willmott (eds), *Critical Management Studies.* London: Sage.

Power, M. and Laughlin, R.C. (1996) Habermas, law and accounting. *Accounting, Organizations and Society.* 21(5): 441–65.

Preston, A.M. (1989) The taxman cometh: Some observations on the interrelation between accounting and Inland Revenue practice. *Accounting, Organizations and Society.* 14(5/6): 389–414.

Preston, A., Cooper, D.J. and Coombs, R. (1992) Fabricating budgets: A case study of the production of management budgeting in the National Health Service. *Accounting, Organizations and Society.* 17(6): 561–93.

Preston, A., Chua, W.F. and Neu, D. (1997) The diagnostic related group prospective payment system and the problem of the government of rationing health care to the elderly. *Accounting, Organizations and Society.* 22(2): 147–64.

Puxty, A.G. (1997) Accounting choice and a theory of crisis: The cases of post-privatization British Telecom and British gas. *Accounting, Organizations and Society.* 22(7): 713–35.

Radcliffe, V.S. (1999) Knowing efficiency: the enactment of efficiency in efficiency auditing. *Accounting, Organizations and Society.* 24(4): 333–62.

Radcliffe, V.S., Cooper, D.J. and Robson, K. (1994) The management of professional enterprises and regulatory change: British accountancy and the Financial Services Act, 1986. *Accounting, Organizations and Society.* 19(6): 601–28.

Roberts, J. (1996) From discipline to dialogue: Individualizing and socializing forms of accountability. In R. Munro and J. Mouritsen (eds), *Accountability: Power, Ethos and Technologies of Managing.* London: International Thomson Business Press.

Roberts, J. and Scapens, R. (1990) Accounting as discipline. In D.J. Cooper and T. Hopper (eds), *Critical Accounts.* London: Macmillan.

Robson, K., Willmott, H., Cooper, D.J. and Puxty, T. (1994) The ideology of professional regulation and the markets for accounting labour: Three episodes in the recent history of the UK accountancy profession. *Accounting, Organizations and Society.* 19(6): 527–53.

Shank, J.K. and Govindarajan, V. (1989) *Strategic Cost Analysis: The Evolution from Managerial to Strategic Accounting.* Homewood, IL: Irwin.

Shapiro, B.P. (1998) Toward a normative model of rational argumentation for critical accounting discussions. *Accounting, Organizations and Society.* 23(7): 641–84.

Shapiro, B.P. (2002) Rash words, insincere assurances, uncertain promises: Verifying employers' intentions in labor contracts. *Critical Perspectives on Accounting.* 13(1): 63–88.

Sikka, P. and Willmott, H. (1997) Practicing critical accounting. *Critical Perspectives on Accounting.* 8(1/2): 149–65.

Solomons, D. (1986) *Making Accounting Policy.* Oxford: Oxford University Press.

Swieringa, R. and Waterhouse, J. (1982) Organizational views of transfer pricing. *Accounting, Organizations and Society.* 7(2): 149–65.

Tinker, A.M. and Neimark, M.K. (1987) The role of annual reports in gender and class contradictions at General Motors: 1917–1976. *Accounting, Organizations and Society.* 12(1): 71–88.

Tinker, A.M., Merino, B.D. and Neimark, M.K. (1982) The normative origins of positive theories: Ideology and accounting thought. *Accounting, Organizations and Society.* 7(2): 167–200.

Tinker, A.M., Lehman, C. and Neimark, M. (1991) Falling down the hole in the middle of the road: Political quietism in corporate social reporting. *Accounting, Auditing and Accountability Journal.* 4(2): 28–54.

Townley, B., Cooper, D.J. and Oakes, L. (forthcoming) Performance measures and the rationalization of organizations. *Organisation Studies.*

Wambsganss, J.R. and Sanford, B. (1996) The problem with reporting pollution allowances. *Critical Perspectives on Accounting.* 7(6): 643–52.

Watts, R.L. and Zimmerman, J.L. (1986) *Positive Accounting Theory.* New York: Prentice-Hall International.

Weber, M. (1978) *Economy and Society.* Berkeley, CA: University of California Press.

Winch, P. (1964) Understanding a primitive society. *American Philosophical Quarterly.* 1: 307–24.

Wright, M. (1994) Accounting, truth and communication: The case of a bank failure. *Critical Perspectives on Accounting.* 5(4): 361–88.

Zeff, S. (1978) The rise of economic consequences. *Journal of Accountancy.* Dec.: 56–63.

Chapter 8

Greening Organizations: Critical Issues

John M. Jermier and Linda C. Forbes

> All our leaders now call themselves environmentalists. But their brand of environmentalism poses very few challenges to the present system. Instead they propose to spruce up the planet with a few technical fixes or individual lifestyle changes: scrubbers on coal plants, eating 'all natural' cereals, and so on. (Ivan Illich, 30 May 2001, personal correspondence)[1]

Taking a critical approach to management studies opens up a rich literature that includes several academic disciplines and traditions of research. It also brings forward a number of key economic, social and environmental issues that are marginalized in conventional management research. The subject of this chapter, organizations and the natural environment, has not been marginalized as much as other contemporary topics in need of serious attention, probably because so many people throughout the world believe that we now face an environmental crisis. But, as a relatively new area of study in the field of management, more conceptual development is needed and, equally importantly, more attention is needed from scholars interested in critical approaches to management. Well-developed, critical perspectives should be available to those who want to think more radically about this urgent and politically salient subject.

Thinking critically about management means thinking more comprehensively and systematically but also involves thinking politically – or more precisely revealing and making explicit the political content and implications of all conceptual approaches (Jermier, 1998). In line with this, we set out in this chapter to examine some prominent conceptualizations of organizational 'greening' and to address the controversial question of whether the greening of business, industrial, governmental and other organizations supports or detracts from taking a more radical approach to green politics, one that demands (as Ivan Illich suggests above) fundamental, system-wide as well as incremental organizational change. Some critics question whether any 'managerial' approach to solving environmental problems can be authentic and substantive enough to respond properly to the environmental crisis and correspond with the transformational ideals of committed environmentalists (e.g., Dobson, 1990). They view sceptically the limited type and amount of change prescribed by those heralding eco-efficiency and other technical solutions and even question whether approaches advocating more sweeping reform, such as the greening of organizational cultures, are adequate. They are concerned that by endorsing organizational greening initiatives, especially those that are undertaken voluntarily, we unwittingly facilitate the 'hijacking' of the environmental movement and undermine transformational green politics (Welford, 1997).[2] This is an important debate that can benefit from re-examination and further thinking through the lens of Critical Theory, the approach to Critical Management Studies we take in this chapter.

As with many other Critical Management scholars, we use the term Critical Theory not to refer precisely to the Frankfurt School critique but to represent a broad range of literature that challenges the status quo and is sceptical of piecemeal, liberal reformism. Thus, in the course of our analysis, we draw on several critical resources. We do, however, single out Herbert Marcuse's (1964) classic work as our touchstone throughout the chapter because we believe that the integrative power of his critical analysis can help students of management think more systematically about the macro forces in contemporary society that permit domination of 'man by man through the domination of nature' (1964: 158). *One-dimensional Man* (*ODM*) is a valuable resource that facilitates making connections among seemingly diverse forms of domination. We also rely on Marcuse (1964) because of the relentless warnings issued in his book about the 'weakening and even disappearance of all genuinely radical critique' (Kellner, 1991: xi), a theme highly relevant to thinking critically about organizational greening in the context of green politics. Moreover, we think *ODM* presents a point of view that has not been adequately appreciated by critical organizational and environmental theorists and want to call attention to its value as a foundational resource for radical ecology (cf. Luke, 2000). When analysing the causes of environmental destruction, finding resources that are sufficiently comprehensive and integrative can be difficult. We appreciate the renaissance in studies of Marcuse (see Herf, 1999) and think *ODM* offers amazing insights for those studying the politics of various possible solutions to the environmental crisis.[3]

In the first section ahead, we discuss the idea of an environmental crisis. We note the severity of the various individual symptoms of the crisis and the magnitude of global ecosystem stress. We also turn our attention to some of the major factors that are usually blamed for the environmental crisis: the population explosion; capital accumulation exigencies; totally administered, high-consumption lifestyles and the ascendancy of degraded forms of reasoning; and anthropocentric and other anti-ecological social paradigms. In the second section of the chapter, we consider the thesis that it is organizations that are the primary cause of and, therefore, the primary solution to the crisis. We present four prevalent types of greening initiatives (regulatory, ceremonial, competitive and holistic) and critically examine them. At the end of the section, we sketch a promising direction in which a form of holistic greening could be developed, one based on subcultural pluralism, sensitive dialogue and critical reflection. In the conclusion, we address the question of whether or not organizational greening can match up in any meaningful way to the gravity of the environmental crisis.

The main contribution of the chapter lies in our critical analysis of organizational greening. Owing to space constraints, we do not attempt to provide an encyclopaedic review of the organizational greening literature or of practical experiments in greening. Instead, we use Critical Theory to assess the conceptual adequacy and political content of some influential organizational greening research and initiatives. Our purpose is to help generate more systematic and critical thinking in this emerging and crucial area of management studies.

THE GLOBAL ENVIRONMENTAL CRISIS

Symptoms of the global environmental crisis

According to 'The World Scientists' Warning to Humanity', a document signed by 1,575 scientists, including more than half of all living scientists awarded the Nobel Prize, human beings and the natural world are on a collision course:

> Human activities inflict harsh and often irreversible damage on the environment and on critical resources. If not checked, many of our current practices put at risk the future we wish for human society and the plant and animal kingdoms, and may so alter the living world that it will be unable to sustain life in the manner that we know. Fundamental changes are urgent if we are to avoid the collision our present course will bring. (World Scientists, 1996: 242)

This warning, issued by many of the world's most distinguished scientists, is clear and foreboding:

> We the undersigned, senior members of the world's scientific community, hereby warn all humanity of what lies ahead. A great change in our stewardship of the Earth and the life on it is required if vast human misery is to be avoided and our global home on this planet is not to be irretrievably mutilated. (1996: 244)

Lester Brown, founder and past President of the Worldwatch Institute (arguably the world's most respected source of analytical information on the environment – see Wallis, 1997), issued his own warning to humanity. In a recent edition of *State of the World*, the Institute's widely circulated annual report, Brown cautioned:

> collapsing fisheries, shrinking forests, and falling water tables illustrate how human demands are exceeding the sustainable yield of natural systems. Exactly when these sustainable yield thresholds are exceeded is not always evident…The risk in a world adding nearly 80 million people annually is that so many sustainable yield thresholds will be crossed in such a short period of time that the consequences will be unmanageable. (Brown, 2000: 13)

In the same report, Brown's colleague Chris Bright (2000) contends that an even greater danger is looming than most people realize because so many trends are 'spiking' in combination, leading to very rapid shifts or 'discontinuities' that are difficult to anticipate. The potential 'super-problems' that result from such negative synergistic forces can set off even more daunting second, third or higher order effects. Such system-level changes are, for all practical purposes, 'irreversible' (2000: 37). This sentiment is echoed in another current report written by the staff members of the United Nation's Environment Programme (2000) who contend that time has already run out on a number of problems that have escalated into full-scale emergencies. Among the emergencies they cite are: depletion of aquifers and water shortages; soil degradation; destruction of tropical rainforests; extinction of species; collapse of marine fisheries; endangerment of coral reefs; urban air pollution; and global climate change.

Even more extensive lists of urgent environmental problems have been compiled (e.g., Foster, 1997), but the point that is difficult to avoid is that despite remarkable achievements in mitigating environmental degradation in some areas (e.g., chlorofluorocarbon emissions), in the big picture, humanity faces circumstances that threaten the very survival of the species (Gardner, 2002). Perhaps this accounts for the frequent use of the phrase 'global environmental crisis' to refer to the present era. Crisis refers to a crucial stage or a turning point in an unstable period and it refers to a point in a process when a crucial decision has to be made (Bandarage, 1997). What other label describes as well a period characterized by a confluence of significant environmental problems that are loaded with danger and unpredictability, individually, and even more so in combination?

Causes of the global environmental crisis

Many analysts and commentators hold strong beliefs about the causes of the crisis. Experts and the lay public alike attribute environmental problems to a variety of sources. One of the more frequent explanations offered is human population, which is projected to reach a minimum of 9 billion by the year 2050 (Brown, 2000). There is no doubt that ecosystems are strained by increases in human population. But, the crisis is not explained by simply listing population statistics. A critical study must also consider how people interact with the rest of nature and the macro forces that shape everyday lives.

Some macro critics contend that the environmental crisis is best understood by understanding capitalism and its accumulation exigencies, either those impacting financial managers responsible for pooled investments, such as retirement, trust and mutual funds (Korten, 1998), or those impacting executives and other elites who have internalized the profit maximization ethic through years of responding to lucrative compensation and reward systems designed by a variety of capitalist owners (Herman, 1998). With either process, especially in the global corporation, all resources (including human and natural) are exploited in the service of accumulation imperatives. Hawken (1993) agrees that corporate capitalism is the fundamental cause of the environmental crisis, dwarfing all other forms of international power and destroying the world by pillaging the earth and standing in the way of restorative options and possibilities. He argues, however, that it must be understood as a complex system that implicates more than just capitalist elites:

> The world is being destroyed – no doubt about it – by the greed of the rich and powerful. It is also being destroyed by popular demand. There are not enough rich and powerful people to consume the whole world; for that, the rich and powerful need the help of countless ordinary people. (Hawken, 1993: 15)

Thus, each citizen consumer has a role to play in reproducing commercial culture and environmental degradation.

Marcuse (1964) challenged the affluent to re-examine their cultures, lifestyles and concepts of the good life. He acknowledged that techno-industrial society, through rationalized administration of all aspects of life, provided a high standard of living (for many but certainly not for all). This was widely thought to be the royal road to happiness and well-being. Marcuse was convinced, however, that despite unprecedented material abundance, scientific developments, and political consensus in the Western world, contemporary societies could not provide true happiness, a state he felt was related to improvement in the potential of humanity. For Marcuse, the road paved with consumer goods led only to the fulfilment of wants not needs and to soft totalitarianism in society because people confused superficial choice in the realm of consumption with democracy and freedom.

Although happiness has been glorified in fantasy as the bottom line of desire and the ultimate intrinsic goal of life, it has proven to be elusive

(Csikszentmihalyi, 1999). For many of those seeking it by marching directly down the culturally prescribed path of the standardized (fast-paced, competitive, high-consumption) lifestyle, distressing and disorienting effects have often overshadowed whatever modicums of real happiness may have been experienced. In one particularly uncompromising critique of a kind of one-dimensional society, social researchers for public television in the United States proclaimed the present, the age of 'Affluenza', an era in which the disease of consumerism is spreading rapidly, accompanied by an epidemic of stress, overwork and debt. It is argued that the cause of this malaise is the dogged pursuit of narrow, materialistic goals in the mistaken belief that the secret of happiness lies therein. The irony in the era of Affluenza is that the culturally prescribed lifestyle, in its own terms, does not and cannot sustain individual happiness and also has increasingly tragic consequences. For example, from overwork, rampant consumerism and escalating debt, we reap spiritual impoverishment, family disintegration, communities that are plagued with crime, and a natural environment that is being rapidly degraded and destroyed (see website for US Public Broadcasting System, http://www.pbs.org/kcts/affluenza/).

It is difficult to know whether such cautions are being heard and heeded in everyday life or in the institutions of society. Marcuse feared that people would lose perspective and not be able to devise lifestyle alternatives because of the seemingly 'rational character of [society's] irrationality' (1964: 9). In the one-dimensional society, citizens often lack the motivation to lead an examined life because the totally administered lifestyle is engineered to eliminate the desire for soul-searching. In the face of incessant technological change and material abundance, exercising good judgement, sound sense and intelligence, or 'being rational', is achieved by embracing what is, and enjoying the benefits. Thus, alternatives tend to seem, at best, utopian and unattainable or, more probably, simply irrational.

A similar type of reasoning is postulated to hold sway in the institutional realm in which 'rationality' is demonstrated by developing and learning to apply techniques for fine-tuning a macro system that is accepted as basically sound. 'Being rational' means *not* emphasizing political and moral considerations that can make one seem ideological, extremist, and even out of touch with current reality. The 'totally administered' institution is engineered to eliminate the need for political and moral reasoning because the rationality lies in the technology (and the science behind it) that is implemented. Marcuse (1964) used the concept of technological rationality to refer to the process in which the political content of technology becomes invisible, leaving the appearance that the interests of all are served by whatever elites choose to implement. Of course, technology is never neutral because it cannot be isolated from the uses to which it is put. The power of technological rationality lies in its capacity to appear value-neutral while suppressing alternatives that are made to appear ideological (Jermier, 1982). In effect, technological rationality becomes all of political and moral rationality because critical thinking is stultified. According to Marcuse, 'When this point is reached, domination – in the guise of affluence and liberty – extends to all spheres of private and public existence…[It] integrates all authentic opposition [and] absorbs all alternatives' (1964: 18). It also permits unbridled growth and leads to environmental degradation, in part because it sees future technologies as capable of restoring whatever is destroyed.

Other radical critics offer comprehensive explanations of the environmental crisis that focus attention on dominant social paradigms and values that degrade non-human nature. For example, for deep ecologists, spiritual ecologists and social ecologists, the fundamental cause of environmental destruction is anthropocentrism – a set of taken-for-granted assumptions that privilege humans as the central fact or final aim of the universe. Anthropocentrism is entrenched in the human psyche and is the ideological cornerstone of techno-industrial domination (Egri and Pinfield, 1996). Ecofeminist scholars also focus attention on dominant social paradigms and values, but particularly on those that reproduce patriarchal culture and other macro forms of domination. For example, Carolyn Merchant's (1998) classic focuses on interconnections between the mechanistic worldview (with its root metaphor that nature is, in essence, 'dead', resembling a machine more than a living organism) and capitalist economy, patriarchal culture, and hegemonic science and education.

We recognize that the environmental crisis cannot be explained fully without reference to the causes discussed above. They will be woven into the analysis that follows. We focus now, however, on the management of organizations because it is in this field that we find an explanation for the crisis that is advanced with increasing frequency and conviction – the idea that corporations and other organizations are primarily responsible for the degraded state of the environment and also, through their own initiatives, are the best hope of turning things around.

GREENING ORGANIZATIONS TO MANAGE THE GLOBAL ENVIRONMENTAL CRISIS?

During the past decade, scholars began publishing research dedicated to understanding the greening of organizations as a unique and fundamental area of inquiry, one separate from the field of social issues in management. This work heralds the pivotal role of *organizations* in preventing and solving environmental problems. While no common definition of the green organization emerged, it was generally agreed that both organizational processes and outcomes needed to be considered in assessing various approaches to greening. Indeed, virtually every organizational component, process, product and by-product has been related in theory (or more casually) to the process of organizational greening. For example, Shrivastava's (1996) framework for the greening of business is centred on green production, but it also emphasizes green resource use (from procurement to recycling), green energy conservation, green facilities, green transportation, green products and green employees.

While several scholars have developed frameworks that specify components of the green organization, the predominant way organizational greening has been conceptualized is with typologies that classify organizations along a continuum of forms ranging from superficial to high involvement approaches (see Schaefer and Harvey, 1998). Strategy theorists have taken the lead in developing these typologies, often defining the stage of organizational greening based on factors such as top management commitment and characteristics of the programme.

The approach to organizational greening that we adopt in this chapter begins with Hoffman's statement: 'there is no such thing as a "green company". The best one can do is describe the progression of how companies are "going green"' (1997: 14). Accordingly, we conceptualize greening as a multi-dimensional *process* and observe that different forms of greening can be emphasized at different points in time, and even in different parts of an organization at the same time. We depart from the notion of stages of greening because we believe this oversimplifies complex organizations. We specify four basic types of greening initiatives: regulatory greening; ceremonial greening; competitive greening; and holistic greening. Our approach is at odds with the tendency among some researchers to advocate monolithic, system-wide culture change in support of greening. Even though this tendency is appealing in some ways, we are concerned that it is not viable and that it oversimplifies both the concept of culture and the process of organizational change. We will discuss these problems at the end of this section.

Regulatory greening

Governmental approaches to environmental protection vary widely throughout the world but regulatory enforcement of organizational compliance with legal statutes is a significant part of organizational greening everywhere. Regulatory demands can be met with evasion, begrudging compliance, enthusiasm, or any point along a continuum (Kagan and Scholz, 1984). Some actors respond to regulatory demands with calculated non-compliance. They intentionally circumvent the law and resign to pay fines if worst-case scenarios occur. Others accept regulation, staying in compliance even when they regard requirements as somewhat onerous and arbitrary. Still others respond enthusiastically, however, because they believe that competitive advantage results from meeting regulatory demands more efficiently than their competitors (Porter and van der Linde, 1995).

There are, of course, limitations to relying on regulation and regulators. Based on data from the UK, Fineman (2000: 71) argued that while we are better off with mandatory regulation than without it, when 'unmasked,' regulation may be 'far less substantial, and far less green than it appears.' Moreover, he contended that regulators' values are often much closer to the interests of industry than those seeking deeper transformations. Often organizations leave decisions about the toxic aspects of production to legal and technical staff that supposedly have the expertise required to understand environmental problems. As Marcuse (1964) warns, however, technological rationality can sidetrack ethical concerns in favour of technical, formulaic analysis of problems. This process can lead employees who are otherwise capable of political and moral reflection to defer to technical experts who 'depoliticize' the process.

Obviously, regulatory enforcement is, inherently, a political process, whose effectiveness depends on legislative initiatives and administrative systems capable of curtailing the power of commercial and other regulated entities. But, given the difficulty of writing technically comprehensive statutes that safeguard the environment, and given how politically volatile and varied the process of enforcement is (May and Winter, 1999), even when organizations comply fully with environmental regulation, critics contend that they usually fall far short of what is needed. One of the main reasons that many environmentalists are reluctant to endorse greening through regulation is that politics create dangerous inconsistencies in standards and patterns of compliance.

Ceremonial greening

A second type of organizational greening stems from what seems to be actors' good intentions to practise sound environmental management. In some cases, however, actors do not move much beyond 'lip service'. They are content to operate at the level of appearances and ceremonial practices symbolizing 'rational' management. This type of greening runs parallel to the practice of superficial corporate environmentalism that has been criticized by numerous scholars (e.g., Greer and Bruno, 1996; Tokar, 1997; also see http://www.corpwatch.org/). In this work, the theme of *'greenwashing'* is developed and evidence is provided showing that despite their self-congratulatory rhetoric and projection as eco-friendly, actors adopting this approach continue to endanger the world with their products and operations. According to the greenwashing perspective, some organizations use public relations and related activities to manage the threats to reputation that result from substandard environmental performance. At the same time, they trumpet minor accomplishments as evidence of deep greening.

In most typologies of organizational greening, there is a category reserved for the practice of surface-level environmentalism (e.g., Coulson-Thomas,

1992). While these frameworks lack the muckraking mentality and hard political edge of the greenwash approach, they are similar in some ways in their suggestions about how organizational greening can take the form of public, ceremonial displays, obscuring the alternative reality of organizational minimalism, inaction or even malfeasance. When managing public impressions so that an appearance of environmental stewardship is projected (regardless of the actual type of greening being practised), organizations may construct a *green ceremonial façade*, focusing attention on one or a small number of highly visible green criteria and neglecting all others (Forbes and Jermier, 2002).

From a critical perspective, some forms of organizational greening may qualify the organization as 'green' at the level of expressed commitments and even formal programmes, but will fall far short as a response to the global environmental crisis. For example, some scholars have observed both positive and negative outcomes in the important area of assessing the effects of environmental management systems, particularly concerning the International Organization for Standardization's ISO 14001 approach (Steger, 2000). In developing a key point about ISO 14001, Switzer and colleagues state, 'because the standard lacks minimum environmental performance requirements and does not [even] require full legal compliance as a condition of registration, some companies may use it to garner "an easy A", while continuing to operate in illegal or irresponsible ways' (2000: 3). As Newton and Harte point out, creating an appearance of technical sophistication and 'objective' greenness hardly guarantees benign impacts: 'it is perfectly feasible for an organization to adopt BS7750 [a forerunner of ISO 14001 and other comprehensive environmental management systems] and do very little about their environmental performance' (1997: 92).

Greenwashing is a sophisticated form of symbolic management through which actors engineer impressions of environmental stewardship. They seek to leave the impression that certain surface-level criteria really matter when it comes to evaluating the degree of greenness of an organization. When successful, greenwashing activities can create structures that resemble a more general process that unfolds when 'the tangible source of exploitation disappears behind the façade of objective rationality' (Marcuse, 1964: 32).

Competitive greening

A third type of organizational greening is widely promoted in both practitioner and scholarly literatures and can involve a considerable investment in greening. At its core is the 'green-green hypothesis' or the belief that it pays financially to be more environmentally oriented. Set in the context of the competitive business model, it is argued in this vein that it is in the best interests of organizations to implement green technologies and practices but to do so following the logic of traditional business calculations. Actors following this model of greening seek to establish competitive supremacy by going *'beyond compliance'* (see Prakash, 2000) but are driven by financial criteria and consider ecological criteria only secondarily.

This type of greening is based primarily on top-down planning and elite initiatives. The main emphasis is on the development and implementation of green production technologies and on studies of pollution prevention and waste minimization, recycling and product design and packaging. But, actors that attempt to develop competitiveness through greening might also establish systems for environmental auditing and reporting, communication and public relations, and distribution and marketing. And, they may institute board-level environmental management committees and other environmental management positions and functions, or comprehensive management systems (e.g. ISO 14001 or the Eco Management and Audit System – EMAS – developed by the European Union). Decisions about embarking on any of these *technical* approaches to environmental management involve cost comparisons among alternatives and projected returns on investment – usually calculated with much heavier weightings on short-run returns. Thus, they centre on perceptions of how competitiveness can be enhanced from the decisions and not on primary desires to alleviate environmental destruction. For example, Bansal and Roth (2000) reported that a firm in their study installed pipelines to transport oil throughout the United Kingdom but the decision to lay the pipeline rather than use freighters was motivated by cost savings, not ecological considerations which were only realized later. Similarly, Madu (1996) notes that the Honda Corporation's decisions to invest in more environmentally friendly technologies, build more efficient cars, and integrate environmental goals into their priorities were based on concerns about survival and calculations of competitive advantage – criteria consistent with the logic of traditional cost-benefit analysis. It is important to point out that the increasing pressure to operate according to such a formula affects all organizations today and not just those in business and industry.

Some critics contend that competitive greening, while appearing to be sound and sensible, is ordinarily a trivial response to the global environmental crisis. They argue that by merely adding the environmental dimension to the development path without allowing that dimension to alter the path in any substantial way is far too limited (Newton and Harte, 1997). Competitive advocates of eco-efficiency encourage reliance on 'business as usual', accepting incremental improvements, while sidestepping bigger issues and opportunities. Critical questions having to do with, for example, continuation of a toxic product line, the desirability of continued growth, or promotion of environmental democracy, are derailed in favour of discussions about the cost effectiveness of incremental changes in the system of production. Moreover, if the changes are not financially profitable using short-run criteria, they are readily abandoned. Critics are concerned that when environmentalism is reduced to a core business issue, it is practised only when time and other resources permit or when there is a pressing public or regulatory initiative (Welford, 1997).

Critics are also concerned that blind faith in new technology is naïve and dangerous because it can lead to the acceptance of toxic systems and irremediable problems we erroneously imagine can be 'fixed' later. In addition, the over-reliance on technology in greening can destroy culturally diverse ways of producing goods and services as productive forces are homogenized and human scale problem-solving is rendered obsolete (Leff, 1995). Returning to Marcuse, we garner the insight that 'technology [is] the great vehicle of *reification* – reification in its most mature and effective form' (1964: 168–9). Systems that are easily naturalized and deified (or reified in other ways) because of their apparent technological progressiveness or rationalist (calculative) sophistication can be mistaken for more sustainable approaches that require deeper greening of the people involved – greening that stimulates higher forms of human discourse and reasoning and, perhaps, ecocentric values and structures of emotion, thus evincing what Di Norcia (1996) refers to as 'a deep caring for nature'.

Holistic greening

A fourth type of organizational greening is aimed at developing a system that elicits deep caring through a well-resourced environmental mission – one that is fully integrated throughout the organization. In principle, advocates of holistic greening aspire to institutionalize a *system-wide environmentalist or ecocentric culture*. Several theorists working with this theme contend that establishing green organizational cultures that inculcate employees with green analytical skills, values, emotions and unconscious motives is the essential ingredient in developing more restorative practices and ecological balance (e.g., Callenbach et al., 1993). They tend to be optimistic that through the development of green cultures, organizations can be genuinely changed at the most fundamental levels, producing a major contribution to transformational green politics.

Holistic green initiatives appeal because they correspond with ecocentric philosophy and appear to advocate an uncompromising, bona fide environmentalism. In this model, organizational elites espouse the idea that comprehensive greening of the organization is a moral imperative. Using techniques of normative control, including rhetorical and evangelical fashioning of the organization's mission, this approach focuses on the total behaviour and collectivist identity of the individual (Willmott, 1993). As can be seen in religious sects and reformist groups (as well as some workplace settings), there are circumstances where organizational ideology is so captivating that it promotes tendencies towards blind loyalty, total commitment and programmed conduct. Like Newton and Harte (1997), we confess to having some mixed feelings when it comes to engendering moral commitment to green causes and encouraging programmed conduct in the service of green ideals. Developing more employees devoted to environmental protection (and some deep green organizations) seems desirable in many ways but also presents some problems.

The main problem is that even if ecocentric ideals are approximated (see Fineman, 1996 on the difficulty of implementation), it is not clear that the system would have long-range viability. Value-centred organizations can take a serious toll on employees in a number of ways that are disturbing in the sense that, when persuasive, they create structures of control that dominate the total life-space of employees (Martin et al., 1998). Total commitment of the individual's body, mind, heart and soul to the organization's cause may be good for greening the economy but can also wreak havoc on individual lives, families and communities as all other life activities are subordinated to the needs of zealous managers and colleagues. Even participation in charitable and community volunteer activities (ironically including environmental activism outside of work) might suffer. Again we see the relevance of Marcuse's (1964) concerns about soft totalitarianism emanating from the workplace.

Greening complex organizations

We raised concerns about regulatory, ceremonial and competitive greening, and even questioned the feasibility and desirability of holistic greening as it manifests in monolithic ecocentric culture. We agree that cultural perspectives on greening are useful, but believe it is necessary to move beyond portraits of organizations as uniform and highly integrated systems in which culture is seen as a clear, consistent, organization-wide force orchestrated by top management initiatives. The project of greening organizations is much more complicated than managerial approaches aimed at engineering culture typically suggest. Such images are not good reflections of the research on culture and organizational analysis (see Alvesson, 2002; Martin, 2002). It is important that cultural research on organizational greening be infused with concepts that better embrace the complexity of the phenomena.

Space does not permit either a full illustration of how this complexity can be handled or a presentation of a new model of organizational greening through culture change, but we do want to identify some key ideas that should be helpful in developing the next generation of critical approaches to organizational greening. To begin, culture should not be reduced to 'a set of espoused and vague values that do not vary that much between organizations, thus conflating rather different phenomena', but should instead be understood as referring to 'deep-level, partly non-conscious sets of meanings, ideas, and symbolism that may be contradictory and run across different social groupings' (Alvesson, 2002: 14). Thus, taking a cultural approach to organizational greening should result in a heavily textured portrait, one that recognizes the ambiguity and contradictory qualities of cultural fields as well as the homogeneity found within various subcultural and other formations (Martin, 2002). It should represent the probable uncertainty, confusion and tension experienced by employees and others as greening initiatives unfold, as well as whatever insight and inspiration employees might experience. To illustrate, Luke (2001) points out that the Ford Motor Company's push to green its culture and lead the automobile industry towards more sustainable practices, is compromised by its standing as the world's largest producer of big, heavy, fuel-inefficient sports utility vehicles. Luke writes: 'The greening of Ford does appear to be sincere, but many of Ford's environmental initiatives are ambiguous' (2001: 321). To the typical employee, especially given that owners of SUVs frequently drive them off-road, damaging and destroying fragile environments along the way, the contradictions between the espoused green values at Ford and at least some of its products must be staggering. To further complicate the portrait of Ford's culture and greening initiatives, President William Clay Ford contends that since there is a big consumer demand for SUVs and since some company will produce them, it is better that Ford take the lead in this market because they are more likely to develop a product that is eco-friendly than any other company.

All organizations, when viewed as cultural fields and examined carefully, contain these diverse and contradictory properties. But given this, what are the implications for understanding and promoting organizational greening through culture change? As greening initiatives unfold, these properties can be papered over but not eliminated. Meaningful organizational change is possible but it is not likely to result entirely from a sweeping mandate from top management. It emerges through a gradual, nonlinear process involving individual and collective (subcultural) actors operating in asymmetrical structures of power. From their respective positions in the relations of power, they negotiate the meanings of various symbolic events and material objects while struggling for awareness of (sometimes taken for granted or unarticulated) paradigmatic assumptions.

This view of organizational greening might be disappointing to those envisioning a new environmental vanguard emerging from elite managerial initiatives. Sinclair (1993) offered a more optimistic perspective, however, arguing similarly that it is difficult or impossible to create a unitary organizational culture except at the surface level of symbols due to the fact that some organizational subcultures are deeply rooted in broader national, racial, religious and other cultures. This fact can, but need not, paralyse an organization with internal conflict. Sinclair's key point is that the strength of any organization is found in its subcultural pluralism, especially when it comes to ethical decision-making. This is because being ethical requires ongoing self-examination and deep reflection and these processes are enhanced from the discourse about values that is inevitable when subcultural diversity is respected. In her model of organizational ethics (which is easily adaptable to issues of environmentalism – see Jones and Welford, 1997), Sinclair recommends enhancing subcultural autonomy and solidifying the connections between wider community groups and organizational subcultures in order to increase the organization's resources. The promotion of cultures in which new discursive processes are enabled, processes that provoke sensitive dialogue and critical reflection among diverse participants, makes sense in light of the danger inherent to regimes of monolithic ecocentric organizing discussed above.

SUMMARY AND CONCLUSION

We called attention to the hypothesis of a looming, global environmental crisis. The crisis has many causes and few apparent solutions but, increasingly, responsibility is placed in the domain of organizations and their managers – the subject of this chapter. Throughout the chapter, we critically examined the popular belief that commercial organizations and others that produce goods and services can act as the vanguard of the environmental movement or provide a panacea for environmental problems. We assessed greening through compliance with environmental regulations in light of how politically volatile and porous enforcement can be. We pointed to environmental management through greenwashing, and other ceremonial ways that organizations can signal deep greening without actually engaging substantively in it. We identified limits of competitive greening by noting that when environmentalism is reduced to a core business issue, it is practised only when resources permit or pressures are heavy. And we questioned the feasibility and desirability of fundamentally and monolithically greening organizations through culture change.

Despite these critical observations, it is clear that organizations have a tremendous impact on the natural environment. Accordingly, they must be harnessed and turned towards promoting greater ecological balance. We believe that the focus on organizational greening through culture change is a useful step in this process but have argued that it is beneficial to redirect this work using more contemporary concepts of culture and a critical perspective on greening. Of course, culture theory provides no simple methods or easy fixes. It reminds us that organizations are not systems controlled easily by top-down commands and initiatives or easily described well with only the views of top management. As Martin (2002: 11) observes, cultural perspectives also 'give voice to the perceptions and opinions of those who are less powerful or marginalized'. What culture theory does provide is a more realistic model of complex organizations and a more promising way to approach transformational green politics in the workplace – one that embraces and takes advantage of subcultural and other forms of diversity.

The main thing added by adopting a critical perspective on greening is a clear emphasis on the question of how organizational and other micro greening initiatives support or undermine transformational green politics. Greening initiatives that animate new discursive processes with emancipative potential for people and the rest of nature should be a high priority for critical scholars but it is easy to confuse greenwashing or other organizational manoeuvres with initiatives that genuinely address the problem and promote a greener future.

We recognize that meaningful transformation, especially that involving culture, is unlikely to occur entirely from within organizations. Voluntary organizational greening can be genuine and beneficial, but external social and political forces in the form of governmental and non-governmental environmental advocates also have a crucial role to play. Neale (1997), for example, used the Brent Spar incident to illustrate how political initiatives are central to organizational change. Shell, it was argued, was only able to re-think its cultural assumptions about its decisions after considerable pressure from Greenpeace, customer boycotts and governmental pressure.

There are important roles to be played by many external groups and we wish to conclude by endorsing the importance of vigilant regulatory enforcement and continued adversarial relations of power between environmental activists and commercial and other organizations. To combat the increasingly destructive effects of contemporary organizations, we favour voluntary internal green transformation (to the extent this is possible, following the sketch above of the model of subcultural pluralism) but also counter-organizing by those groups who believe that nature's fragility demands that we not trust even well-intentioned corporate managers and other organizational elites to set the environmental agenda on their own.

Returning once more to Marcuse (1964), we recognize that narrow conceptions of rationality will continue to propel most sectors of commerce, government and the rest of society:

> We live and die rationally and productively. We know that destruction is the price of progress as death is the price of life, that renunciation and toil are the prerequisites for gratification and joy, that business must go on, and that the alternatives are Utopian. This ideology belongs to the established societal apparatus; it is a prerequisite for its continuous functioning and part of its rationality. (Marcuse, 1964: 145)

We also recognize that business as usual will continue in at least some domains, meaning that environmental degradation and destruction will be with us, affecting humans and other elements of nature in palpable but often insidious ways.

We depart from Marcuse's (1964) views, however, on two fundamental points. First, technological rationality does rule but not completely, even in the bastions of institutionalized greed. A turning point has been reached even among some organizational elites who now see the need for alternative forms of reasoning and transformational green politics. Second, for Marcuse, transformational resistance (the 'Great Refusal', 1964: 255–7), if it were to arise at all, would arise from the most advanced consciousness of humanity in the face of barbarous exploitation. That is, from the extreme margins of society raging against the destructiveness of 'the machine'. We think green transformation can occur but, unlike Marcuse, believe it is unlikely to emanate entirely from the margins. We are also sceptical about the likelihood of it emanating entirely from the dead centre. We have stated our reservations about holding out hope that organizations, through hierarchically managed cultural change, would assume a vanguard position in the new green politics. Indeed, we tend to agree with Welford (1997) and others that this approach is too limited and, if unchecked, might lead to a 'hijacking' of the environmental movement by commercial reformists.

Where we place our faith is in a complex combination of traditional and non-traditional green politics. We emphasized the importance of traditional action such as regulatory vigilance and adversarial counter-organizing in grassroots and environmental organizations. But we also see the importance of the new forms of organizing that are possible in business, industry and government – forms that bring a deep understanding and appreciation of culture change to discussions about power, discursive processes and organizational greening, as well as forms that attempt to enact collaborative problem-solving involving all relevant parties.[4] The Critical Theory approach to organization and management studies has never been better situated to critique green impostors and promote transformational green politics.

NOTES

1 This statement by Ivan Illich appeared in a book called *Dictionary of Environmental Quotations* (B. Rodes and R. Udell, eds, New York: Sunon & Schuster, 1992). The source of the quote was given as the journal, *New Perspectives Quarterly*, Spring, 1989. To read more about Illich's views on environmentalism and to authenticate the quote, we looked for the article in the designated issue of *NPQ* but did not find the quote in that issue or any prior or subsequent issues. To clear this up, we contacted Illich. He remembered making the statement, said he still held this opinion about contemporary leadership and environmentalism, and gave us permission to use the quotation.

2 The notion of green politics first began gaining widespread attention in the early 1980s when green parties emerged in Germany and elsewhere. Today, there is a tendency to associate green politics only with idealistic, uncompromising and sweeping environmental activism, which we refer to as transformational green

politics. This tendency should not obscure the fact that there are many varieties of green politics, including some that are reformist and that favour incremental change (see Torgerson, 1999). The range is instructive for interpreting what it means to green corporations and other organizations.

3   *ODM* (and the work of the Frankfurt School more generally) can be criticized for its seeming neglect of crisis tendencies and contradictions in contemporary society. While it is true that Marcuse downplays conflict, dissent and resistance in *ODM*, in his introduction he stated that his study vacillates between two contradictory hypthotheses: '(1) that advanced industrial society is capable of containing qualitative change for the foreseeable future; [and] (2) that forces and tendencies exist which may break this containment and explode the society' (cited in Kellner, 1991: xxxiii). Kellner goes on to suggest that *ODM* be read as 'a theory of the containment of social contradictions, forces of negation, and possibilities of liberation' (1991: xxxiii). In personal correspondence with the authors, Kellner also makes the point that Marcuse saw one-dimensional thinking and action as the antithesis of critical, dialectical reason. It is this higher form of reasoning that Marcuse hoped to call attention to and promulgate by presenting its antithesis.

4   A metaphor we find useful for framing the project of green transformation comes from American labour history, as reinterpreted by social critic, Max Cafard (1990, *The Surre(gion)alist Manifesto*, *The Exquisite Corpse*, 8(1): 22–3 [http://www.corpse.org]): 'The Wobblies, the most radical of American labor movements (the only labour movement to appeal to hobos and surrealists) said it was "creating the new world within the shell of the old". Today, the old one is an even more dried-out shell than ever. It's time to begin growing a new world! This is the meaning of green politics.'

REFERENCES

Alvesson, M. (2002) *Understanding Organizational Culture.* London: Sage.

Bandarage, A. (1997) *Women, Population and Global Crisis.* London: Zed Books.

Bansal, P. and Roth, K. (2000) Why companies go green: A model of ecological responsiveness. *Academy of Management Journal.* 43: 717–36.

Bright, C. (2000) Anticipating environmental 'surprise.' In L. Starke (ed.), *State of the World 2000: A Worldwatch Institute Report on Progress Toward a Sustainable Society.* New York/London: W.W. Norton.

Brown, L.R. (2000) Challenge of the new century. In L. Starke (ed.), *State of the World 2000: A Worldwatch Institute Report on Progress Toward a Sustainable Society.* New York/London: W.W. Norton.

Callenbach, E., Capra, F., Goldman, L., Lutz, R. and Marburg, S. (1993) *Ecomanagement.* San Francisco: Berrett Koehler.

Coulson-Thomas, C. (1992) Strategic vision or strategic con: Rhetoric or reality? *Long Range Planning.* 25: 81–9.

Csikszentmihalyi, M. (1999) If we are so rich, why aren't we happy? *American Psychologist.* 54: 821–7.

Di Norcia, V. (1996) Environmental and social performance. *Journal of Business Ethics,* 15: 773–84.

Dobson, A. (1990) *Green Political Thought.* London: Unwin Hyman.

Egri, C.P. and Pinfield, L.T. (1996) Organizations and the biosphere: Ecologies and environments. In S.R. Clegg, C. Hardy and W.R. Nord (eds), *Handbook of Organization Studies.* London: Sage.

Fineman, S. (1996) Emotional subtexts in corporate greening. *Organization Studies*. 17: 479–500.

Fineman, S. (2000) Enforcing the environment: Regulatory realities. *Business Strategy and the Environment*. 9: 62–72.

Forbes, L.C. and Jermier, J.M. (2002) The institutionalization of voluntary organizational greening and the ideals of environmentalism: Lessons about official culture from symbolic organization theory. In A. Hoffman and M. Ventresca (eds), *Organizations, Policy and the Natural Environment: Institutional and Strategic Perspectives*. Stanford: Stanford University Press.

Foster, J.B. (1997) *The Vulnerable Planet: A Short Economic History of the Environment*. New York: Monthly Review Press.

Gardner, G. (2002) The challenge for Johannesburg: Creating a more secure world. In L. Starke (ed.), *State of the World 2002*. New York: W.W. Norton.

Greer, J. and Bruno, K. (1996) *Greenwash: The Reality behind Corporate Environmentalism*. New York: Apex Press.

Hawken, P. (1993) *The Ecology of Commerce*. New York: HarperBusiness.

Herf, J. (1999) Review of One Dimensional Man: Technology, War and Fascism: Collected Papers of Herbert Marcuse, Volume 1. *The New Republic*. 38 (1).

Herman, E.S. (1998) Comments on David C. Korten's 'Do corporations rule the world and does it matter?' *Organization & Environment*. 11: 399–401.

Hoffman, A.J. (1997) *From Heresy to Dogma: An Institutional History of Corporate Environmentalism*. San Francisco: New Lexington Press.

Jermier, J.M. (1982) Infusion of critical social theory into organizational analysis. In G. Salaman and David Dunkerly (eds), *International Yearbook of Organization Studies*. London: Routledge.

Jermier, J.M. (1998) Critical perspectives on organizational control. *Administrative Science Quarterly*. 43: 235–56.

Jones, D. and Welford, R. (1997) Culture change, pluralism, and participation. In R. Welford (ed.), *Corporate Environmental Management 2: Culture and Organizations*. London: Earthscan.

Kagan, R.A. and Scholz, J.T. (1984) The criminology of the corporation and regulatory enforcement strategies. In K. Hawkins and J.M. Thomas (eds), *Enforcing Regulation*. Boston, MA: Kluwer Nijhoff.

Kellner, D. (1991) Introduction to the second edition. In H. Marcuse, *One-dimensional Man*. Boston, MA: Beacon Press.

Kellner, D. (1999) *Collected Papers of Herbert Marcuse*. London: Routledge.

Korten, D.C. (1998) Do corporations rule the world? And does it matter? *Organization & Environment*. 11: 389–98.

Leff, E. (1995) *Green Production: Toward an Environmental Rationality*. New York: Guilford.

Luke, T.W. (2000) *One-dimensional Man*: A systematic critique of human domination and nature–society relations. *Organization & Environment*. 13: 95–101.

Luke, T.W. (2001) SUVs and the greening of Ford: Reimagining industrial ecology as an environmental corporate strategy in action. *Organization & Environment*. 14: 311–25.

Madu, C.N. (1996) *Managing Green Technologies for Global Competitiveness*. Westport, CT: Quorum.

Marcuse, H. (1964) *One-dimensional Man: Studies in the Ideology of Advanced Industrial Society*. Boston, MA: Beacon Press.

Martin, J. (2002). *Organizational Culture: Mapping the Terrain*. Thousand Oaks, CA: Sage.

Martin, J., Knopoff, K. and Beckman, C. (1998) An alternative to bureaucratic impersonality and emotional labour: Bounded emotionality at the Body Shop. *Administrative Science Quarterly*. 43: 429–69.

May, P.J. and Winter, S. (1999) Regulatory enforcement and compliance: Examining Danish agro-environmental policy. *Journal of Policy Analysis and Management.* 18: 625–51.

Merchant, C. (1998) *The Death of Nature:* A retrospective. *Organization & Environment.* 11: 198–206.

Neale, A. (1997) Organizational learning in contested environments: Lessons from Brent Spar. *Business Strategy and the Environment.* 6: 93–103.

Newton, T. and Harte, G. (1997) Green business: Technicist kitsch? *Journal of Management Studies.* 34: 75–98.

Porter, M. and van der Linde, C. (1995) Green and competitive: Ending the stalemate. *Harvard Business Review.* 73: 120–34.

Prakash, A. (2000) *Greening the Firm: The Politics of Corporate Environmentalism.* Cambridge: Cambridge University Press.

Rennings, K., Brockmann, K.L. and Bergmann, H. (1997) Voluntary agreements in environmental protection: Experiences in Germany and future perspectives. *Business Strategy and the Environment.* 6: 235–63.

Schaefer, A. and Harvey, B. (1998) Stage models of corporate 'greening': A critical evaluation. *Business Strategy and the Environment.* 7: 109–23.

Shrivastava, P. (1996). *Greening Business: Profiting the Corporation and the Environment.* Cincinnati, OH: Thompson Executive Press.

Sinclair, A. (1993) Approaches to organizational culture and ethics. *Journal of Business Ethics.* 12: 63–73.

Steger, U. (2000) Environmental management systems: Empirical evidence and further perspectives. *European Management Journal.* 18: 23–37.

Switzer, J., Ehrenfeld, J. and Milledge, V. (2000) ISO 14001 and environmental performance: The management goal link. In R. Hillary (ed.), *ISO 14001: Case Studies and Practical Experiences.* Sheffield: Greenleaf Publishing.

Tokar, B. (1997) *Earth for Sale: Reclaiming Ecology in the Age of Corporate Greenwash.* Boston, MA: South End Press.

Torgerson, D. (1999) *The Promise of Green Politics.* Durham: Duke University Press.

United Nations Environmental Programme (2000) *Global Environmental Outlook 2000.* London: Earthscan Publications.

Wallis, V. (1997) Lester Brown, the Worldwatch Institute, and the dilemmas of technocratic revolution. *Organization & Environment.* 10: 109–25.

Welford, R. (1997) *Hijacking Environmentalism: Corporate Responses to Sustainable Development.* London: Earthscan Publications.

Willmott, H. (1993) Strength is ignorance; slavery is freedom: Managing cultures in modern organizations. *Journal of Management Studies.* 30: 515–52.

World Scientists (1996) World scientists' warning to humanity. In P.R. Ehrlich and A.H. Ehrlich (eds), *Betrayal of Science and Reason.* Washington, DC: Island.

Chapter 9

Building Better Worlds? Architecture and Critical Management Studies

Gibson Burrell and Karen Dale

In this chapter, we move through the particular in order to consider the general. We travel from the sixteenth-century passage of the Vasari Corridor in Florence to the passages of the Parisian Arcades in the nineteenth century. We take from the twentieth century the daylight mass production factories of Albert Kahn and the hermetically sealed offices of Skidmore, Owings and Merrill. What we are interested in is not simply the building of buildings but, more significantly, the building of the social through buildings. Using Henri Lefebvre (1991), we suggest that these particular architectural designs are more than representations of space. They are important 'representational spaces' that 'appropriate the imaginary'.

Critical Theory has shown how today's world is one that is caught up in administration, where the rationalizing effect of organization is virtually total. Rationalization stretches well beyond the arena of production, into consumption and thence the world of culture and cultural artefacts. Culture has become an industry and is co-opted in modes of controlling most aspects of productive and consuming life. Adorno debates this relationship in his provocative essay 'Culture and Administration' where he maintains that: 'whoever speaks of culture speaks of administration as well' (Adorno, 2001: 107). Architecture is just such a cultural practice. Architecture has conventionally been seen as part of the creative arts, and as linked with aesthetics rather than management. As with other artistic endeavours, it is often associated with radical change. However, Critical Theorists have shown that if art is not the mere pawn of capitalism neither is it simply autonomous. Following a visit to General Motors in 1958, Eero Saarinen commented that architecture was the only one of the arts that was *not* at war with society (Peter, 2000: 81). The clear implication is that architecture is not necessarily socially progressive. It may well be reinforcing of corporate power. Today, well-known 'signature' architects still portray their work as Art, and the very way that individual architects' names are associated with prestigious buildings works to mask the closely knit relationship between architecture and big business.[1]

We approach architecture as not simply providing the material environment of organization but as a part of the corporate activities that 'shape and promote needs, wishes, beliefs and identities' (Alvesson and Willmott, 1992: 5). In this, we employ the work of Walter Benjamin, a theorist whose relationship with Critical Theory was always intimate but never smooth. Benjamin wanted to produce an awakening from the dazzling images and commodified illusions of the contemporary world, to be achieved by turning the energy of modern images back upon themselves. And since the work of the Critical Theorists and the agenda of Critical Management Studies (CMS) are both focused towards the awareness of illusion and subsequent liberation, the chapter asks whether an emancipatory architecture of organization is possible.

ARCHITECTURE AND CRITICAL MANAGEMENT STUDIES

We start by exploring a number of connections between architecture and the concerns of CMS. First, part of what we are trying to do is to *recover the 'material conditions, production sites and place boundedness'* (Sassen, 2000: 169) of modern organization and management. This, we would argue, is an important task for CMS, as traditional management thought has treated the reified concept 'organization' as the significant unit of analysis, presenting this as the collective endeavours of people working together towards a common goal in a neutral way. Such a framework obscures, inter alia, both social and material conditions of organizing, including spatial and embodied aspects of organization. Thus, we need to regain a sense of space and place in our understandings of management and organization. The number of studies in this area is to date relatively small (e.g. Baldry et al., 1998; Hatch, 1998; Pfeffer, 1982; Williams et al., 1994). The place-boundedness of early organizational forms has long been recognized by radical commentators to facilitate control of workers through the greater opportunities for surveillance and supervision (e.g. Marglin, 1974). In a more recent piece, Baldry and colleagues, in their discussion of 'Bright Satanic Offices' (1998: 163) argue for a 'reincorporation of the physical work environment into any analysis of the labour process'. They say that it is customary to look at factory, office, hospital, warehouse as neutral shells unconnected to social dynamics. The key point of their analysis is that buildings are all about control (Baldry et al., 1998: 164). One of the key effects of achieving control, in part through spatial arrangements, is that power relations become obscured. Architectural forms are often taken for granted and therefore are not seen as being easily changed. Indeed, in comparison to other more obvious forms of management control, there is a degree of inertia built into the very solidity of architectural structures (Alvesson, 1995: 134). In this, spatial control can be compared with the bureaucratic and technological forms of control that Edwards (1979) argues provide a distancing mechanism for managers. Thus spatial control requires elaboration through the examination of how architectural and spatial forms of organization come to seem normal. Architecture indeed offers conventional management a number of solutions to perceived managerial problems. So, for example, there are issues of cost-reduction and efficient use of resources through the recycling of air and heat that buildings require, which impact upon the inhabitants of work-spaces. The tradition of *Burolandschaft* (Hofbauer, 2000) takes this further to consider the most effective use of space and furniture positioning to create effective organization of white-collar work.

As we shall show, architectural practices can be very large-scale organizations that mirror the enterprises they serve as suppliers of space and place. Closeness to the client in terms of mimetic properties of style, structure and procedure means that the large architectural practices often resemble big business themselves, and deliberately so. Bureaucracy meets bureaucracy. Manager meets with manager. Architecture is big business and it is managed. One significant question is how this integration of culture and management is achieved, and the need to explore some of the conflicts and contradictions thus produced. This aim fits with the research agenda set out for CMS by Alvesson and Willmott in 'breaking the mythic spell of conventional management theory' through exposing power asymmetries and critiquing the assumed 'neutrality of management theory and the impartiality of management practice' (1992: 4).

In linking the CMS agenda to architecture and space, we need to move beyond the labour process emphasis on power, to consider further connections between architecture and organization. Thus our second theme is to consider how architecture and spatial arrangements *'produce people'* (Alvesson and Willmott, 1992: 5). We argue that architectural arrangements actively construct the experiences and subjectivities of different groups of people in different ways. In this chapter, and this needs to be stressed given the emphasis in CMS on shopfloor experience, we will *not* be approaching the question of organizational spaces from the micro-perspective of individuals' experiences, although this interpretivist approach is obviously important. Rather, we will consider attempts to construct certain categories or classes of people (cf. Jacques, 1998) through the manipulation of buildings and space.

We shift the focus from relations of production to consider issues of consumption and culture as also important for exploring the links between architecture and organization in a critical way, and, as part of this, for our understanding of the multitude of ways that architecture and space contribute to producing organizational and organized subjectivities. Architecture represents a cultural activity in which the transcendence of the everyday world is promised. Architectures that deal in dreams, such as those found at the Disney sites, play a key role in the management of consumption. They allow 'people processing' to occur on a vast scale, where the person walking around is encouraged to consume and believe in the myth on offer. Monuments perform a similar function in that they speak of a memory of a mythical past where lionization of a person or a group is undertaken for political and economic reasons. Thus architecture is about the construction of the mythical as well as the building of the concrete. It makes appeals to higher values on many occasions in the guise of it being 'high art'. Critical Management Studies recognizes the attempted play on subordinate consciousness that is made in many managerial attempts to invoke culture and history. Architecture is a cultural form by no means closed to such attempts and deciphering some of these is in order.

In doing this we overlay the material, physical aspects of space – the sorts of dimensions discussed by Baldry and colleagues – with *social and representational space*. Here the work of Henri Lefebvre[2] is fundamental. Lefebvre points to the tendency to see space as a neutral vacuum within which things happen. Instead, he theorizes the way that space is socially produced, actively created. He argues that: 'space is produced by social relations that it also reproduces, mediates and transforms' (Natter and Jones III 1997: 149). Within his work Lefebvre describes a number of different sorts of spaces, including 'abstract space' – logico-mathematical, cognitive spaces, typified by Cartesian thought (1991: 24), but also linked to the social experience of abstract space through alienating relations of production under capitalism (1991: 49) and 'lived space' which Lefebvre connects intimately with the body (1991: 40, 405). These are not unconnected, but are a part of social space. Lefebvre does not homogenize social space, but provides a number of different ways of understanding how space is produced. One aspect that is of particular interest to us is the distinction he makes between 'representations of space' and 'representational spaces'. The first of these, dominant in modern societies, is the 'conceptualized space' (1991: 42) of planners, scientists, politicians and of course architects: we might characterize this as 'organized space'. Representational spaces are those of the imaginary, the symbolic, the aesthetic. This is 'space as directly lived through its associated images and symbols' (1991: 39; cf. Shields, 1997: 190).

This relates closely to what Benjamin describes as *phantasmagoria* – the wish symbols or ideals, the 'century's magic images' which blur and transform the conditions of commodification and exploitation that underlie the social organization of production, so that people are inured to them (Tiedemann, 1999). The phantasmagoria was a form of projection that became popular in the early nineteenth century:

> Painted slides were illuminated in such a way that a succession of ghosts ('phantasms') was paraded before a startled audience…[I]t used back-projection to ensure that the audience remained largely unaware of the source of the image: Its flickering creations thus appeared to be endowed 'with a spectral reality of their own'. Benjamin used the phantasmagoria as an allegory of modern culture, which explains both his insistence on seeing commodity culture as a projection – not a reflection – of the economy, as its mediated (even mediatized) representation, and also his interest in the visual, optical, 'spectacular' inscriptions of modernity. (Gregory, 1994: 231–3)

The commodity character of late-nineteenth-century culture could thus be comprehended through this concept. The term is actually in *Das Kapital* but Benjamin brings it to bear on consumption, as *a deceptive image designed to dazzle*, in which use value is hidden behind exchange value. He recognizes that such features may be deceptive yet promising of social change at the same time. He is interested in the surface 'lustre' of beautiful aesthetics used to sell and produce commodities in order to find some transcendence of capitalism. As we shall see, Benjamin plays on the 'tension between concretisation and the dream' (Tiedemann, 1999: 933) in architecture, for his own metaphysically informed historical materialism saw that 'Capitalism was a natural phenomenon with which a new dream-filled sleep came over Europe, and, through it, a reactivation of mythical forces' (in Tiedemann, 1999: 935). In his first sketches for the Arcades Project in the early 1920s, Benjamin calls the arcades a 'Dialectical Fairyland'. Here Benjamin reveals his interest in the mythic and the magical that he shares in part with the Surrealists, whose focus on dreams he finds compelling. In contemplating the Real he relies upon some notions from psychoanalysis and treats the concrete as a very deep level of sleep. He sees architecture as central to this dreamworld: 'Construction plays the role of the subconscious' (Benjamin, 1999: 4). Thus, in Benjamin's Parisian Arcades Project we can see the significance of representational space. He sees the Arcades as the creation of a transformative space where 'the artistic designs of architecture are laid like dreams over the framework of physiological processes' (1999: 22). They are architectures of power in their disciplinary effects on producers and consumers, but more than this they allow for the appropriation of the imaginary. They facilitate the construction of the consumer through the fantasy experience of buying.

Part of this fantasy experience of space, we emphasize, is that while the phantasmagoria dazzles, it simultaneously desensitizes. Benjamin recognizes this 'deadening effect', but we wish to take this notion further. In his discussion of what is meant by 'aesthetics', Welsch (1997) indicates the importance of *anaesthetics*. Herein, the human subject is seen as desensitized to other events that are taking place at the very same time as he or she experiences aesthetics. To the extent that one of the human senses is highly stimulated, the others become under-stimulated. The human sensorium is wide and the aesthetic experience never plays on all five simultaneously or to the same intensity. This is not only the case for the individual sentient human, but can be seen in the relationship between those categories who contribute to the phantasmagoria. It necessitates, to a greater or lesser extent, the desensitization of those who labour to produce the dazzle where it happens, desensitization of those many miles away who labour to produce the material used to dazzle, and desensitization of those who produce the original designs for constructing the bedazzlement. Importantly, the consumer's experience is often very different from that of the aesthetic or emotional labourer. These labourers often survive the 'switching on' of the spectacle by 'switching off' themselves.

Carrying this set of notions with us – representational space, phantas-magoria and anaesthetization – we are ready to begin our analysis of specific architectural forms. For us, the key issue is not solely the physical and symbolic management of architectural space, but the *appropriation of the imaginary*.

BUILDING POWER

We want to start with an example of the *construction of superiority*: of how the powerful can, through architecture, create spaces, construct connections and achieve distances that serve their purposes. The Vasari Corridor in Florence, although it dates from the proto-capitalist sixteenth century, is a major representational space providing links to characteristics of the more modern organizational forms we will talk about later. The 'Vasari Corridor' links the Uffizi to the church of Santa Felicia, the Palazzo Pitti and on to the Boboli Gardens in Florence via an elevated passageway that leads out of the first floor of the Uffizi, down the street and turns a corner to become the upper storey of the Ponte Vecchio across the Arno. The Uffizi was not built as an art gallery but as the administrative and judicial centre of the Dukes of Medici; the highly influential rulers of Tuscany, widely credited as important patrons of the arts, instrumental in creating the context for the Renaissance blossoming of culture. These days it forms part of the cultural experience of the tourist to Florence – although the inside of the corridor is only available to those few who know to arrange a visit in advance, not to the masses who queue to peruse the works of art in the Uffizi.

It was Vasari, predominantly known as the biographer of the Renaissance artists, who designed the Uffizi in 1560 and who was requested five years later to develop the elevated gallery and thus create 'a unique urban relationship' which 'unites the nerve centres of the city' (Fossi, 1999: 8). Of course, this unification is only for the aristocracy: the powerful few of

Florence could perambulate from the Uffizi all the way – almost a kilometre – to their transfluvial gardens thereby integrating mind, body and soul in the form of home, work, river crossing, prayer and leisure pursuits.

As well as creating unifications, the corridor creates distances, both physical and symbolic. The Vasari Corridor separated those in power from those who were not, and provided views where the court could look down on their inferiors. The separation was further produced by the forced ejection of the original butchers who traded on the Ponte Vecchio to the more refined (and less smelly!) trade of the jewellers who retain their position there today. The separation was also marked by the presentation of high art along the walls of the corridor, so that the powerful could avoid any reminder of the world outside their own ranks and concerns. Indeed, the art works consisted primarily of portraits of the aristocrats, so the whole effect is one of reflection of the powerful back to themselves: a sealed off and closed existence in which the aesthetics of the corridor anaesthetize the courtier to what is going on below. In terms of representational space, the corridor symbolizes hierarchy and cloistering, high art for those high in the sky, a superior access to church for those closer to God, interests and pursuits that are not base, an aesthetic sensibility that would go over the head of the Florentine mob: the creation of the fantasy of unfettered power over the 'inferior'.

Some comparisons may be made with the tendency of modern organizations to also use the spatial symbolism through the most senior directors and managers being placed at the top of the building, often surrounded by reminders of their own or the organization's successes. The urban linkages can also be seen in the modern creation of 'mixed use' spaces, for example, Canary Wharf in London, where work, leisure and domesticity are brought together in one area, with protection of this enclave from unwanted elements of society (see Frampton, 1992: 301, and Ghirardo, 1996: 192 for further discussion). The city heights in *Bladerunner* and the *ResidenSea* cruise liner project reflect similar constructions of superiority. Using Lefebvre's terms, Vasari had produced a representation of space (in his corridor) that became a model for shaping the imaginary by and for a novel form of representational space.

BUILDING CONSUMPTION

It is to 'representational spaces' of consumption that we now turn. This is in a deliberate reversal of the usual flow of production to consumption, for as we seek to show here, relations of consumption and the culture industry – of which architecture is a key player – help to produce the taken-for-granted attitude towards production spaces and buildings. The production of luxury goods and their merchandising certainly preceded industrial capitalism and this needs to be recognized. What we are about to see are the twin processes of switching on and switching off – between constructing phantasmagoria but at the cost of an-aesthetization. Twin processes which become fully developed in the twentieth century in production sites but which reflect earlier forms of representational space in the *construction of the consumer*.

Benjamin's *Passagen-Werk*, known in English as the 'Arcades Project', starts with pen-pictures of the shopping arcades, the glass-roofed passages that he saw as having such an important architectural and social significance for the nineteenth century in their transformation of cultural and economic life under capitalism. He quotes from an *Illustrated Guide to Paris* of 1852:

> These arcades, a recent invention of industrial luxury, are glass-roofed, marble-panelled corridors extending through whole blocks of buildings, whose owners have joined together for such enterprises. Lining both sides of these corridors, which get their light from above, are the most elegant shops, so that the arcade is a city, a world in miniature. (Benjamin, 1999: 31)

In architectural terms, their significance rests on their combination of materials: they are made possible by the new technology of iron girder construction filled in by large areas of glass and illuminated in the hours of darkness by the first gas lighting. Their social significance is in the collective organization of the small-scale capitalists who joined together to create an urban environment that was more attractive to customers, gaining greater value both in terms of property and profit. An excerpt from the prospectus for one arcade development illustrates how all would contribute in the costs in order to have shares in the 'future company' (1999: 52). Of even greater social significance is the nascent development of marketing techniques to seduce the customer and thence to construct a whole new category of the modern consuming subject.

The 'passages' became a mecca for the metropolitan populace and a 'must-see' item for foreign visitors. Many of the shops purveyed luxury products, items of fashion and interior design. Benjamin comments: 'in fitting them out, art enters the service of the merchant' (1999: 4). One source of 1867 that he draws on, estimates 20,000 sales clerks were at work in Paris, many of them using knowledge of the arts or classics to construct displays and create new fashions. Another quotation describes how the Parisian shopkeepers found commercial success through the display of goods, even where that meant sacrificing some goods to the display, through the employment of male assistants and having a known, fixed price where customers did not have to haggle (1999: 52). All these techniques were designed to appeal to the new female shape of consumerism. In many ways, the arcades and the commercial tricks used within them were the forerunners of the department stores. Although historians see this as too simplistic a continuity, the juxtaposition of multitude sources provided by Benjamin builds up a rich picture of the construction and then seduction of the 'consumer' through art and artifice. 'Welcome the crowd and keep it seduced' is the primary analysis presented (1999: 40). The Arcades are Benjamin's phantasmagoria where the economic and material relations of consumption and production are hidden behind a dazzling façade.

For all that the Arcades were revolutionary enclosures, they have indeed become commonplace as a site of consumption. Most metropolitan cities have acres devoted to the arcade form of architectural enablement of consumption. Glass and steel adorn shopping malls the world over. In what has become known as 'postmodernism' in architectural style, West Edmonton Mall, the hotels and casinos of Las Vegas, Disney and Disneyfied sites all over the world use the methods first developed in the Arcades as light-centred phantasmagoria. These are dazzling aesthetic experiences for the 'guests'. But we know, the Disney 'cast' have to deal with the anaesthetizing experiences of daily work on the rides (Van Maanan, 1991), the labour turnover rate in McDonalds is exceptionally high, and the 'pole-dancers' in Las Vegas need to anaesthetize themselves with drugs and drink. But whether the tension between these twin processes of anaesthetization and aesthetization will transfigure capitalism remains a very moot point indeed.

BUILDING PRODUCTION

Here, we concentrate on mass production because in some senses this is a defining impeller of the twentieth century and stands at a central point in the management and organization discipline. The processes within the factory have been widely studied but in our field little has been said about the architectural framework in which these take place. We now take factory spaces for granted but these had to be achieved as revolutionary edifices in the face of many extant practices. Thus, the innovative factory designs discussed below open up significant possibilities in the building of the relations of capitalism and for the *construction of the mass-produced mass producer*, a specific new category of worker.

It may be thought that the design of a building does not determine the social relationships of what happens inside it (Brand, 1994). Our point is not that the inside can be simply read from the outside of any building but that they are folded upon each other (Deleuze, 1993). The very concepts of 'inside' and 'outside' are deeply problematical. One interpellates the other. We are not arguing that external and internal factory designs determine social relationships, but they do provide a dazzling image for those for whom industrialization is the way forward. They shape and morphologize what can take place successfully within a massed material framework. Large factories with their mass production technologies and a workforce used to the rhythms of the industrial day are associated of course with Ford and with Taylor but our understanding of how organizations work spatially needs to be based on an awareness of the impact of one architect.[3]

This individual is Albert Kahn, born in Germany in 1869, domiciled in the USA but whose influence was to become global. Beginning with contracts with the Packard Motor Company in 1903 and thence working for Ford and GM, including the development of the Ford Highland Park site which is generally regarded as the first locus of the mass production of cars, Kahn established a huge reputation for meeting corporate needs. By the late 1930s, Gossel and Leuthauser (1991: 404) reckon that Kahn controlled and was responsible for 19 per cent of all US industrial construction: an incredible influence at a time of great industrial growth and change. Perhaps even more staggering was the fact that he had been entrusted with *all* industrial building projects in the Soviet Union until the mid-1930s. On the strength of a huge $40 million contract with Stalin, he set up office in Moscow in 1929. Kahn excelled in the design of buildings for mass production, in that the construction of single-storey buildings covering many acres, illuminated by saw-tooth roofs was his trademark. This became known as the 'daylight factory' (Ackermann, 1991). What he developed through his firm was no more and no less than a new *Kahnian paradigm* of factory construction. What he offered to Ford, the US Department of Defense and to Stalin was a brilliant phantasmagoria in which the consumed image was of huge populations of industrial labourers producing almost limitless amounts of goods and *materiel* under one roof and one central controlling command structure. He allowed a material appropriation of this imaginary.

Kahn was a professionally trained architect but the lure of the business of mass production meant he turned his back on the aesthetic imagination associated with architecture as art. Most (in)famously, his 1905 design for 'Building Ten' of the Packard Motor Company's site in Detroit is seen by some as a defining moment in twentieth-century architecture. The building has been described as 'zero architecture'. In *A Concrete Atlantis*, Banham says it was:

> a zero term in architecture, and hardly any other architect or builder with a professional conscience could have done it. Few could have brought themselves down (or up?) to this level of cheese paring economy – or ruthless rationality, if you prefer – even if they had to affect such an attitude to keep the attention of profit-oriented entrepreneurs whom they had hoped would commission buildings for their offices. (Banham, 1986: 86)

Constructed of concrete, it excluded any decoration or even extraneous trimmings for Building Ten was stripped of any art whatsoever. Looking at the coarse-grained photographs of Building Ten from offices in Europe, Packard's commission to Kahn's practice looked as if it had produced a new and exciting architectural form with appeal to corporate interests. Yet even Kahn could not reject his aesthetic training entirely and all factories with public frontages had to be given some decoration. Architecture was no longer for art's sake but architecture for industry's sake. With it came the anaesthetization of the factory worker in 'automobile factories of despair' (Kamata, 1974).

The production of these factories itself reflected the new world of mass production. Kahn used concrete, and later prefabricated steel, as perfect for cheapness, standardization, lighting, fireproofing, ventilation and unobstructed, flexible interiors through which any assembly line might be threaded. These requirements may seem to social scientists as taken-for-granted mundanities, but for Kahn they had to be achieved through innovative organizational design. As Curtis tells us, concrete 'recommended itself for the design of wide-span factories to accommodate the new techniques of "Taylorization" whereby all steps of fabrication were submitted to a scientific rationalization for the mass production of goods' (1996: 81). It is no cheap pun to say that Kahn made concrete the organizational world of industrialism in the first half of the twentieth century.

This description highlights Kahn's role in the creation of a new culture, a new built environment, to allow the progress of mass production. Huxley's (1994: 5) *Brave New World* argues that undifferentiated replication (Dale, 2001) is a major instrument of social order and control: it brings 'Community, Identity, Stability'. These elements were important in the new representational spaces of that epoch for it is important to realize that many of the new entrants to the plants of Detroit and Stalingrad came straight from agrarian roots, may not have spoken the language of the metropolis, and were unused to the rhythms of the factory day. The control of their workspace allowed the efficient socialization of the worker in programmes of re-education: they were constructed as a new category of industrial employee (Jacques, 1998).

Kahn's designs, then, represented the archetypical structure of the industrial factory and have contributed, through this phantasmagoria of docile, undifferentiated workers, to the employers' appreciation of how to control large groups of people under one roof. The dazzling apparition he conjured up was a mirror to their corporate desire for huge controlled productive spaces of mythic proportions.

BUILDING ADMINISTRATION

As the service sector and the state both developed in the postwar period, there was a burgeoning of bureaucracy and a huge growth in the space constructed for their staffs. Building administration took both the form of

Kahnian methods applied to office space in what was effectively the 'back' of the corporation and the construction of the organizational 'front' for those running the corporation, with its relatively aesthetized spaces and overtones of monumentalism. The requirement for successful architectural practices to be aware of these desires for big business to be associated with death-defying beauty, as well as everyday functionality, is by no means hidden. But of course, it was possible to use Kahnian techniques even in head offices and still have some notion of 'impression management' in terms of aesthetic impact on the city below. Yet the balance between these is being constantly negotiated between client and architect within an institutional context. This negotiation led to the development of a new representational space: that of the large-scale bureaucratic office, especially reflected in company headquarters.

One company that played a key part in perfecting this postwar creation was the firm of Skidmore, Owings and Merrill (SOM), originating in Chicago in 1936 but becoming global in its later activities. They invented, at least in part, domineering buildings which contained production workers grinding away at the labour of bureaucracy but also through design tricks, profitably represented the sales and marketing function the corporation had to perform. In short, SOM connected the circuits of capital in clearer, much more efficient ways. SOM, by a variety of methods (Owings, 1973), by the 1980s, and by a considerable margin, had achieved a position as a leading architectural and engineering firm in the USA and abroad. In 1980, it had $95 million worth of commissions of which 80 per cent came from commercial headquarters and administrative buildings. Our discussion of a prime example of Lefebvrian 'representational space' will focus on one landmark building: Lever House.

Glancey comments that: 'the Lever building is one of the most influential of all 20th century buildings. From the perspective of the end of the century it might look like any other office block, but that's the point: countless thousand office blocks look like the Lever building' (1999: 192). In the 1950s SOM mirrored the rise of Corporate America, and gave it an architectural projection of its power. SOM's design of the Lever Building in 1952 became the prototype of the office building to come and marked a new generation's phantasmagoria. It was a glass lantern within New York.

The buildings of administration became part of an attempt to bridge the world of production and the world of consumption through the construction of a new representational space. The masking of this duality of function is achieved through the utilization of another phantasmagoria. These huge buildings are phantasmagorias of modern capitalism in that they project dazzling images of the glamour of corporate life, while the source of this, the mundanities of mass white-collar record keeping, is hidden. The 'staging' of events is professionally and permanently undertaken so that the attempt to aestheticize the routine is more and more likely to be realized.

Madison Avenue, because of its expertise in marketing, acted as a huge draw to incoming corporate headquarters (Owings, 1973: 108). Importantly, Lever Brothers at this time was spending 85 per cent of its outgoings on advertising (Owings, 1973). The use of acres of glass in buildings again became part of this move towards phantasmagorian spectacle. Taking the Crystal Palace as the model, subsequent architects have repeatedly seen the capacity for glass and light to mesmerize. As Alvesson comments (1995: 133), corporate architecture has significant expressive and symbolic purposes, perhaps especially so where the product is intangible. With the offices in the Lever Building, SOM 'had managed to get under the skin of the newly emerging post war corporate America and, in the process, created a house style for it' (Glancey, 1999: 192). This corporate house style, however, is different from the Kahnian paradigm. Such postwar buildings reflect back the client's desires through the growing emphasis on marketing and image-creation. For example, SOM learnt that it was possible to advertise the client company's product in the architecture of head offices so that the Inland Steel building of 1955 in Chicago used stainless steel columns on the *outside* of the building to signal its own commodities. This tendency for incorporating corporate projection went down very well with clients. It struck a 'monumental' note and expressed confidence in the American tradition (Lampugnani, 1988: 307; Owings, 1973).

By standing between the world of consumption and the world of production, the skyscraper blocks such as the Lever Building created the category of the mass bureaucrat. Within the massification of administration, corporate constructions reflected the idea that organizational power and authority are best represented by height above the ground. But another theme is recognizable here. In the 1950s, the notion of 'Organization Man' was being articulated in Corporate America (Gouldner, 1957; Whyte, 1957). This glamorous individual, played on celluloid by Rock Hudson, was devotedly loyal to the firm and in recognition of that service was amply rewarded through career and hierarchical perks. The notion of fixity in place but vertical ascent in space became enshrined in the new architectures. Entry to the buildings of the corporate world was to be made difficult – but so was exit. The entrapment of the top floor was always something to aim for and the mystique of those 'elevated' only reinforced this.

The Lever Building exemplifies these themes in its 'forward thinking commercial architecture' (Curtis, 1996: 410), with its thin high-rise block built on a low flat building at its base with a metal and glass curtain wall. It relied totally on mechanical systems for ventilation and air-conditioning. It was transparent but closed. Since the building was where many could see it, separation was sought and maintained through closed doors and sealed windows. Indeed, the buildings were *meant* to be highly visible to the urban non-organizational public. Being bathed in internal light and the required absence of curtains both meant that the employees and what they stood for shone out into the metropolitan night. But this building was going to be difficult for anyone or anything to enter. So the Lever Building was closed off to the public physically but open to them visually.

The success of SOM rests not only on the brilliant projection of corporate capitalism, but also its mimicry of these forces in its own methods and organization. As a house style, the model of the Lever Building came cheap. Handlin describes SOM as the 'inheritors to Kahn's utilitarianism' (1997: 246). Walter Gropius (1955, quoted in Peter, 2000: 39) said that the Lever Building relied upon prefabrication so that 85–90 per cent 'of the whole building was component parts ready-made in a factory, brought to site and assembled there'. It used mass production methods and components. What also went down well with clients was the opposition in SOM to union or craft power.[4] SOM followed this logic of efficiency and cost-consciousness through into the organization of their own business. Architecture as expressed through firms such as SOM is mimetic of the demands of capital rather than ideals of creative individuality. As Lampugnani argues, 'from the beginning, the office was organized on novel principles taken over from the office organization of the American business world. Team work and individual responsibility along with appropriate motivation of employees on the one hand were combined with anonymity of the individual and a strictly economic working method on the other' (1988: 305). SOM might be seen as an expression of unalloyed corporate growth: the reflection of the vertical integration of large multinational companies. It embodies a large bureaucratic structure based on hierarchy and a division of labour. It was quite clear to its founders that architecture of this corporate kind was mainstream and lucrative (Owings, 1973). It did not attack the status quo but reinforced it.

Skidmore, Owings and Merrill provide a fantasy for the owners of capital in which executive space is aestheticized with expensive art (Massey, 1990; Owings, 1973) but below, anaesthetization is designed in through certain colour schemes and noise abatement. Throughout, space is meant to be controlled and policed within a closed area of total sanitization.[5] Many of their buildings offer the fetishization of avoiding leakage. They are monuments to conservative accounting conventions where transparency and openness are promised but never delivered. They achieved the innovative blueprint of a spatial form for *constructing the mass bureaucrat*. And by no means least, SOM designs entighten the circuits of capital by bringing production and consumption functions closer together in the very fabric of the head-office building. This particular appropriation of the imaginary is very important indeed.

BUILDING EMANCIPATION

To change life… we must first change space. (Lefebvre, 1991: 190)

Throughout this chapter we have looked at the part architecture plays in the construction of categories of people, especially through phantasmagoria, and at its key representational spaces. In accord with the interests of Critical Theory, we will now consider briefly the possibility of emancipatory buildings and spaces. In line with our Foucauldian leanings (WOBS, 2001: 1591–3), we draw out some of the ambivalences of such 'emancipation'.

'Representational' buildings can express power relations through closure and separation – the cloistered Vasari Corridor and the sealed-off Lever Building, for example. If these buildings represent architectures of exclusionary containment, might an architecture of emancipation then be expressed through both greater *openness and transparency?* Immediately these notions raise the question of glass and what it signifies. As mentioned earlier, there has been great emphasis in the twentieth century upon the building properties of glass, in that in forming a protective membrane against the weather, it allows some things inside to be seen outside. Glass opens up yet closes down. A glass wall is a sensory contradiction (Aldersey-Williams, 1999). It is an inherent part of the property of the crystal panel to stand as a source of transparency but also of occlusion. Every piece of glass, thus conceived, is a source of distortion.

Of course, spaces have been made open and transparent without the presence of glass. The agora of Athens (Sennett, 1994: 55–61) was an area of unpaved open ground of about ten acres into which all citizens, whether rich or poor, could come and meet and participate in Athenian democracy. Of course, 130,000 others were excluded by dint of not being citizens, but the point is that an architectural expression of democracy was conceived of as open and flat. Much utopian imagery thereafter revolves around city life made more open and rendered egalitarian. The utopia described by Harvey in *Spaces of Hope* (2000: 263–79) would be one such attempt. In his provocative appendix called 'Edilia', 'the insurgent architect' describes the organizational details of this new Eden. The basic units of habitation are the 'hearth' made up of 25 or so adults and children while the largest social unit is the 'regiona' of 3 million people, which is an independent self-supporting bioregion. This manner of organization is symbolized by the physical layout of the units. Whole city blocks have been knocked through to create communal living spaces yet still respecting the privacy of the individual. Cultivation occurs within the city. While there are arbours and closed gardens for recreation, there is intense horticulture. Probably based on contemporary Baltimore, Harvey's highly organized and static structure takes the nature of the city for granted and says little about the dynamic processes of human interaction. His 'insurgent architect' is more a builder of static social mores than of the lived-in environment. But so too have been many 'Utopias' – including the 'original' by Thomas More.

Utopian spaces aside, there have been significant attempts to create a consciously open and transparent architecture for explicitly democratic buildings. Thus, we have in the work of Norman Foster the exploration of democratic architecture. Politicians within the Berlin Reichstag are now overseen by the public who care to take the spiralling walkway to the top of the building and look down, literally and metaphorically upon their 'leaders'. The same principles are being applied to the Welsh Assembly in Cardiff. Aldersey-Williams (1999) goes so far as to claim that 'Glass is now the material of choice for democrats in Strasbourg, in Berlin, in Edinburgh'. The Reichstag with its glass cupola gives the impression that no boundaries exist between the people and the elites who are supposed to represent them. The architecture gives the impression of bringing down spatial barriers, while hiding the real barriers that obviously do exist to the attainment of full democracy. The Visitors' entrance, for example, is carefully screened from the politicians. We might argue, Orwell-like, that 'democratic architecture' renders institutions more non-democratic because it represents closure as openness and occlusion as transparency. Thus, 'glass appears revolutionary while achieving conservative ends' (Aldersey-Williams, 1999).

There is a strand of historically informed scholarship that may be relevant at this point. At Versailles in the court of Louis XIV, the architecture reflected perspectivalism (Hoskin, 1995), glass and mirrors. The notion of living one's life in public without privacy became a key part of the culture of Absolutism. As Poggi relates, 'The ruler's person...was continuously displayed in the glare of the condensed and "public" world embodied in the court' (1978: 68). Louis XIV was born in public, ate in public, went to bed in public, was clothed and groomed in public, urinated and defecated in public, perhaps copulated in public, and when he died was messily chopped up in public so that his body parts could be held in public by his closest courtiers. Versailles' architecture and gardens encouraged a visibility of the King's person but also of his courtiers. And through this openness he sought to maintain his search for absolute power. This remarkable period then seems to suggest that openness and transparency are *not* necessarily associated with democratic forms of government but rather with Absolutism. But it is not so straightforward as this. While Versailles was a p(a)lace of enhanced courtier visibility, the better to render control, Louis XIV developed a series of ceremonies and events whence he made spectacular entrances from hidden locations where he could lay undisturbed in topiary labyrinths, the eye was fooled by extravagant *tromp l'œils* and the masqued ball gave him some temporary anonymity. In other words, Absolutism too is about increased transparency and openness but accompanied by countervailing processes of reduced transparency and reduced openness.

So any talk of buildings that permit, encourage or enhance translucency and therefore reflect some 'progress' towards something judged more emancipatory by Critical Theorists needs to be seen in the light (sic) of these contradictory pressures. Democratic structures, in other words, need not be judged solely on the basis of their avoidance of opacity. One needs to be wary of seeing such representational spaces through a glass – darkly.

Other architects, meanwhile, seek to provide environmentally sound buildings that do not require wholesale pillage of the environment for unsound non-sustainable materials (Jodidio, 2001: 204–6). Harvey (2000) makes this point too. It is now becoming recognized that 'concrete' is one of the most damaging building materials, as it requires the most energy to produce it, before it liberates the greatest amount of CO_2 gas and particulate air pollution. What this says for large engineering projects may well be ignored of course. But green architects often eschew high-technology solutions for this reason (Edwards, 2001) and seek a return to vernacular forms of building that are much more in harmony with the extant landscape. Even the Arts and Crafts Movement, which sought this return to vernacular forms and traditional craft skills against the nascent mass production of the late-nineteenth century, indicates the difficulties of producing emancipatory spaces and buildings without much wider changes in social and economic structures. For example, Morris, Marshall, Faulkner and Co. was founded in 1861 to produce high-quality crafts using pre-industrial forms of production, but its products and services were too expensive for the ordinary people, its 'target market', to afford. The company itself struggled between its artistic and political values and the need to control costs for company survival. Its very inception and continuance depended, rather ironically, on the investments of William Morris's father in the mining industry and an aristocratic clientele (Cumming and Kaplan, 1991; Massey, 1990).

Are we left with only irony then? Is it possible to build a better world? Are all buildings edifices of power and manipulation of one sort or another? Although SOM has done much to promulgate non-emancipatory architecture, Owings predicted that humans would come to inhabit the spaces between buildings, enjoying the oldest form of human place – the plaza – when he said, 'Nonarchitecture – open spaces – will be the objective and the buildings will simply frame them' (1973: ix). Perhaps Owings is representing a space here that will become a key representational space. Perhaps only *nonarchitecture* is the way of escaping our emplacement in the built environment. But we are not suggesting in some Deleuzian way that permanent nomadic life with concrete-less and glass-less temporary shelters placed on the open steppes represents a utopian or even 'better' lifestyle. To some extent, that too is a built environment that is not often associated with egalitarianism. We conclude that a built environment which offers us spaces and places for more democratic and egalitarian experiences of power, consumption, production and administration remain yet to be explored. But it might have to be 'nonarchitectural', both in appearance and function, within a fundamentally changed form of our understanding of 'space'.

What we have sought to show in this chapter is that the architecture of organization is neither *simply* the creation of taken-for-granted spaces for our everyday employment *nor* the construction of monolithic citadels of power. Using the concepts of Benjamin, Adorno and Lefebvre, we have tried to explore how these spaces are intimately linked with our imaginaries and with our identities: not only are they constructed by architects of buildings and of capitalism, but by us, the diverse inhabitants of organizational life. Within these organizational places there are yet spaces whose production we all contribute to, although not in circumstances of our own choosing.

NOTES

1   Ashly Pinnington and Tim Morris's work (Morris and Pinnington, 1998; Pinnington and Morris, 1996, 2000) shows the heterogeneity and segmentation of architectural practices, from the 'art-architects' to the 'design and build' corporations.
2   Lefebvre can be seen as having many points of connections with the school of Critical Theory, coming from a broadly Marxist perspective but also going beyond materialism and a narrow conception of relations of production, into representational and cultural practices.
3   And as with Ford and Taylor, we are not arguing that all mass production spaces can be seen as pure Kahnian. As with Fordism and scientific management, what we need to appreciate is the pervasive influence and diffusion of Kahn's design, which now means that we often take its effects for granted.
4   Gordon Bunshaft who designed the Lever Building said at the time that 'The building industry as a whole, not just the architectural aspect of it, is a slow moving device and it is full of trades, guilds, and what not. These move very slowly' (quoted in Peter, 2000: 40–3).
5   SOM also built Canary Wharf: perhaps the best and most overscaled example hitherto of the connection between development and architectural practices, at least in the UK.

REFERENCES

Ackermann, K. (ed.) (1991) *Building for Industry*. UK: Watermark.
Adorno, T. (2001) *The Culture Industry*. London: Routledge.
Aldersey-Williams, H. (1999) Cracking form: glass architecture. *New Statesman*. 17 February.
Alvesson, M. (1995) *Management of Knowledge-Intensive Companies*. Berlin: de Gruyter.
Alvesson, M. and Willmott, H. (1992) Critical Theory and management studies: An introduction. In M. Alvesson and H. Willmott (eds), *Critical Management Studies*. London: Sage.
Baldry, C., Bain, P. and Taylor, P. (1998) Bright satanic offices. In P. Thompson and C. Warhurst (eds), *Workplaces of the Future*. Basingstoke: Macmillan.
Banham, Reyner (1986) *A Concrete Atlantis*. Cambridge, MA: MIT Press.
Benjamin, W. (1999) *The Arcades Project*. Cambridge, MA: Harvard University Press.
Brand, S. (1994) *How Buildings Learn*. London: Phoenix.
Cumming, E. and Kaplan, W. (1991) *The Arts and Crafts Movement*. London: Thames & Hudson.
Curtis, W. (1996) *Modern Architecture since 1900*. London: Phaidon.

Dale, K. (2001) *Anatomising Embodiment and Organisation Theory*. Basingstoke: Palgrave.

Deleuze, G. (1993) *The Fold*. London: The Athlone Press.

Edwards, B. (ed.) (2001) *Green Architecture*. Architectural Design 71:4, New York: Wiley.

Edwards, R. (1979) *Contested Terrain*. New York: Basic Books.

Fossi, G. (1999) Introduction to *The Uffizi: The Official Guide*. Florence: Giunti.

Frampton, K. (1992) *Modern Architecture: A Critical History*. London: Thames & Hudson.

Ghirardo, D. (1996) *Architecture after Modernism*. London: Thames & Hudson.

Glancey, J. (1999) *20th Century Architecture*. London: Carlton.

Gouldner, A. (1957) Cosmopolitans and locals: towards an analysis of latent social roles. *Administrative Science Quarterly*. 2: 281–306.

Gössel, P. and Leuthäuset, G. (1991) *Architecture in the Twentieth Century*. Cologne: Taschen.

Gregory, D. (1994) *Geographical Imaginations*. Oxford: Blackwell.

Handlin, D. (1997) *American Architecture*. London: Thames & Hudson.

Harvey, D. (2000) *Spaces of Hope*. Edinburgh: Edinburgh University Press.

Hatch, M.-J. (1998) *Organization Theory: Modern, Symbolic and Postmodern Perspectives*. Oxford: Oxford University Press.

Hildebrand, G. (1974) *Designing for Industry: The Architecture of Albert Kahn*. Cambridge, MA: MIT Press.

Hofbauer, J. (2000) Bodies in a landscape. In J. Hassard, R. Holliday and H. Willmott (eds), *Body and Organization*. Sage: London.

Hoskin, K. (1995) The viewing self and the world we view: Beyond the perspectival illusion. *Organization*. 2(1): 141–62.

Huxley, A. (1994 [1931]) *Brave New World*. London: Flamingo.

Jacques, R. (1998) *Manufacturing the Employee*. Thousand Oaks, CA: Sage.

Jodidio, P. (2001) *New Forms: Architecture in the 1990s*. Cologne: Taschen.

Kamata, S. (1974) *Toyota: Factory of Despair*. New York: Random House.

Lampugnani, V.M. (1988) *Encyclopaedia of 20th Century Architecture*. London: Thames & Hudson.

Lefebvre, H. (1991) *The Production of Space*. Oxford: Blackwell.

Marglin, S. (1974) What do bosses do? The origins and functions of hierarchy in capitalist production. *Review of Radical Political Economics*. 6: 60–112.

Massey, A. (1990) *Interior Design of the Twentieth Century*. London: Thames & Hudson.

Morris, T. and Pinnington, A. (1998) Evaluating strategic fit in professional service firms. *Human Resource Management Journal*. 8(4): 76–87.

Natter, W. and Jones III, J.P. (1997) Identity, space, and other uncertainties. In G. Benko and U. Strohmayer (eds), *Space and Social Theory*. Oxford: Blackwell.

Owings, N.A. (1973) *The Spaces In Between: An Architect's Journey*. Boston, MA: Houghton Mifflin.

Peter, J. (2000) *An Oral History of Modern Architecture*. New York: H.N. Abrams.

Pfeffer, J. (1982) *Organizations and Organization Theory*. Marshfield, MA: Pitman.

Pinnington, A. and Morris, T. (1996) Power and control in professional partnerships. *Long Range Planning*. 29(6): 842–9.

Pinnington, A. and Morris, T. (2000) Transforming the architect: Ownership form and archetype change. Unpublished paper.

Poggi, G. (1978) *The Development of the Modern State*. London: Hutchinson.

Sassen, S. (2000) Excavating Power. *Theory Culture & Society*. 17(1): 163–70.

Sennett, R. (1994) *Flesh and Stone*. London: Faber and Faber.

Shields, R. (1997) Spatial stress and resistance: Social meanings of spatialisation. In G. Benko and U. Strohmayer (eds), *Space and Social Theory*. Oxford: Blackwell.

Tiedemann, R. (1999) Dialectics at a standstill. In W. Benjamin, *The Arcades Project*. Cambridge, MA: Harvard University Press.

Van Manaan, J. (1991) The smile factory: Work at Disneyland. In P. Frost, L. Moore, M. Louis, C. Lundberg and J. Martin (eds), *Reframing Organizational Culture*. Newbury Park, CA: Sage.

Warwick Organizational Behaviour Staff (WOBS) (eds) (2001) *Organizational Studies: Critical Perspectives on Business and Management*, Vol. 4. London, Routledge.

Welsch, W. (1997) *Undoing Aesthetics*. London: Sage.

Whyte, W.H. (1957) *The Organization Man*. Garden City, NY: Doubleday.

Williams, K., Haslam, C. and Williams, J. (1992) Ford versus Fordism. *Work, Employment and Society*. 6(4): 517–55.

Chapter 10

Business, Ethics and Business Ethics: Critical Theory and Negative Dialectics

Martin Parker

Over the last twenty years or so, 'Business Ethics' has become an accepted part of the management canon. First in the USA, and now in Europe, there are a growing number of books, journals, chairs, institutes, consultants and courses. Much like all the other management subdisciplines, there is an implicitly imperialist claim in this expansion. Just as marketeers claim that everything follows from marketing, or accountants that organizations would be nothing without the numbers, so do Business Ethicists seek to subordinate academic and practical matters to arguments about the values and purposes of business organizations. The rise of Business Ethics is an interesting case study in the history of ideas, and of the claims to expertise and legitimacy that are needed in order to launch a putatively 'new' area of inquiry. Constructing such legitimacy means that certain questions need to be addressed. Were businesses not ethical before Business Ethics? What expertise do professional ethicists have that ordinary mortals do not? And, perhaps most importantly, will Business Ethics actually make businesses ethical?

These are the kinds of questions I will be dealing with in this chapter, but there is a further question here too. What is 'Critical Management Studies' to make of Business Ethics? At first sight, both positive and negative responses seem justified. Positively then, since Business Ethicists claim to be concerned about abuses of managerial power, the protection of workers and consumers' rights, the harm that business does to the environment and so on, then surely they are fellow travellers on the rocky road to a better world? To chide them for having read Kant and Bentham rather than Habermas and Foucault would seem to be splitting hairs (and heirs) if the goals of the intellectual projects are so similar. Yet, negatively, Business Ethics could be seen to represent the managerial colonization of emancipatory projects, what Tester has nicely termed the 'motorised morality' of mission statements and organizational procedures (1997: 124; see also Kjonstad and Willmott, 1995; ten Bos, 1997; Willmott, 1998). In a strange and potentially catastrophic reversal, the very words that might be used to sponsor radical change are appropriated and placed in the service of a globally rapacious capitalism. Politics disappears, and the casuistical ethics of the bottom line claims its place.

In the chapter that follows, I will begin by interrogating some Business Ethics texts in order to lay out some of the conventional assumptions, and absences, that underpin this area of inquiry. I then go on to explore some of the arguments that two of the neo-Marxist Frankfurt School Critical Theorists – Max Horkheimer and Theodor Adorno – have made about the contrasts between 'traditional' forms of understanding and 'critical' or 'dialectical' methods. The chapter then considers Business Ethics through the lens of Horkheimer's Critical Theory, Adorno's quasi-deconstructive 'negative dialectics', as well as a more conventional form of economic determinist Marxism. I argue that, while all these approaches are critical in some sense, and Marxist in some sense, they position the subjects and objects of criticism in very different ways. Finally, I work these understandings back on to Critical Management itself, and open up the possibility that the differences between Business Ethics and Critical Management Studies might be less than often assumed, or perhaps hoped. It might be that neither form of thought can easily avoid assuming that which it wishes to counterpose itself against. But then, why should the activity we call criticism end up by giving us a clear point of view on things?

HISTORY, EXPERTS AND EFFECTS

I will begin by outlining the forms of legitimation and argument that can be commonly found in Business Ethics texts. That being said, I will be treating Business Ethics as if it were a unified field, which it is not, and hence drastically oversimplifying a series of complex arguments. There is a real danger of simply constructing straw targets here, but I hope the generalities of the argument will still make some sense nonetheless. So let me begin. As I suggested above, the case of Business Ethics is an interesting recent example of the legitimation of a 'new' area of intellectual and practical activity. To profess Business Ethics – or anything else for that matter – is to claim (at least) three things. First, that something is needed; second, that you are the kind of person who can do it; third, that you can achieve something with your expertise. Taken together, these ideas form what ten Bos (2002), following Bauman, calls a theory of 'insufficiency'. That is to say, Business Ethicists must claim that the various customers of their knowledges do not have the resources to deal with moral matters on their own, and hence need guidance from experts. So how is such a claim made?

A very common opening gambit in texts on Business Ethics is to suggest, implicitly or explicitly, that there is some kind of crisis of ethics. Put simply, this is a diagnosis of the present age which compares it unfavourably with the past. It is suggested that people don't trust businesses anymore, that negative images of organizations are common in the media, that hyper-competition is making employees and organizations perform whatever the costs, that globalization is causing competing belief systems to collide, or that the environment can no longer sustain unbridled capitalism (Cannon, 1994: 1; Hoffman and Frederick, 1995: 2). Now if this is the case, then managers are in a different and potentially dangerous world and are sorely in need of guidance. As is clear, this is a diagnosis that essentially relies on a narrative of ethical decline. I have elsewhere written about this as a version of the long-standing tension between nostalgia and modernization which can be located in many accounts of the transition to modernity, perhaps most notably Durkheim's version of anomie and the division of labour (Parker, 1998: 29). This kind of story suggests that modernization involves the loss of community and traditional forms of moral regulation. The small-scale, high-trust and face-to-face interactions that once constrained market exchanges have now been replaced with anonymous and huge corporate structures. The players in global marketplaces now have no meaningful responsibilities to people or places. Indeed, to even admit such responsibilities is seemingly to court disaster because capital, like a nervous bird, can flee so rapidly at the slightest sign of conscience.

In a sense, the empirical accuracy of this kind of history is unimportant, what seems to matter is that it helps to legitimize the need for Business Ethics. In practice, sustained historical analyses of capitalism over the last few hundred years are rare in the Business Ethics literature.[1] Indeed, the very notion of a 'new' ethical crisis often requires that historical continuities are denied by, for example, dismissing Marx by claiming that he was writing about bad old nineteenth-century capitalism (Stewart, 1996: 22). Whatever the accuracy of the history, what is important for my argument is that the story provides a space for Business Ethics to step into. Ethical analysis, education and regulation is now needed, when previously it was not. Importantly, this is a history that is also very often used to legitimize management and the business school in general with talk about 'hyper-competition', 'globalization', and change being the only constant. More effective business and management then becomes the answer. This is rather like being told that we 'need' estate agents, or pet psychologists, or better deodorants. The creation of the need is an essential move in legitimizing the product. Businesses, and busy-people, now 'need' ethics, when presumably they did not before. And if the abstractions of this argument are not enough to persuade, then they can be supported by a simple assertion that it is important for all businesses to think hard about ethics because state legislation and heightened public awareness demand it (Clutterbuck et al., 1992: 15;

Drummond and Bain, 1994: 2). This is what Griseri calls the 'compliance function' (1998: 216) – which is akin to saying that ethics is a part of contemporary business practice, and whether you like it or not, it is something you must know about. In a strangely performative way, the fact that people talk about Business Ethics proves that it is needed.

And so, the need created, the question that then arises is who is to fill it. Or, as Jackson puts it in the introduction to her text – 'I have to show that business people…have something to learn that they do not know already and that they need to know' (1996: 1). Business Ethicists have two cards to play here. The first is a body of ethical knowledge which it largely inherits from moral philosophy. This is a substantial piece of cultural capital, stretching back to Plato and Aristotle, and incorporating big words (utilitarianism, deontology) and big names (Immanuel Kant, John Stuart Mill). The usefulness of such language should not be underestimated, since it is sufficiently arcane to impress, and allows the putative business ethicist to be a gatekeeper to the knowledges that are the province of the academy. To put it simply, without moral philosophy, it would have been more difficult to legitimate Business Ethics as a discrete and credible domain of enquiry. Virtually all Business Ethics texts hence contain references to Kantian conceptions of duty, particularly the implications of the categorical imperative – 'do as you would be done by'. Such arguments are then usually counterposed to utilitarian notions of the greatest good for the greatest number, often connecting these to their contemporary formulations in stakeholder theory. Often there is also reference to virtue theory and discussions of the importance of individual or organizational character. However, there are also some interesting blind spots in what counts as the relevant intellectual capital. The moral philosophies which are incorporated largely comprise the classics of the analytical canon, and it is rare to find references to twentieth-century 'continental' philosophy here. Nietzsche, Heidegger, Gadamer, Sartre, Foucault, Derrida, Lyotard and so on, are largely absent from the Business Ethics text,[2] as are many references to the various forms of twentieth-century Marxism (of which much more below). In addition, there are also some clear absences in terms of the intersections between moral philosophy and political theory. Detailed interrogations of law, the state, power, justice, equality, liberty, democracy, human rights and so on are also absent from the centre of Business Ethics. Rather ominously, 'politics' does not seem to be part of 'ethics'.

The second card that Business Ethicists have to play is in stressing the application and relevance of their knowledges. Tactically, this is important in order to avoid accusations of irrelevance by a busy, practically minded audience, or what Sorell has called the 'alienation problem' (1998: 17). This issue largely boils down to stressing the role of Business Ethics as a form of mediation between the intellectual capital of the academy and the pragmatism of management decision-making in the real world. This is clearly a delicate balancing act between 'ethics' and 'business' which answers the question 'why business needs ethics' (Stewart, 1996: 5). Too far in the direction of ethics and there is little connection to the lifeworld of business; too far in the direction of business and the discipline becomes a rehearsal of management common sense with no 'unique selling proposition', as the marketeers put it. As a result, most Business Ethics texts stress their applied and practical nature – 'straight talk about how to do it right' (Treviño and Nelson, 1999; see also Jackson, 1996; Ottensmeyer and McCarthy, 1996); the experience of their authors in business or running an ethics consultancy (Drummond and Bain, 1994); or even contain inspiring photographs of (and quotes from) CEOs at the start of every chapter (Stewart, 1996).

Perhaps most importantly though, virtually all of these texts use the usual repertoire of case studies and discussion questions that are common in management teaching texts. Such cases, often copyrighted as being 'owned' by a particular person or institution, are almost always framed as a person-alization of the issue concerned. 'What would *you* do in this situation? Give reasons for your decisions.' I suppose this stress on the agency of the indi-vidual is hardly surprising, given the absence of consideration of what is nor-mally termed 'politics'. That is to say, an emphasis on individualism seems to obviate consideration of structural constraints, even to the extent of filling in questionnaires to determine 'your cynicism quotient' and an exercise on 'walking my talk' (Treviño and Nelson, 1999: 18, 169). Indeed, the philo-sophical resources most commonly deployed – deontology, utilitarianism, and a curiously de-socialized version of virtue ethics – encourage precisely these kind of individualized thought experiments. Whether interrogating one's moral duties; evaluating potential means and ends; or considering traits of character such as wisdom, fidelity and so on, the emphasis is on active consciousness-informing personal choices. The management decision-maker collects the evidence, models a set of potential algorithms, and then makes a decision on what actions should be taken. Further, these decisions are also often then framed within chapters on key business issues – sexual harassment and diversity, health and safety, whistleblowing, intellectual property, the environment, and so on. This is, of course, both eminently 'practical' by definition, but it also succeeds in excluding many matters which are then deemed beyond the remit of the case in point. Rather like the *ceteris paribus* of economics, only certain matters are defined as relevant, and everything else becomes a form of background noise. Everything else is somehow 'outside' Business Ethics.

Finally, and perhaps most importantly, there is the question of whether Business Ethics will actually make businesses more ethical. Do the means – studying Business Ethics – have any demonstrable effect on the desired ends – more ethical businesses? Here, the texts are generally more cautious, and justifiably so. For a start, since the ends very rarely include the overthrow of managerial capitalism, or even radical state intervention, the centre of the project is amelioration rather than revolutionary change. It is rare to find analyses that suggest alternative understandings of markets, of hierarchical organization, or the work-effort bargain. Instead the emphasis is on working within contemporary business organizations in order that their worst excesses can be tempered. Indeed, since the vast majority of ethics texts tend to assert that ethics makes for better business, or at least that there is no contradiction between ethics and business, sometimes even amelioration seems irrelevant. Ethics becomes a specific part of a business and marketing strategy. Second, and as I discussed above, the personalization of ethical problems leads to an emphasis on individual rationality within a satisficing mode of decision-making. The reader of these texts is assumed to be an individual who will meet, or has met, everyday dilemmas and might have to make decisions that they are not completely comfortable with. Different stakeholders have 'rights' that need to be balanced (Ottensmeyer and McCarthy, 1996), and people in business must operate within the rules of the game. The rhetorical mode of the practical and personalized case study is hence to position a set of unmovable assumptions, and then ask the reader to work within these. This means that Business Ethics is rarely utopian, or even moderately ambitious, in its aims. Its mode of address is to suggest personal development, or perhaps sensible reform, as reasonable ends. Such modesty is laudable in the often breathless arena of management in general, but if so little is expected, then little is likely to be achieved.

In summary then, the field of Business Ethics is an interesting example of the construction of a problem, the legitimation of certain forms of knowledge, and firm but modest claims about its utility. Even interesting and critical books which are sceptical about the usefulness of conventional Business Ethics on the grounds of practicality or its potentially dysfunctional effects (Griseri, 1998; Pearson, 1995) end up in similar places. Yet, and this is my concern in the rest of this chapter, Business Ethics manages to systematically exclude much that might potentially assist projects of emancipation and social change. Indeed, it might be argued that its particular form of pro-managerial rational individualism is dangerously seductive precisely because it is a 'noble lie' that assumes so much (Castro, 1996: 267). If this is ethics, then business (and all that is attached to it) seems to be here to stay. It is with this in mind that I will now turn to Critical Theory in order to think through some of the insights that it might give into 'business' and 'ethics', as well as 'Business Ethics'.

ETHICS AND DIALECTICS

Given the context of this chapter, I'm not going to spend any space here documenting the history or legitimizing the key concepts of Critical Theory or Critical Management Studies. The book's introduction and the other chapters already do that perfectly well.[3] In addition, I am going to concentrate almost entirely on what might be called classical Critical Theory – particularly Horkheimer and Adorno. This means that I will not be discussing the second generation of Frankfurt School writers and neo-Marxists, or the developments in French structuralism, poststructuralism, feminism and psychoanalytic theory – all of which are often nowadays included as part of Critical Theory (Tallack, 1995). Further, my concern is really to work through 'business' and 'ethics', so my treatment of these writings is (as with Business Ethics above) extremely selective and abbreviated. This section of the chapter will begin by looking at Horkheimer's early formulations of the distinctiveness of Critical Theory, then discuss his collaboration with Adorno in the *Dialectic of Enlightenment*, and end with Adorno's rather deconstructive conception of 'negative dialectics'. In the following section, I will then move on to apply some of these ideas to Business Ethics.

One of the key moves that Max Horkheimer makes in his early essays for the Frankfurt Institute of Social Research is to distinguish 'traditional' from 'critical' theory. In doing this, he suggests that the distinction between 'facts' and 'values', or between the 'is' and the 'ought', which sustains traditional theory is a flawed one (Horkheimer, 1989; see also Bottomore, 1984: 16; Jay, 1996: 46). This leads to two claims that define early Critical Theory. The first is to insist, like Karl Mannheim's sociology of knowledge, that the distinction between fact and value is not an objective transhistorical artefact that can be wrestled from the world through 'positivist' methods. What we know and want to know is always connected with who we are, with our interests as particular human beings positioned within specific social contexts. Further, but unlike Mannheim, Horkheimer suggests that it is only the dialectical method that can grasp this historical embeddedness fully. Dialectics (in the sense developed by Hegel) explores the logical relation between opposing propositions in an argument, and hence the interconnectedness of supposedly separate terms. In social terms it therefore presumes a relationality between things which suggests that individuals are produced intersubjectively, and that individual and context, particularity and generality are necessarily made in conjunction. In philosophical and political terms, this adds up to a radical attack on any approach which assumes a separation between the austere Kantian subject and their object of inquiry, or between the knower and the known.

Now it seems that this immediately brings into question the stability of words which attempt to make values into facts – such as 'ethics'. The very idea of ethics is all too often premised on the assumption that this word means something, that it refers to a form of life or body of knowledge that has some kind of permanence outside certain historical contexts. Thinking and writing about ethics, in business or anywhere else, is often assumed to be an activity which has coherence in and of itself. Yet for Horkheimer such an approach objectifies, makes the distinctions between the subjects who study and their objects of study into something timeless and reified. It rehearses the founding myths of impartiality in bourgeois science. But for Horkheimer

> When an active individual of sound common sense perceives the sordid state of the world, desire to change it becomes the guiding principle by which he organises given facts and shapes them into a theory...Right thinking depends as much on right willing as much as right willing on right thinking. (in Bottomore, 1984: 16)[4]

Or, in other words, what we know depends on our conception of what is right. By 'right' here, there seems to be some call to an ethical standpoint, to an approach to the world that begins with a sensitivity to the condition of others. But this is no abstraction based on the application of a golden rule from moral philosophy, since for Horkheimer such sensitivity is a precondition of active engagement with the world. 'Ethics' is not separate from the world, and therefore nameable as a distinct domain of inquiry, but (following Hegel's notion of *Sittlichkeit*, or ethical life) is an inescapable part of an inextricably dialectical entanglement with that world. Ethics cannot be something we have, or do not have, but is a relationship that we sometimes name in order to articulate features of our particular relationships to (what we understand as) our history, our present and our possible futures. Naming some/thing 'ethics' cannot subtract ethics from the rest of the world, however many times it is said, but neither can the name simply summon the ethical life into being.

For Horkheimer then, traditional theory is flawed precisely because it trades on the myth of 'identity thinking' which characterizes positivist versions of theory. Identity thinking applies a misplaced concreteness to the objects produced by thought and, in so doing, assumes that they stand outside the dialectic. Positivism, as the general description for such thought, assumes that the subject can stand in an external relationship to the object, that the 'ethicist' can comment dispassionately on 'ethics' as if this were merely a collection of facts. Yet, as Horkheimer insists, his stance does not lead to the moral abyss that he sees in Mannheim's sociology of knowledge. It is not a form of 'this impartial relativism [*that*] reveals itself as the friend of what exists at any given time' (in Hoy and McCarthy, 1994: 12). Rather, and because of Horkheimer's debt to Hegelian progressivism, he understands dialectical inquiry as a gradual form of reconciliation with a rational totality – 'an unchangeable will to unflinchingly serve the truth!' (Horkheimer, 1989: 36). Notions such as freedom, truth, justice and so on should not be surrendered to the debasements of the present impurities of reason, but brought more fully into existence precisely by revealing their current partiality and incompleteness. So, when Horkheimer critiques the individualism of Kantian morality in his essay 'Materialism and Morality', he does so in order to reveal its accommodation to market mechanisms. For Horkheimer, capitalist possessive individualism necessarily leads to self-interest, and thus does not sit easily with a concern for the general welfare. Kant's 'categorical imperative' – do as you would be done by – can then be seen as an awkward and unworkable attempt to make individuals responsible for collective matters. This kind of individualizing rationalism shifts the focus of attention from totality to 'conscience', a ghostly sign for impossible duties. Narrow egoism then reigns in the heart and in the head, while the collective iniquities of the public sphere become no longer a matter for what has now been so restrictively defined as 'ethics' (see Hoy and McCarthy, 1994: 24).

While it would be difficult to argue that these early essays add up to a positive or optimistic programme in critical reconstruction, they are certainly based on a broadly Hegelian sense of dialectical reason fulfilling its historic potential, of a 'denunciation of what is currently called reason' (Horkheimer in Jay, 1996: 253). Imagination, fantasy, even utopianism, are the desires which drive this work, and the various problems with industrial civilization that Horkheimer identifies are addressed by the early Frankfurt scholars in a variety of ways through forms of empirical and theoretical research which are intended to contribute to progressive social change. However, following from the wartime move from Frankfurt to the USA, the tone of some of this Critical Theory begins to change.[5] Perhaps the best-known document of this development is the 1947 book Horkheimer co-wrote with Theodor Adorno, *Dialectic of Enlightenment*. This work is a radically pessimistic diagnosis of (among other things) the power of the culture industries to subdue discontent. Ominously, and paradoxically, critical thought now 'does not abandon its commitment even in the face of progress' (1997: ix). Here, 'progress' is not Hegelian reconciliation, but a North American version of consumer capitalism which appeared to be rapidly satisfying human desires. Yet Adorno and Horkheimer write of an entirely classified and colonized world, one in which the 'needs' of consumers are predetermined by the 'needs' of capital. While the consumer may consider themselves to be free, in fact their freedom is almost entirely circumscribed to choosing product X or product Y. It is a meaningless freedom within which 'pleasure promotes the resignation which it ought to help to forget' (1997: 142).

Such is the power of the mass culture industries that they manage to classify, organize and label all possible forms of consumption so that there is no way out.

> Something is provided for all so that none may escape…Everybody must behave (as if spontaneously) in accordance with his previously determined and indexed level, and choose the category of mass product turned out for his type. (Adorno and Horkheimer, 1997: 123)

Of course, this is not merely a matter of material commodities, but of other choices as well. The decisions that constitute politics and ethics are colonized by business too, because this is a social order within which genuine freedoms are no longer possible. Choosing how to live one's life, or how to exercise one's imagination, are matters that are effectively re-presented as mundane alternatives between one similar attitude and another, between McDonald's and Burger King. There is no 'outside' to this world, no utopian dream that cannot in some way be captured, manufactured and re-marketed as yet another lifestyle choice. While Herbert Marcuse's later quasi-Freudian popularization of this diagnosis adds the possibility that repression might be avoided through the liberation of the imagination (1972: 195), such optimism – however moderate – is hard to discern in *Dialectic of Enlightenment*. Instead it seems that there is no escape, and everything is colonized, or colonizable. Even 'official philosophy' adds up to a 'Taylorism of the mind' which seeks 'to help improve its production methods, to rationalize the storage of knowledge, and to prevent any wastage of intellectual energy' (1997: 242). Such is the dreadful promise of the dialectic in social terms. The 'instrumental reason' necessary for industrial civilization and mass enlightenment merely produces the practical and conceptual tools for further repression. Or, in terms of this essay, business subsumes ethics because the exercise of power and the alienation of those subjected to it go hand in hand (1997: 9).

If Adorno and Horkheimer's book is pessimistic, it still forms a recognizable example of 'ideology critique' (see also Horkheimer, 1947). However, the development of dialectical thinking in Adorno's later work is even more radical in that it essentially refuses any notion that what Horkheimer was originally terming 'right' could even be specified. The Hegelian sense of the dialectic, as developed in early Frankfurt School work, relied on some sense in which contradictions could be (at least partially) reconciled. Critique, for the early Horkheimer, had a purpose, some kind of future state of affairs in mind. This might be a better representation of knowledge within the social totality, or a specification of the shortcomings of present ideologies, or even an attempt to formulate alternatives to the present 'sordid state of the world'. Yet in Adorno's later work, in his *Negative Dialectics* (1973) in particular, all such claims become articulated as further examples of 'identity thinking'. That is to say, even Critical Theory's claims take themselves to be true and hence slip back into an undialectical reification of negation itself. Or, to put it another way, that the distinction between traditional and critical theory is solidifying into a tradition itself. Against this ossification of knowledge, Adorno's negative dialectics refuses completion or synthesis, and hence sponsors a continual attitude of scepticism to all forms of totalizing knowledge claim. Turning Hegel's ontology on its head, Adorno claims that 'the whole is the false' (1974: 50) and hence that the reification of negation, as a celebration of a pious high moral ground, should itself be negated. This means that dialectical criticism becomes its own reward, but a poisonous and melancholy reward since it can only lead to further critical engagements which attempt to avoid either handwringing about the dreadfulness of the present or grand utopian dreams of the future. Both radical interiority and radical exteriority are positions that assume the whole (from 'inside' or 'outside') but 'dialectics means intransigence towards all reification' (Adorno, 1995: 294).

In a sense, this negative dialectic is no longer Hegelian in the progressive sense, but given the radical historicity that is at the heart of Hegel's philosophy, it would be perhaps better to say that this is the only form of the dialectic that Adorno believes to be supportable within advanced capitalist societies. It necessarily involves the refusal to attach thought to something that could be positively specified, on the grounds that the very solidity of 'positions' is the problem. 'No theory today escapes the marketplace...all are put up for choice; all are swallowed' (Adorno, 1973: 4). To take a position, a stance, on a particular matter is immediately to concede the ground to a rapacious form of philosophy which seeks to close things down.

> We like to present alternatives to choose from, to be marked True or False. The decisions of a bureaucracy are frequently reduced to Yes or No answers to drafts submitted to it; the bureaucratic way of thinking has become the secret model for a thought allegedly still free. (Adorno, 1973: 32)

As soon as an identity is claimed, for self or for other, then it becomes a solidified reification – and this holds just as much for resistance as it does for compliance. Hence Adorno's thought, in *Minima Moralia* (1974) for example, becomes a series of paradoxical aphorisms which seek to avoid both resting on either thesis or antithesis, positive or negative. He refuses the clarity of administered linear thought; the proof or logic which allows the reader to digest thought as if it were a commodity to be consumed. Instead he embeds thought (including his own) in history, and insists that it is never finished, and always compromised.

> He who stands aloof runs the risk of believing himself better than others and misusing his critique of society as an ideology for his private interest....His own distance from business at large is a luxury which only that business confers. (Adorno, 1974: 26)

Despite their common designation as 'Critical Theorists', there are evidently some crucial differences between the early Horkheimer and the late Adorno. Horkheimer insisted that Critical Theory must be distinguished from positivism on the grounds that there are no pure domains of fact. Adorno wishes to radicalize even this distinction, and hence to question the critical separation that 'standing aloof' relies upon. My aim in this chapter was to try and 'read' Business Ethics through the Frankfurt School and that is what I intend to do in the next section. Yet, the question now arises, through which Frankfurt School?

CRITIQUE AND BUSINESS ETHICS

Even that question is a little premature however, and this is simply because there is another ghost of Marx implicit in some of these arguments. This is what might be called (to borrow Horkheimer's designation for positivism) a 'traditional' Marxism that relies on a broadly realist understanding of science in order to describe the 'facts' of capitalist economies (Thompson et al., 2000). For these traditional theorists, the Frankfurt School's version of Critical Theory is misguided and a distraction from understanding the historical mechanics of capitalism. Tom Bottomore, for example, characterizes the development of the school's thought as a move from Marx to Weber, from a modernizing progressivism that attempts empirical studies of capitalism in order to change things, to the nostalgic pessimism of 'radicals in despair' (1984: 37). He deploys these arguments largely because he is hostile to the drift to a liberal revisionism that he sees exemplified in these ideas. For Bottomore, Marxism must involve a progressive analysis of capitalist economy and history, and he sees these commitments weakened and eventually abandoned altogether in the Frankfurt School material that he surveys. It is worth noting that Bottomore wishes to conflate two potentially different lines of distinction here – the divide between Marxists and Weberians, and the divide between progressive politics and nostalgic politics. The implication seems to be that Bottomore's Marxism is inherently progressive, while Weberian alternatives are introverted and incapable of sponsoring radical change. While I have no wish to adjudicate on this claim here,[6] it does raise an important issue for my analysis of Business Ethics and opens up the possibility of at least three ways in which critical studies of management might engage with Business Ethics.

The first would be the kind of traditional Marxism that Bottomore wishes to sponsor. As Wray-Bliss and Parker argue (1998), this is an approach deriving from the mature Marx which would tend to treat Business Ethics as an oxymoron, or a meaningless example of hypocritical ideology (see also Wood, 1991). Business Ethics would be treated in a similar way to all other legitimations of capitalist organization, no different in its aims than human resource management, strategy, accounting, marketing and so on. All such arguments and ideas are generated by the ruling classes merely to provide further support for a form of production that dispossesses the vast majority and benefits very few. Its legitimation, intellectual resources and practitioners are of no substantive interest in themselves, except insofar as they provide further examples of the superstructural generation of ideology. There is almost no sense in which this traditional Marxist approach could be called dialectical, apart from any grand historical periodizations that it might claim as an article of faith. It is an attitude that would resolutely situate itself on the 'outside' of bourgeois Business Ethics, precisely because 'value' is self-evidently given by the 'facts' of industrial capitalism. Collecting better facts than the opposition serves to further demonstrate the inequities of the present, and hence to further armour the righteous in their fight against injustice (Parker, 1999; Thompson et al., 2000).

Horkheimer's Critical Theory would have problems with this kind of transcendent version of Marxism. While its aims may be laudable, the mechanisms by which it attempts to articulate them simply mirror traditional theory's reliance on the subject–object dichotomy and the false certainties of scientific knowledge. The identity of objects – capitalism, the proletariat, the economy – is assumed in what is effectively a trans-historical manner. That is not to say that traditional Marxism has no sense of history, but rather that it is so entangled within the identity thinking of capitalism that it views its knowledge claims through the lens of positivist science. It is, in a sense, unaware of just how deeply compromised its most fundamental assumptions already are. Horkheimer, on the other hand, 'refused to make a fetish of dialectics as an objective process outside man's control' (Jay, 1996: 54). His dialectical approach would therefore be rather more careful about assuming that we can know in advance what truth, justice and emancipation might look like, simply because knowledge and human interests are so deeply intertwined. While this is extremely unlikely to mean that Business Ethics would be given a clean bill of health, it is likely that the positive and progressive elements in its constitution will be dialectically contrasted with the actuality of business organizations. So when Business Ethicists gesture towards a more responsible and reflexive version of management, or greater accountability to a variety of stakeholders, these articulations will be further sponsored and encouraged by situating them in their current 'sordid' context. The point is not to reach truth as if it were a collection of facts, but to explore the openings that historically embedded reason provides for a gradual reconciliation with a more rational totality. If traditional Marxists follow the Marx of *Capital*, then Horkheimer follows the young Marx, the materialist Hegelian who is attempting to provide a form of knowledge that was adequate to his times. Business Ethics as it is currently constituted may be an example of impure reason, but lurking within it might be the possibility of emancipation from its own constitution, and hence the further possibility of a more meaningful sense of ethics approach emerging from its ruins.

Finally then, Adorno's 'negative dialectic'. The distinctiveness of this approach is its absolute insistence on the contingency of all identity thinking, including that which identifies itself as 'for' or 'against' Business Ethics, and which also includes the positions that might be adopted by any thinker. The logical move here is to stress the historicity of any negation of negation, and hence the contingency of something called 'logic' itself. Where Horkheimer wishes to preserve the possibility of negation as a progressive reconciliation of reason, Adorno suggests that negation cannot stand outside its conditions of possibility either. The great refusal then rapidly loses any purity, any moral superiority, that might be claimed for it within (what I have called) either 'traditional' or 'critical' versions of Marxism. All that can be done is to rehearse categories of thought in order to establish that there can be no escape into either the immanence of the particular (Business Ethics' handwringing about the present) or the transcendence of the whole (traditional and radical dreams of a more reasonable world). So, Business Ethics must both presuppose and negate itself continually, and it cannot be summarized as either positive or negative in its implications. Business and ethics both concern forms of exchange, and they can be both taken to task for perpetuating various forms of cruelty, yet business and ethics can also only be criticized, or negated, from the viewpoint of the bourgeois intellectual whose conditions of possibility are also concepts like business and ethics. To put it another way, people in ivory towers shouldn't throw stones, yet (if they want to be 'critical') throwing stones is all that they can ever do. Adorno is a melancholic Nietszchean ironist in the sense that his aphoristic logic performs its impossibility. He suggests that neither 'critical' or 'theory' are sustainable positions, but this does not prevent the negative dialectician from aiming their venom at the actually existing world that constitutes them.

> The barbaric success-religion of today is consequently not simply contrary to morality: it is the homecoming of the West to the venerable morals of our ancestors. Even the norms which condemn the present world are themselves the fruit of its iniquities. All morality has been modelled on immorality and to this day has reinstated it at every level. (Adorno, 1974: 187)

Adorno's position is a ridiculous one, yet in its sheer severity and seriousness, it is perhaps the purest form of critique. There is no way out, just an endless rehearsal of being critical of being critical.

Let me try to illustrate these differences with reference to a (generalized) Business Ethics case, since they are rather abstract as they stand. There are plenty of these in the texts I have summarized above, so I don't propose to be specific here. Whatever the details, the case will state some facts about an organization, outline the ethical problem (corruption, pollution, discrimination or whatever) and then ask the reader what they would do in this situation. The 'correct' Business Ethics answer will involve some reference to ethical theories and economic imperatives in order to justify some form of management action. So how would the case be treated by each of the three 'Marxisms' I have covered above? For the traditional Marxist critic, the local details and motivations would be irrelevant since the problem is an outcome of structural processes. Because business organizations are constituted by the rules of a capitalist mode of production, their members are coerced (both ideologically and more directly) into acting in ways that conform with these rules. If an organization knowingly makes defective products, it does not mean that individuals or organization are acting 'unethically', just that they are conforming to the laws of profitability. Whatever the case, the solution is radical social change. Minor philosophical quibbles about 'ethics' are mere distractions. Indeed, talk about ethics is merely a symptom of the ways in which consciousness is structured by historical context. Change the context and the symptoms will no longer be relevant.

Horkheimer's version of Critical Theory might well share such doubts, but would take the language of ethics more seriously. A better world is implicit in discussions about 'duty', 'character', 'good' and so on, even if it is manifested in imperfect and distorted ways though the language of Business Ethics. So encouraging reflection and discussion on the meaning of such concepts would be crucial. However, the aim of such reflection would be to show how the meaning of 'ethics' is highly circumscribed by the business context from which it emerges. If we think hard about what it means to be good in an organization at the present time, that understanding can become a bridge into the future. It is by exploiting the tensions between grand words and sordid reality that the former can encourage us to reject the latter. Negating the current meaning of the good opens a space for a fuller version of the good to emerge. For example, imagining what a really empowered employee might be shows just how entrapped current versions of empowerment are. Conceiving a genuinely environmentally friendly organization illustrates the partiality of current attempts at incorporating greenwash. In each case, the aim would be to stimulate the imagination of alternative possibilities by showing what kind of world is potentially hiding within certain concepts.

Finally then, Adorno. A negative dialectic would have, as its first move, something like the stance I have suggested for Horkheimer above. But this would not be enough. In order to claim that there is a better version of the good waiting in the wings of history, the critic must inevitably set themselves up above the here and now. For Adorno, this faith in negation is misconceived on two grounds. First, because these golden ethical words are then effectively treated as referring to something that exists somewhere outside the language of the here and now. If criticism is set up as being a transcendent principle, then it is removed from its own complicity with the present times. Second, because through that move the critic, like their concepts, becomes a hero who also stands outside history. For these reasons, the second move in the negative dialectic would be to insist on criticizing the idea of the critic, and the words they express faith in. So imagining what a really empowered employee might be can only be done from the standpoint of an intellectual with certain assumptions about reason, autonomy, emancipation and so on. Exposing greenwash can only be done with the present state of knowledge and understanding of words like nature, production, consumption and so on. The point here is not that criticism should be avoided, but that it should be criticized too and situated within its historical conditions of possibility. The Business Ethics case is partial and individualizing, but so is any attempt to set up a position outside the case which acts as a commentary upon it.

I've outlined three positions here, all deriving from some version of Hegel and Marx, all insisting on some version of the historicity of knowledge, all in some way impatient with the present and offering 'critical' analyses of a technocratic consumer society. Further, all would surely treat 'Business Ethics' as it is presently constituted as an example of 'ideology', 'false consciousness' and so on. Yet their articulation is radically different in terms of the position they provide for the critic. Bottomore's traditional critic is an external one who uses the tools of science precisely because they assume that there is a position beyond ideology, a form of consciousness that is (demonstrably) not false. Horkheimer's critical theorist assumes that ideology and consciousness are historically determined matters, but that certain terms contain positive possibilities that can be encouraged through their negation. Adorno's negative dialectician is intractably hostile to the ways in which ideologies form consciousness, but refuses any faith in a reified negation of these terms either. There are no alternatives to the traps of language, and the dreadful seductions of the high moral ground. In summary, the issue at stake here seems to be whether the theorist is an ideologue too, whether their consciousness can escape from its own conditions of possibility in order to aim at something else. To put it another way, is critique beyond critique?

CONCLUSION

> The injunction to practise intellectual honesty usually amounts to sabotage of thought. The writer is urged to show explicitly all the steps that have led him to his conclusion, so enabling every reader to follow the process through and, where possible – in the academic industry – to duplicate it. This demand [*is*] wrong in itself as a principle of representation. For the value of a thought is measured by its distance from the continuity of the familiar. (Adorno, 1974: 80)

In suitably reflexive terms, I want to conclude this chapter by thinking about its own conditions of possibility, and hence what it might mean to be critical of Business Ethics. This chapter appears in a book which is part of an emerging body of writings usually termed 'Critical Management'. To profess Critical Management – like Business Ethics – is to claim (at least) three things. First, that something is needed; second, that you are the kind of person who can do it; third, that you can achieve something with your expertise. Once again, to borrow the term from ten Bos (2002), this is an account of 'insufficiency'. I'll take each of these issues in turn, but more briefly this time around.

The diagnosis of the present is that capitalist or industrial societies are unjust. Their divisions of labour and wealth are inequitable, their governance and organizational structures biased towards the powerful, the subjectivities they generate are individualized and insecure, and their conceptions of nature are instrumental. It then follows, for those people who care about such matters and don't consider them inevitable, that such injustice must be resisted. And so, the need created, the question that then arises is who is to fill it. The answer seems to be those academics, mostly resident in business schools, with an interest in work and organizations, who have access to a wide range of 'critical' intellectual resources. Here the picture becomes a little more complex, because some of those who have deployed these resources for a considerable time – labour process Marxists in particular – are reluctant to let them be co-opted by the upstart Critical Management academics (Parker, 1999). However, other resources, which have only more recently been applied to problems of organization and management, are rapidly becoming canonical: to whit, structuralism and poststructuralism, postmodern cultural critique, feminism, postcolonialism, environmentalism and so on. Perhaps most importantly, a key position is provided here for 'Critical Theory', though there are some important questions about which critical theory this might be. I will deal with this in a little more detail below. Finally, the question of what can be achieved. Here, Critical Management is rhetorically expansive but short on detail. While words like 'emancipation', 'justice' and so on are often used, there has been a general reluctance to make programmatic interventions in the constitution of organizations and capitalism generally. Critical Management has been fairly successful in erecting an academic superstructure of conferences, sympathetic journals and even key texts (such as this one), but the dissemination of these ideas more generally, and their translation into practical interventions, has been notable by its absence (Parker, 2002). Hardly surprisingly, Sorell's 'alienation problem' for Business Ethics seems to apply to Critical Management as well.

The parallel between Business Ethics and Critical Management, as academic 'subdisciplines', should be fairly obvious. Both have made their own justifications of need, their own claims about expertise, and their own (modest) claims about effect. Both claim that the managed world has ethical/political problems, and that they have knowledge that sheds some light on these matters. The similarities between the two seem, in that sense, to be quite considerable. So the question I posed at the start of the chapter returns. Why are they not considered to be allies? Why is there so little productive engagement between the two positions? I want to answer this question in two ways. The first is a sociological diagnosis of the institutionalization and segmentation of knowledge, the second is a more philosophical diagnosis of differing versions of 'critique'. In terms of the former, it could be said that there is (for a variety of reasons, and despite optimistic claims about interdisciplinarity) a growing separation between distinct domains of enquiry which ensures that cross-border exchange becomes ever more difficult. An obvious example of this is that there are now different journals, conferences, discussion lists, formal and informal networks, and even departments and research centres, which make it increasingly unlikely that the practitioners of either Business Ethics or Critical Management Studies will often actually meet. However, even if they do, different assumptions about the status of their respective gurus, what counts as canonical knowledge, appropriate forms of methodology and language and so on, will make translation between either side difficult. As I have argued elsewhere with regard to 'organizational behaviour' and the 'sociology of organizations' (Parker, 2000), the construction of a domain of inquiry necessarily means that it must both practise amnesia and construct 'others'. Internal coherence seems to rely on some notion of 'us' and 'them', and this kind of gradual concretization makes talking to 'them' more and more difficult. These processes make abstract arguments about 'reification' become very real indeed. On both sides, if 'they' are bad and 'we' are good, then why should we bother talking to them?

But, as I'm sure many readers will agree, this is not all that is at stake here. The forms of critique deployed within either field differ too, which leads me back to some sort of distinction between my three neo-Marxisms and an individualized form of liberalism. It is precisely because Business Ethics usually employs a conception of the rational individual subject making various constrained choices that it is usually regarded with suspicion by those who demand a more structurally informed type of analysis. At base, this is some form of dispute between Kantians and Hegelians, between those who wish to trade on the modern notion of the sovereign individual and those who wish to stress that the subject can only ever achieve meaning in relation to social and political context. As Wood (1991) has pointed out, Marx was often contemptuous of what he called 'morality' because he regarded it as an apology for the actually existing form of capitalism. So it is with much of Business Ethics. Even those Business Ethicists who do develop a more collectivist version of sociality and politics – virtue theorists or communitarians for example – tend to treat this as a precondition for the exercise of individual moral choice or character traits. Not that this is true of all communitarianism, which in political theory is often opposed to liberalism (see Mulhall and Swift, 1992), but the translation of these ideas into Business Ethics is more consensus functionalist than communitarian in its formulations. Hegel's holistic *sittlichkeit* decomposes into separate constituent elements, charismatic managers, ethical codes to guide practice, and strong culture organizations. If these components can be placed into a functional alignment, organizations can achieve engineered consent and managers be given clear guidelines while profits are still being made (for example, Jackson, 1996).

Yet a simple opposition between Marxists and liberals is not sufficient here, because there is a real question about which form of Marxism Critical Management academics are sponsoring. And, even if the Frankfurt School is distinguished from traditional Marxism, there is a further question about which Frankfurt School we might be referring to. On the one side, there is a tradition that leads from Horkheimer's early essays to Habermas. This is a form of critique that attempts to build powerful arguments that rely heavily on some notion of immanent reason. Not, to be sure, the transcendent vision of positive inquiry that can be found in both Business Ethics and traditional Marxism, but a version of human potential that is secreted within the structures of the everyday. So, when Horkheimer refers to a Hegelian sense of overcoming, or Habermas contrasts various forms of communicative reason, the common assumption is that there is a positive purpose in critical inquiry. To put it very crudely, an active attempt to understand the world is premised on the idea that using reason can bring about a more reasonable world (for an application of this kind of thought, see Alvesson and Willmott, 1996). Yet there is a very different version of Critical Theory too, one that might begin with the *Dialectic of Enlightenment* and lead to Adorno's negative dialectic. Here, reason is no longer seen as a utopian principle of negation since its very reification also becomes a problem to be dealt with. David Hoy (in Hoy and McCarthy, 1994) wishes to claim that this is a lineage that is better understood through Nietzsche than Marx, and can be extended to Derrida and Foucault as inheritors of this tradition (see also Jay, 1996: xvi passim). For Adorno, there is no special place for 'reason' at all, it is merely one of the colonizing technologies produced by the modern world. It can neither be negated nor should it be affirmed. Indeed, to assume that one might have a position on all the objects produced by reason or unreason is to capitulate to the commodification of thought.

> If thought is not measured by the extremity that eludes the concept, it is from the outset in the nature of the musical accompaniment with which the SS liked to drown out the screams of its victims. (Adorno, 1973: 365)

In other words, Business Ethics might be the accompaniment which drowns out corporate indecency, but its negation (in essays like this) can often add up to pretty much the same thing.

Now this tension, which I am personalizing as a distinction between Horkheimer and Adorno, has some clear resonances in contemporary debates in social theory (see Hoy and McCarthy, 1994), and has particular importance for the question I began this chapter with. When posed with the kind of case study that Business Ethicists are so fond of, Horkheimer might wish to show how its very questions presuppose the actuality of capitalist social relations, and of the bourgeois decision-making subject. In doing so, he would be attempting to show that the social arrangements which are reflected in the constitution of the case study are unreasonable, that they contain hidden assumptions that should be negated. If the critique is sufficiently persuasive, then the possibility for more reasonable arrangements opens up. This will almost certainly involve some revision of what the word 'ethics' might be taken to mean, perhaps with the aim of attaching an ethics (of a private character) to a politics (of the public sphere). However, while Adorno might engage in similar tactics, his negation of Business Ethics must (of necessity) display suspicion of the very terms on which such a critique takes place. It would be, in a sense, a critique that undoes itself too, that always refuses the smug subject position of 'outsider' with sure and certain knowledge of the world. Adorno's critique has no transcendent aim, other than to display the inexorability of subject positions that are already constituted by the objects of business, ethics, and Business Ethics. It cannot go beyond, and it cannot stay within. All that remains is restlessness, impatience and melancholy (ten Bos, 2003).

> And then the salaried philosophers come along and reproach us with having no definite point of view. (Adorno, 1974: 74)

Given that this chapter has been dealing with the weightiest of matters – ethics, politics, theory, history, philosophy – it seems deeply ironic that it might end with not having a definite point of view. One might want to think that thinking leads somewhere, to a definitive and defensible attitude towards its object. So that 'we' might know what 'Business Ethics' is, and what 'Critical Management' is, and what sort of relationship holds between the two terms. Are these 'good' or 'bad' things, and how do we avoid the bad and get closer to the good? The aim of thought might then be a set of reasonable principles by which we might live our lives; or even some form of revealing, an uncovering of some orientation to others or social arrangement which is self-evidently better than this 'sordid' state of affairs. But sometimes thought doesn't go that way, and instead it ends up dethroning its own logic of 'and' and 'if' and 'therefore', or even revealing its own passionate intentions as the shallowest examples of self-interest. It is easy then for others to climb onto their high moral grounds (via readings of Kant, or Hegel, or Marx) and declaim such thought as irrelevant, as unconcerned with the pressing practical problems of people who live their lives in splendour or in poverty, and the everyday problems of people who work in business organizations. As Lukács put it:

> many of the leading German intellectuals, including Adorno, have installed themselves in this 'Grand Hotel Abyss'…It is a hotel provided with every modern comfort, but resting on the edge of the abyss, of

> nothingness, of the absurd. The daily contemplation of the abyss, in between the excellent meals and artistic entertainments, can only enhance the residents' enjoyment of this superlative comfort. (in Bottomore, 1984: 34)

But then the trap of agreeing, or disagreeing, with Lukács, and claiming that such thought is necessarily guilty or innocent opens wide. To concede this would, in Adorno's terms, sabotage thought and bring it to a premature, impossible and violent conclusion.

As René ten Bos has argued (1997, 2002, 2003), avoiding final conclusions is an attitude that rests on an assumption about the inherent messiness of the world, and the impossibility of providing final adjudications or solutions that will lead to order. For Business Ethics, and for Critical Management, this must mean that critique is never beyond critique. Just as Business Ethics can be argued to be a social technology which assumes capitalism and therefore perpetuates it, so can an intransigent opposition to Business Ethics become replete with alternative assumptions about what counts as 'real' ethics, or 'real' knowledge. While my, rather deconstructive, understanding of Adorno does not avoid such problems, I think it has the merit of revealing them. Not revealing in the sense of providing an answer to the question of what 'we' 'should' do next, but instead accepting that neither 'we' or 'should' are terms that have any final adjudication outside of the messy problems and politics that constitute both Business Ethics and Critical Management. On the basis of what I have argued above, and following Adorno, permanent suspicion about the activities of Business Ethicists and Critical Management academics is the only 'definite point of view' that I can cling on to. Which is to end by doing no more than paradoxically exemplifying the endless movement of dialectical thinking.

NOTES

Thanks to Mats Alvesson, Phil Hancock, Campbell Jones and Hugh Willmott for their comments on earlier drafts of this chapter.

1 Though see Castro (1996), the brief opening chapters in Cannon (1994), and some chapters in Frederick (1999) for exceptions.
2 A US version of the beginnings of such an engagement can be found in Freeman and Phillips (1999).
3 Though see Wiggershaus (1994) or Jay (1996) for excellent reviews of the Frankfurt School's thought.
4 A quote with historically acceptable sexism that further underlines the general point about the historical contingency of knowledge.
5 Though see the other book that Horkheimer published that year, *Eclipse of Reason*, echoes his earlier work in terms of a measured faith in a reasoned critique of impure reason. It might be that Adorno's influence on *Dialectic of Enlightenment* is more important than Horkheimer's.

6 Though the fact that Weber's distinction between 'facts' and 'values' is certainly not shared by Horkheimer or Adorno makes any deep similarities between the Frankfurt School and Weber very difficult to sustain.

REFERENCES

Adorno, T. (1973) *Negative Dialectics*. London: Routledge & Kegan Paul.

Adorno, T. (1974) *Minima Moralia*. London: New Left Books.

Adorno, T. (1995) Cultural criticism and society. In D. Tallack (ed.), *Critical Theory: A Reader*. Hemel Hempstead: Harvester Wheatsheaf.

Adorno, T. and Horkheimer, M. (1997) *Dialectic of Enlightenment*. London: Verso.

Alvesson, M. and Willmott, H. (1996) *Making Sense of Management*. London: Sage.

Bottomore, T. (1984) *The Frankfurt School*. Chichester: Ellis Horwood.

Cannon, T. (1994) *Corporate Responsibility*. London: Pitman.

Castro, B. (ed.) (1996) *Business and Society*. Oxford: Oxford University Press.

Clutterbuck, D., Dearlove, D. and Snow, D. (1992) *Actions Speak Louder. A Management Guide to Social Responsibility*. London: Kogan Page.

Drummond, J. and Bain, B. (eds) (1994) *Managing Business Ethics*. Oxford: Butterworth-Heinemann.

Frederick, R. (ed.) (1999) *A Companion to Business Ethics*. Malden, MA: Blackwell.

Freeman, R. and Phillips, R. (1999) Business Ethics: Pragmatism and postmodernism. In R. Frederick (ed.), *A Companion to Business Ethics*. Malden, MA: Blackwell.

Griseri, P. (1998) *Managing Values*. Basingstoke: Macmillan.

Hoffman, W. and Frederick, R. (1995) *Business Ethics: Readings and Cases in Corporate Morality*. New York: McGraw-Hill.

Horkheimer, M. (1947) *Eclipse of Reason*. New York: Oxford University Press.

Horkheimer, M. (1989) The state of contemporary social philosophy and the tasks of an institute for social research. In S. Bronner and D. Kellner (eds), *Critical Theory and Society: A Reader*. New York: Routledge.

Hoy, D. and McCarthy, T. (1994) *Critical Theory*. Oxford: Blackwell.

Jackson, J. (1996) *An Introduction to Business Ethics*. Oxford: Blackwell.

Jay, M. (1996) *The Dialectical Imagination*. Berkeley, CA: University of California Press.

Kjonstad, B. and Willmott, H. (1995) Business Ethics: Restrictive or empowering? *Journal of Business Ethics*. 14: 445–64.

Marcuse, H. (1972) *One-dimensional Man*. London: Abacus.

Mulhall, S. and Swift, A. (1992) *Liberals and Communitarians*. Oxford: Blackwell.

Ottensmeyer, E. and McCarthy, G. (1996) *Ethics in the Workplace*. New York: McGraw-Hill.

Parker, M. (1998) Business Ethics and social theory: Postmodernizing the ethical. *British Journal of Management*. 9: 27–36.

Parker, M. (1999) Capitalism, subjectivity and ethics: Debating labour process analysis. *Organisation Studies*. 20(1): 25–45.

Parker, M. (2000) The sociology of organisations and the organisation of sociology: Some reflections on the making of a division of labour. *Sociological Review*. 48: 124–46.

Parker, M. (2002) *Against Management*. Cambridge: Polity Press.

Pearson, G. (1995) *Integrity in Organisations: An Alternative Business Ethic*. Maidenhead: McGraw-Hill.

Sorell, T. (1998) Beyond the fringe? The strange state of Business Ethics. In M. Parker (ed.), *Ethics and Organisations*. London: Sage.

Stewart, D. (1996) *Business Ethics*. New York: McGraw-Hill.

Tallack, D. (ed.) (1995) *Critical Theory: A Reader*. Hemel Hempstead: Harvester Wheatsheaf.

ten Bos, R. (1997) Business Ethics and Bauman ethics. *Organisation Studies*. 18(6): 997–1014.

ten Bos, R. (2002) Machiavelli's Kitchen. *Organisation*. 9(1): 51–70.

ten Bos, R. (2003) Business Ethics, accounting and the fear of melancholy. *Organisation*. 10.

Tester, K. (1997) *Moral Culture*. London: Sage.

Thompson, P., Smith, C. and Ackroyd, S. (2000) If ethics is the answer, you are asking the wrong questions: A reply to Martin Parker. *Organisation Studies*. 21(6): 1149–58.

Treviño, L. and Nelson, K. (1999) *Managing Business Ethics*. New York: Wiley.

Wiggershaus, R. (1994) *The Frankfurt School*. Cambridge: Polity Press.

Willmott, H. (1998) Towards a new ethics. In M. Parker (ed.), *Ethics and Organisations*. London: Sage.

Wood, A. (1991) Marx against morality. In P. Singer (ed.), *A Companion to Ethics*. Oxford: Blackwell.

Wray-Bliss, E. and Parker, M. (1998) Marxism, capitalism and ethics. In M. Parker (ed.), *Ethics and Organisations*. London: Sage.

Author Index

Subject Index